Qoheleth

Studies on Personalities of the Old Testament
James L. Crenshaw, Series Editor

Qoheleth

The Ironic Wink

James L. Crenshaw

The University of South Carolina Press

Published by the University of South Carolina Press
Columbia, South Carolina 29208

www.sc.edu/uscpress

Manufactured in the United States of America

22 21 20 19 18 17 16 15 14 13   10 9 8 7 6 5 4 3 2 1

Library of Congress Cataloging-in-Publication Data

Crenshaw, James L.
    Qoheleth : the ironic wink / James L. Crenshaw.
      pages cm. — (Studies on personalities of the Old Testament)
    Includes bibliographical references and index.
    ISBN 978-1-61117-257-7 (alk. paper) — ISBN 978-1-61117-258-4 (epub)
    1. Bible. Ecclesiastes—Criticism, interpretation, etc. I. Title.
    BS1475.52.C74 2013
    223'.806—dc23

                                                      2013005006

This book was printed on a recycled paper with 30 percent postconsumer waste content.

Contents

Series Editor's Preface

Critical study of the Bible in its ancient Near Eastern setting has stimulated interest in the individuals who shaped the course of history and whom events singled out as tragic or heroic figures. Rolf Rendtorff's *Men of the Old Testament* (1968) focuses on the lives of important biblical figures as a means of illuminating history, particularly the sacred dimension that permeates Israel's convictions about its God. Fleming James's *Personalities of the Old Testament* (1939) addresses another issue, that of individuals who function as inspiration for their religious successors in the twentieth century. Studies restricting themselves to a single individual—for example, Moses, Abraham, Samson, Elijah, David, Saul, Ruth, Jonah, Job, Jeremiah—enable scholars to deal with a host of questions: psychological, literary, theological, sociological, and historical. Some, like Gerhard von Rad's *Moses* (1960), introduce a specific approach to interpreting the Bible, hence provide valuable pedagogic tools.

As a rule these treatments of isolated figures have not reached the general public. Some were written by outsiders who lacked a knowledge of biblical criticism (Freud on Moses, Jung on Job) and whose conclusions, however provocative, remain problematic. Others were targeted for the guild of professional biblical critics (David Gunn on David and Saul, Phyllis Trible on Ruth, Terence Fretheim and Jonathan Magonet on Jonah). None has succeeded in capturing the imagination of the reading public in the way fictional works like Archibald MacLeish's *J. B.* and Joseph Heller's *God Knows* have done.

It could be argued that the general public would derive little benefit from learning more about the personalities of the Bible. Their conduct, often less then exemplary, reveals a flawed character, and their everyday concerns have nothing to do with our preoccupations from dawn to dusk. To be sure, some individuals transcend their own age, entering the gallery of classical literary figures from time immemorial. But only these rare achievers can justify specific treatments of them. Then why publish additional studies on biblical personalities?

The answer cannot be that we read about biblical figures to learn ancient history, even of the sacred kind, or to discover models for ethical action. But what remains? Perhaps the primary significance of biblical personages is the light they throw on the imaging of deity in biblical times. At the very least, the Bible constitutes human perceptions of deity's relationship with the world and its creatures. Close readings of biblical personalities therefore clarify ancient understandings of God. That is the important datum which we seek—not because we endorse that specific view of deity, but because all such efforts to make sense of reality contribute something worthwhile to the endless quest for knowledge.

James L. Crenshaw
Robert L. Flowers Professor Emeritus
of Old Testament, Duke University

Acknowledgments

The book of Ecclesiastes has fascinated me for as long as I can remember. A Guggenheim Fellowship to study the depiction of old age in Ecclesiastes and in related literature from the ancient Near East and an invitation to be a fellow at St. Edmund's House at Cambridge University in 1984–85 made it possible for me to put the finishing touches on a commentary on Ecclesiastes for the Old Testament Library. Still I could not get over my fascination with the biblical book, and I continued to teach it to graduate students at Duke University and to write articles on various aspects of its thought. In 2006–7 I was named the Joseph McCarthy Visiting Professor at the Pontifical Biblical Institute in Rome with the responsibility of teaching Ecclesiastes to two dozen Jesuits and three sisters. On returning to Duke in the fall semester I taught a seminar on the book to graduate students, thinking it would be my last such offering. That was not to be, even if my interests have broadened considerably in recent years.

My retirement from Duke University in 2008 and move to Nashville to be near our two sons and five grandchildren left me with much free time to continue my research and writing. I was immediately invited to teach a Maymester course on Job and Ecclesiastes at Vanderbilt. My wife and I quickly enrolled in the Osher Lifelong Learning Institute at Vanderbilt, and I have been privileged to learn something from superb teachers about a variety of topics (the Russian revolution, the age of the universe, great thinkers of the nineteenth century, the Civil War, revolutions in the Americas, the Mayan civilization, health reform, social protest, great singers and their songs, and more). Thanks to my friend and former colleague Charles Hamrick, to the marvelous director, Norma Clippard, and to the selection committee, I was invited to join the teaching staff. So far, I have taught classes on Job and Ecclesiastes, which greatly assisted me in writing *Reading Job: A Literary and Theological Commentary* (Macon: Smyth & Helwys, 2011) and the present book on Ecclesiastes. I am also scheduled to teach a class on Psalms in the fall of 2012.

I wish to express my deep appreciation to the more than two hundred adults who made my classes a joy. Their presence constantly challenged me to make the study of biblical texts both intellectually stimulating and, dare I say, fun. I am also grateful for members of Sunday school classes at Westminster Presbyterian Church, Trinity

Presbyterian Church, First Presbyterian Church, and Vine Street Christian Church, all of Nashville, where many of my ideas about Ecclesiastes were tested. This book is dedicated to these lovers of learning.

My thanks also go to my wife, Nita, who for more than fifty-six years has encouraged me to follow my passion to understand ancient literature. As usual, Gail Chappell has typed much of my handwritten prose on a computer, saving me much time and headache. She has my lasting gratitude.

The translations in this book are my own, and I have simplified all transliterations of the Hebrew.

Introduction

Wayfarer, do not pass by my epitaph, but stand and listen, and then, when you have learned the truth, proceed. There is no boat in Hades, no ferryman Charon, no Aeacus keeper of the keys, nor any dog called Cerberus. All of us who have died and gone below are bones and ashes: there is nothing else. What I have told you is true. Now withdraw, wayfarer, so that you will not think that, even though dead, I talk too much.[1]

Like the unknown author of this Greek epitaph, who had experienced a shaking of the foundations of knowledge in his or her day, the protagonist in the book of Ecclesiastes, who called himself Qoheleth (pronounced Qoh-hél-eth) had seen the assumptions of the intelligentsia and the practical guidelines of ordinary citizens give way under the heavy questioning of poets such as the genius behind the book of Job and the vicissitudes of history as empire after empire decimated the Judean countryside.

For authors such as these, truth had become "a pathless land," one that could not be approached "by any path whatsoever, by any religion, by any sect."[2] The human condition, it follows, is accurately depicted in a *New Yorker* cartoon of an individual walking on a treadmill facing a sign on which is inscribed a single word, "TRUTH." And yet, despite their avowed agnosticism, each of these three individuals claimed to have reached solid ground capable of withstanding the crumbling half-truths on which they were nurtured.

"What I have told you is true" matches Job's bold denial that a calculable divine justice exists and Qoheleth's assertion that "everything is vanity," to use a familiar expression that I shall soon challenge as an adequate translation of the Hebrew word *hebel*.[3] In short these thinkers dared to dismiss as lies major givens of society and to offer counter testimony with no authority except the logic of their own arguments.

Leaving aside the Greek epitaph for now, I turn to the conclusions of the two Hebraic wise men. The books of Job and Ecclesiastes belong to the third division of the Tanak, or the Hebrew Bible (Old Testament). The first two divisions are the Torah and the Prophets. The Torah consists of Genesis, Exodus, Leviticus, Numbers, and Deuteronomy. These five books are called Torah because they are presented as the teachings of Moses, spokesman for the deity. As such, they are accorded special revelatory status in Judaism, along with an oral tradition. The Prophets include the "historical" books of Joshua, Judges, Samuel, and Kings, plus Isaiah, Jeremiah, Ezekiel, and the Twelve. These twelve short books, by no means insignificant, are called Minor Prophets because of their brevity.

The third division has less structural and thematic cohesion than the first two. It seems to have been a sort of catchall for the other books that had acquired sufficient popularity and sanctity to be included in a canon of sacred writings some time around the first century B.C.E. The largest of the books is Psalms, usually linked with Job and Proverbs. Traditionally these three have been arranged in two different sequences to yield anagrams indicating either truth or perfection (in the sense of wholeness). That is, the first Hebrew letters of Job, Proverbs, and Psalms make up the word *'emeth* ("truth"), and the order Psalms, Job, and Proverbs produces the word *tam* ("perfection"). In addition five books eventually came to be known as festal scrolls.[4] Listed in order of appearance they are Song of Songs, Ruth, Lamentations, Ecclesiastes, and Esther. The books of Daniel, Ezra, Nehemiah, and Chronicles round out this third division. As a mix of divine and human words, the second and third divisions have secondary authority for Judaism while Christianity accords equal revelatory status to all three divisions.

In the third division three books are generally identified as wisdom literature.[5] They are Proverbs, Job, and Ecclesiastes. A few scholars consider Song of Songs in this group, as well as several psalms that discuss life's injustices and place a premium on moral instruction, most notably 34, 37, 49, 73, and 119.[6] Whereas both Torah and Prophets purport to be directives from God, wisdom literature makes no such claim. In it the wise, as they are called, give their own insights gleaned from observing nature and people. The results of rigorous analogical thinking, these observations and instructions are distilled for those willing to hear, especially the young.

The collected sayings in Proverbs are overwhelmingly prudential.[7] At first parents and later professional teachers instruct the young—and any others who will listen—on how to avoid pitfalls and how to make the most of opportunities presented them. Except for a few cracks here and there, the teachings suggest that individuals can control their destiny and that God oversees a just universe.

The book of Job turns that comforting world upside down.[8] Its fictional hero experiences the collapse of the sacred canopy constructed by earlier sages. The tragic death of his seven sons and three daughters and the rupture in the intimacy with God forced Job to reject the truisms that his friends dished out to a hungry soul. Such revolutionary ideas may have been produced for more sophisticated thinkers than the youthful audience of the book of Proverbs.

Unlike the author of the Joban masterpiece, Qoheleth thought it futile to swim against the stream. In his view it does no good to argue with God, which had been Job's way of dealing with injustice. Qoheleth chose other human beings as partners in conversation. In the entire book, twelve chapters comprising two hundred and twenty-two verses, he never once addressed the deity, never identified him as "my God." Although he had much to say about God, both positive and negative, he was content to talk *about* but not *to* the distant deity.

Like the author of "The Human Destiny," a Ballad of Heroes Long Past, a text discovered at Tell Meskene in Syria (ancient Emar),[9] Qoheleth reached the conclusion that life is a mere breath, brief and insubstantial like the wind. He realized that no human exertion, not even that of a primordial king, Gilgamesh of Uruk, can change the human condition.[10] The sentence of death is an eternal decree with universal application. As the Stoic philosopher Epicurus is reputed to have said, "Against other things it is possible to obtain security, but when it comes to death we human beings all live in an unwalled city."[11]

For his honesty and astute study of human nature and the environment into which mortals have been thrown, Qoheleth has gained a small band of admirers in high places. Among others, they include a Nobel laureate, a recipient of various prizes and a Guggenheim Fellowship for poetry, a newspaper columnist, and a composer of folk songs.

First the Nobel laureate in literature. In her acceptance speech at Stockholm in 1996, Wislawa Szymborska began by expressing admiration for Qoheleth while at the same time questioning his assertion that there is nothing new under the sun: "You were born under the sun, the poem you created is new, as are your readers, and so is the cypress under which you are sitting." She continued, "And Ecclesiastes, I'd also like to ask you what new thing under the sun you're planning to work on now. A further supplement to thoughts that you've already expressed? Or maybe you're tempted to contradict some of them now? . . . Have you taken notes yet, do you have drafts? I doubt that you'll say, 'I've written everything down, I've got nothing left to add?' There's no poet in the world who can say this, least of all a great poet like yourself.'"[12]

Second the Guggenheim fellow. In *Questions for Ecclesiastes* Vanderbilt poet Mark Jarman[13] imagined what it would have been like if his father, a minister, had quoted various teachings of Qoheleth to the grieving parents of a young girl who had just discharged a rifle though the roof of her mouth and the top of her skull.

What if, he asked, his father had said the sun rises and sets; the wind blows south and then north; rivers run into the sea; fourteen-year-old girls would manage to end it all; and nothing is new under the sun? What if the pastor had said the eye is not satisfied with seeing nor ear filled with hearing? Would he then want to see the room in which the suicide took place or to hear the sound of the gunshot?

What if, Jarman continued, the pastor had said he praised the dead more than the living, and the one not yet alive is better than the dead or the living? Or if he had said, "Be not rash with your speech or in a hurry to utter something before God, for God is in heaven"? What if he had said that the dead know nothing because their memory is forgotten, as are their love and hatred, for the dead have no more portion in what is done under the sun? What if, on taking leave of the couple, the preacher had urged them to live joyfully all the days of their vain life, for that is their portion?

After describing his memory of his father, who had visited strangers on that awful night, Jarman concluded that the God who will bring every work into judgment, with every secret thing, good or bad, could have shared his knowledge with those who urgently needed to hear it but kept a secret.

Jarman continued the theme of costly divine silence in another book of poetry, *Unholy Sonnets*.[14] The eighth sonnet describes a murderer's refusal to heed the voice of conscience but an even worse decision on the part of God, who watches the drama play out and sees the victim and killer but "still maintains his vigil and his power, which you and I would squander with a scream." The fourth unholy sonnet in *Questions for Ecclesiastes* celebrates divine absence. Jarman thought of a deity who recedes into the void and demonstrates love through absence, baffling humans but receiving the adoration of the stars.[15]

Third the newspaper columnist. In his book *Against the Grain: Unconventional Wisdom from Ecclesiastes,* Ray Waddle summed up his understanding of the biblical book as follows: "Ecclesiastes is a beaker filled with earthly elements—the passage of time, life's beauty and limitations, the divine silence, the consolations and confusions of our allotted days on earth, the poetry of the human condition. A few drops from Ecclesiastes' beaker into the well water of faith are a healthy thing. Without them religion takes ungodly flights into realms of abstraction, pomposity, hysteria, and murderous purity. These prompt a person to claim too much—visions that turn out to be untrue, moral pronouncements that turn out to be mere bullying, divine errands that turn into blood-baths. An old cycle gets revved up again—religious conflict, violence, disillusion, bewilderment, loss of faith, desecration, the name of God besmirched again and again, taken horribly in vain."[16]

Fourth a song writer. The familiar poem about a time for everything under heaven inspired Pete Seeger to compose "Turn, Turn, Turn," which strikes a familiar chord with many listeners in the same way the words of Qoheleth appeal to those who choose to read them at funerals. There seems to be both promise and finality in the cadence of things that are subjected to fixed times, none of which is under our control. There is indeed a time to give birth and a time to die, just as there is a time for war and a time for peace. And there is a time for everything in between these beginnings and endings.

Like few others, the philosopher Bertrand Russell recognized the promise even in the presence of vanity: "To take into the inmost shrine of the soul the irresistible forces whose puppets we seem to be—death and change, the irrevocableness of the past, and the powerlessness of man before the blind hurry of the universe from vanity to vanity—to feel these things and know them is to conquer them."[17] Less sanguine is Arthur Schopenhauer's sardonic remark about finality: "Time is that by virtue of which everything becomes nothingness in our hands and loses all real value."[18] In a similar vein Jean-Paul Sartre wrote that "All existing things are born for no reason, continue through weakness and die by accident. . . . It is meaningless that we are born; it is meaningless that we die."[19]

Qoheleth's grandeur is that he could hold together the paradox that life is devoid of meaning and that joy abounds, at least for a few. The philosopher Jacques Ellul thinks Qoheleth viewed life as a thread of which one end is vanity and the other is the presence of God. According to Ellul, "In reality, all is vanity. In truth, everything is a gift of God. This represents Qoheleth's position, as I understand it."[20] Nevertheless Ellul concedes that we may not grasp the true intent of the strange teacher: "He may mean what he says, he may be mocking bits of popular 'wisdom,' or, on the contrary, he may mean the opposite of what he says! This ironic tone underlies everything Qoheleth says to us, in my opinion."[21] Of one thing Ellul is certain. Qoheleth "makes visible all the blanks and gaps: the gap in our knowledge, the gap in social reality, and the gap of existence."[22] If this reading of the book is accurate, readers stand face to face with veiled truth. The reason: direct truth leads to despair.

Perhaps Qoheleth's indirect communication explains why one of the most perceptive interpreters of the book in the past generation vacillated when describing its fundamental themes. At one time Robert Gordis said that the two fundamental themes are the essential unknowability of the world and the divine imperative of joy.[23] Later in the same commentary, however, Gordis identified the two basic themes as the inevitability of death and the supreme duty to derive the most from life. As a result Gordis isolated three basic themes instead of two.[24]

While he may have been unable to settle on two themes for the book, Gordis could hardly contain his admiration for Qoheleth. Listen to his words of praise: "Whoever has dreamt great dreams in his youth and seen the vision flee, or has loved and lost, or has beaten bare-handed at the fortress of injustice and come back bleeding and broken, has passed Koheleth's door, and tarried beneath the shadow of his roof."[25] Again: "This cry of a sensitive spirit wounded by man's cruelty and ignorance, this distilled essence of an honest and courageous mind, striving to penetrate the secret of the universe, yet unwilling to soar on the wings of faith beyond the limits of the knowable, remains one of man's noblest offerings on the altar of truth."[26] Qoheleth seems to have been unable to reconcile his innate love of life and his awareness that corruption was eternal, inherent in the scheme of things. Even his love of life flowed from the tragic brevity of existence rather than from a world governed by a good God.

At the heart of Qoheleth's search was the meaning of life in a world from which God had withdrawn into the heavens. The similarities between him and modern existentialists, especially Albert Camus, are easily recognized. Qoheleth would probably have agreed with the following sentiment from Camus: "If the only significant history of human thought were to be written, it would have to be the history of its successive regrets and its impotencies."[27] The myth of Sisyphus is surely an apt description of the human condition; we are condemned to roll a boulder to the top of a mountain, only to have it return to its original position so we have to start the action once more. The task is endless and without profit, something Qoheleth underscored at the outset.

Qoheleth's search for meaning led him to advocate a kind of golden mean. His motto could be: "Nothing in excess." The story of Job's difficulties resulting from excessive righteousness undoubtedly influenced Qoheleth here. Another notable figure, this time from a wholly different cultural context, reached the same conclusion that Qoheleth did. After twenty-nine years of living in luxury, Gautama Buddha embarked on a search to understand suffering. The catalysts were four accidental observations of a sick person, a beggar, an old person, and a corpse. Deeply troubled by what he had seen, the Buddha tried wisdom first, drinking deeply from the fountain of gurus. Six years of asceticism followed, and then he turned inward and achieved enlightenment. He tried to eliminate the cause of suffering, which he took to be desire, and came to the conclusion that the middle way was the right one, neither too passionate nor too cold. Like Qoheleth, the Buddha was caught up in a paradox: in his case the desire to eliminate desire. Once again we come up against a fundamental truth: serious thought about life is always full of contradiction.

Returning to our starting point, we recall that the Nobel laureate gently chided Qoheleth for denying novelty. In *Pensées* Blaise Pascal modestly described his thoughts as rearranging traditional knowledge.[28] In other words, if there is nothing new under the sun, what is the intellectual person to do? One possibility is to restructure thought itself. In this way one can compile thoughts at odds with themselves. The irony is that this approach to the intellectual task allows one to be wholly honest, and human beings are inconsistent if they are anything. Time only multiplies their inconsistencies.

Sometimes even great thinkers are wrong. Consider Qoheleth's denial that anything is really new. Not everyone in ancient Israel thought that way. The prophets Jeremiah, Deutero-Isaiah, and Ezekiel envisioned things wholly new. In Jeremiah's case it was the establishment of a new covenant that required a new heart too (Jer 31:31). Ezekiel's promise of a new spirit and heart amounts to the same thing (Ezek 11:19; 18:31; 36:26), as does the new exodus in Deutero-Isaiah's comforting message (Isa 42:9; 43:19; 48:6). His successor, Trito-Isaiah, imagined a new name (Isa 62:2) and a new heaven and earth (Isa 65:17; 66:22), innovations planned by Yahweh—the special name by which Israel knew its God—for his people. Like these prophets, a few psalmists allowed newness to enter their imagination (Pss 33:3; 40:3; 96:1; 98:1; 144:9; 149:17).

Clearly prophets thought new things came into being. Did the wise also speak about something new? Rarely. The book of Proverbs has little interest in newness because of the power of tradition. Still the author of the book of Job referred to new wine bottles and a new bow (Job 29:20) and the second-century teacher Ben Sira compared a new friend to new wine, suggesting that real friendship takes time to reach its full potential, like wine (Sir 9:10). Nothing in wisdom literature about new things approaches the sublime assessment in Lam 3:23, which praises Yahweh's mercy as new every morning, so great is divine faithfulness.

Getting something wrong does not always condemn one to oblivion. Writers have been known to borrow Qoheleth's language, even when they had to explain it to readers. In *The Sun Also Rises,* Ernest Hemingway wrote an epigraph to inform readers that the reference is to the book of Ecclesiastes. Incidentally he added another epigraph to clarify the source of the sentence, "You are a lost generation," which he borrowed from Gertrude Stein. And literary critics have chosen a theme from Qoheleth, "vanity of vanities," to characterize the ingredients that inform the world's irony. Thus Morton Gurewitch observed "that the vanity of vanities that informs the world's irony is beyond liquidation."[29] In a sense irony is like human existence in that the end result is nothing. Wayne C. Booth wrote: "Since irony is essentially 'subtractive,' it always discounts something, and once it is turned into a spirit or concept and released upon the world, it becomes total irony that must discount itself, leaving . . . Nothing."[30] He added: "What could be more ironic than the making of statements about a world in which the making of statements is meaningless?"[31] And with that question, we have come to look Qoheleth in the face. Small wonder some writers view him as a champion of the absurd, while others think that he had a lover's quarrel with the world, to use the language of Robert Frost.

In this book I engage in a lover's quarrel with Qoheleth not unlike the brief one that took place in Stockholm in 1996. I begin by asking why the author chose the mask of royalty and the enigmatic name Qoheleth. This exploration into authorial conceit is followed by a discussion of literary gaps, the many inconsistences in the teachings attributed to this remarkable wise man. It asks: "Why did he clothe insights in contradictory statements?" I next take up the theme word and refrains that Qoheleth uses to express his fundamental understanding of reality, its existential absurdity. I go on to examine the epistemological inadequacy of basing conclusions on sight, to expose the power of tradition (Qoheleth's many assumptions that have no empirical basis) to show how the concept of time rules everything he says (in other words the finality of death), and treat Qoheleth's practical response to what he takes to be a meaningless world. Finally I reflect on the earliest attempts to counter his radical message. Were his teachings dangerous like those of the supreme ironist, Socrates? Who knows? Qoheleth might respond to our journey with an ironic wink.

Why "ironic"? Because he wants to challenge a reader to ponder the contradictions in his interpretation of reality while thinking the wink conveys the right answer to her or him alone, leaving others in the dark. Qoheleth's wink reminds one of a father or grandfather who weaves a fancy yarn to entertain a child, a story mixing truth and fiction, but in the telling winks occasionally as if to say "but you and I know the truth." One might say the story is wreathed in a cerebral smile.

If irony is, as Quintilian defined it, speech "in which something contrary to what is said is to be understood," or as described by Aristotle, "a pretense tending toward the underside of truth," the book of Ecclesiastes is steeped in irony. The problem is that irony lies in the eye of the beholder. In my view Qoheleth's irony is complex; what is said is and is not meant. I shall return to the notion of irony after introducing the persona of Qoheleth in more detail.

CHAPTER I

Authorial Deceit

E cclesiastes, the strangest book in the Bible,[1] introduces a speaker who twice identifies himself as Qoheleth and is referred to in the third person as Qoheleth five times. Because the book includes a superscription in the opening verse, two inclusios or thematic refrains, in 1:2 and 12:8 that summarize Qoheleth's views about life, and two epilogues that refer to Qoheleth in the final six verses, it is customary to refer to the book as Ecclesiastes and to the speaker behind its core, 1:3–12:7, as Qoheleth. The peculiar variation between first and third person is one of many mysteries in the book. Over the centuries, this extraordinary individual has been known by several names and descriptors.

The word *Ecclesiastes* is the Latinized form of the Greek *ekklesiastes* and comes from the translator of this festival scroll into Greek. At the time of the translation of the entire Hebrew Bible (the Old Testament)—conveniently referred to as the Septuagint because of a legendary story about seventy, or seventy-two, scholars from Jerusalem who were assigned the task of translating the sacred scriptures into Greek for the Jewish community in Alexandria, Egypt—the word *ekklesiastes* indicated a member of a citizens' assembly. Like the first translator of the book, most subsequent interpreters have endeavored to find an appropriate rendering of the Hebrew word *Qoheleth*. They have suggested four possibilities: "Assembler," "Gatherer," "Haranguer," and "Debater."

A fifth option, "Preacher," has found its way into various translations, for example the King James Version of 1611 and the modern Revised Standard Version. This understanding of the Greek *ekklesiastes* originated in the third century c.e. with the Church Father Gregory Thaumaturgos and lies behind Martin Luther's sixteenth-century translation "*Prediger,*" which has become standard in discussions of the book among German interpreters. Unlike the other four, it does not derive from the possible meanings of the Hebrew verb *qahal*.[2]

On the basis of an editorial identification of Qoheleth in 12:9 as a *hakam* ("professional wise man"),[3] some scholars view him as "Teacher." This is the choice of the translators of the New International Version and the Common English Bible. Others use the content of Qoheleth's teachings to characterize him, with varying results. Among other things, he has been described as "Skeptic," "Pessimist," "Hedonist," "Gentle Cynic," "Philosopher," and "Wise Man."

Many readers may sympathize with Qoheleth, for we too go by various forms of address over the years. In my own case, I have been called "Jimmy," "James," "Jim," "Son," "Spouse," "Dad," "Pastor," "Professor," "Doctor," "Little Brother," "Mr. C.," and on rare occasions something less acceptable than any of these. The variety of nomenclature indicates the passage of time and multiple relationships.

The word *Qoheleth* occurs seven times in the Bible, all in Ecclesiastes. In these seven uses, *Qoheleth* is either an appellative or a personal name. Its distribution seems carefully thought out. It occurs three times at the beginning (1:1, 2, and 12) and three times at the end (12:8, 9, and 10). The lone exception in 7:27 is roughly two-thirds of the way through the book and calls attention to the signal importance of the context for Qoheleth's fundamental attitude about life. Because Qoheleth has the definite article in this instance and in 12:8 ("the Qoheleth"), it may originally have been a title, like the word *hassatan* in the prologue of the book of Job and in Zech 3:1–2, which identifies the adversary by his function in service of the deity.[4] The Septuagint also has the article in 1:2; apparently the translator understood the word *Qoheleth* as a title rather than a personal name.

The seven uses of *Qoheleth* are as follows:

The words of Qoheleth, David's son, king in Jerusalem (1:1).[5]

"Utter futility," says Qoheleth, "Utter futility. Everything is futile" (1:2).

I am Qoheleth. I was king over Israel in Jerusalem (1:12).

"Look, I have found this," says the Qoheleth, [adding] one to one to find the sun (7:27).

"Utter futility," says the Qoheleth. "Everything is futile" (12:8).

In addition to Qoheleth's being a wise man, he continually taught the people knowledge (12:9).

Qoheleth sought to find pleasing words and wrote truthful words faithfully (12:10).

Etymologically *Qoheleth* connotes either assembling or gathering. The speaker's self-presentation in 1:12, either "I, Qoheleth, was king in Jerusalem over Israel" or "I am Qoheleth. I was king in Jerusalem over Israel," and the editorial identification of the author in 1:1 as "son of David, king in Jerusalem" can only refer to Solomon, unless "son" bears the extended sense of descendent. Beginning with Midrash Qoheleth Rabbah, scholars have taken a clue from the story in 1 Kings 8:1–5, 22 in which the verbal root *qhl* describes this king's assembling of the people for the purpose of dedicating the newly constructed temple. In this narrative, the verbal form of *qhl* carried both meanings, "to assemble" and "to gather." The story states that King Solomon assembled all the people and that they gathered before him. In addition his fame as wisest of kings in the east and author of many proverbs and songs (1 Kgs 4:29–33 [English, 4:32–34]) makes this king an obvious choice for the author's persona. A reputation as gatherer of more than a thousand wives and concubines lends subtle irony to an epithet for Solomon coined from a verbal root meaning "to gather," and "to assemble."

Within the Bible the verb *qahal* in its various modes is used only with *people* as subjects or objects. The description of Qoheleth in the first epilogue (12:9–12) may justify a wider understanding of the word *qahal* to include collections of proverbial sayings. Here he is characterized as a composer and arranger of maxims, and the resulting "masters of collections" are said to have been given by one shepherd. Who is this source of Qoheleth's wise sayings as envisioned by the author of this statement? Three possibilities have been suggested: Solomon, the shepherd of the people Israel; God as universal Shepherd; and any ordinary tender of sheep and goats.

The noun *Qoheleth* is always written with a feminine ending, although it is treated as masculine except in 7:27. In this instance the feminine verbal form is the result of mistaken division by the custodians of the sacred text during the period from the fifth to the tenth centuries of the Common Era.[6] The manuscripts with which these Masoretes worked had only consonants and consisted of continual script, there being no separation between words. The original indicator of the article that in Hebrew is attached to the beginning of a definite noun was in this case combined with the verb immediately preceding it. Thus *'mr hqhlt* became *'mrh qhlt*.

The usual verb form with Qoheleth as subject is construed as masculine (1:2; 12:9). In the latter verse, Qoheleth is identified as *ḥakam,* a wise man. It is therefore unlikely that the title is patterned after the feminine personification of wisdom (*ḥokmah*) and indicates the collections of wise sayings in this way. Although unusual, a feminine ending on a masculine name is attested elsewhere in the Bible. A certain Alemeth is listed among the sons of Becher in 1 Chron 7:8.

This linguistic phenomenon of a feminine ending attached to a masculine word has been explained on the basis of names for the sons belonging to servants of Solomon as listed in Ezra 2:55 and Neh 7:57 as well as Ezra 2:57 and Neh 7:59. Here we find the feminine ending *eth* on two personal names in a context that specifies males (*sopereth* and *pokereth hassabayim*). Presumably such usage originally indicated occupations, in these two cases a scribe and perhaps a leather worker (literally a binder of gazelles). Moreover, the word for a scribe, *sopereth,* appears both with and without the definite article, just like Qoheleth.

The philosopher Maimonides (1135–1204) came to be known by the cryptogram RMBM, RaMBam, short for Rabbi Moshe ben Maimon, and Rabbi Solomon ben Isaac (1040–1105) was called RSY (*Rashi*). Could Qoheleth have functioned in this manner? After all the medieval commentators Rashbam (Rabbi Samuel ben Meir, 1085–1155) and *Rashi* associated the name *Qoheleth* with the skeptic Agur in Prov 30:1, which they understood to mean "Gatherer" in Aramaic. In this vein Ernst Renan, the Frenchman who is said to have made the highly objectionable remark that Ecclesiastes is the only charming book ever written by a Jew, thought of Qoheleth as a cryptogram for Solomon. Neither he nor anyone else has been able to provide a credible solution to the hypothetical cryptogram QHLT. At least Patrick W. Skehan gave a plausible reading of the name of the father of Agur, Yaqeh, in Prov 30:1. Taking it as a cryptogram, Skehan explained *yqh* as "Yahweh is holy."[7]

Frank Zimmerman added a wrinkle to the theory that the mysterious name *Qoheleth* conceals a cryptogram.[8] Because Aramaic became the everyday language of the empire around the eighth or seventh century, Zimmerman concluded that the many *Aramaisms* in the book indicate that Aramaic was the original language in which Qoheleth taught. That assumption led Zimmerman to propose *knsh* ("Gatherer") as the author's name. How then did the name *Qoheleth* arise? Zimmerman observed that the total value of each of the two names, the first letter of the alphabet being equal to one, the second letter to two and so on, was exactly 375. He believed that the author considered himself an intellectual descendent of Israel's famous king, whose wisdom was said to be unrivaled in the East. Then, when the sages translated the book into Hebrew, instead of transliterating the name they searched for an equivalent. For Zimmerman, *Qoheleth* was the result.

So far I have assumed that the form *Qoheleth* is a participle, although a feminine *qal* (simple) participle of the verb is not attested elsewhere. Michael V. Fox, who knows more about Qoheleth than most scholars, has denied that such a form existed.[9] Instead he views Qoheleth as a nominal derivative of the noun *qahal* in the same way *boqer* ("herdsman") comes from *baqar* ("cattle") and *korem* ("vintner") comes from *keren* ("vineyard"). According to Fox, nouns derived from nouns mostly indicate occupations. They do not necessarily ring true, although they do in both these examples. If he is right, the etymology of *Qoheleth* may not offer a reliable clue about meaning, and interpreters are left in the dark about the precise significance of the enigmatic name *Qoheleth*.

There's More in a Name than Meets the Eye

Qoheleth's laconic self-introduction—"I am Qoheleth. I was king over Israel in Jerusalem"—in 1:12 calls to mind several other dramatic texts with similar semantic features. In Gen 27:19 Jacob responds to a question asked by his blind father, Isaac—"Are you my son, Esau?"—as follows, "I am." Having successfully disguised himself as his "macho" brother, he has managed to trick Isaac into blessing him. Esau's truthful cry "I am your son, your firstborn, Esau" in Gen 27:32 comes too late to repair the damage done by his greedy brother.

A second example of self-disclosure takes place in a foreign country to which brothers have come in search of food. The one who has the power over life and limb states simply, "I am Joseph" and then adds words that would send cold chills through anyone in similar circumstances ("whom you sold into Egypt," Gen 45:3–4).

Whereas Jacob's identification of himself as Esau was a ruse, Esau's was a desperate plea to correct a mistake, and Joseph's disclosure to his brothers was full of suspense, the third instance resembles Qoheleth's in that it both reveals and conceals at the same time. In it a reluctant Moses inquires about the true identity of the one, who according to Exod 3:6, has already said "I am the God of your father Abraham, the God of Isaac, and the God of Jacob." The answer Moses receives is highly ambiguous: *"'ehyeh 'asher 'ehyeh,"* (Exod 3:14). The three words can be translated several ways: "I am that I am"; "I am who I am"; "I shall be who I shall be"—and so forth.

The exact meaning of this clause is debatable. It may refer to the deity's power over nature, to eternal being in a philosophical sense, and to activity as creator of the universe. Its semantic meaning depends on whether the verb is construed as a form of "to blow," or "to be" and whether its mode is causative or simple *qal*. Whatever its semantic range, theologically the clause appears to promise that God will be present and sufficient for all Moses's needs.

The ambiguity of the divine name disclosed to Moses contrasts with many personal names in the Bible that convey a message. Names such as *Elijah* ("*Yah* is El"), *Elihu* ("He is my El"), *Samuel* ("El hears"), and *Daniel* ("El judges") indicate a relationship to the deity, while some names express dismay as in *Ichabod* ("Where is the glory?"), expose flaws in character as in *Nabal* ("Fool"), indicate brevity of existence as in *Abel* ("Breath"), and refer to emotional distress as in *Mara* ("Bitter") and *Lo' Ruhama* ("Not Loved"). Other names characterize the deity (*Elimelek,* "My El is king") and call attention to divine attributes such as power and compassion (*Shaddai,* "Mountain One" or "Breasts," like the Grand Tetons in Wyoming).

Even pen names have been known to carry messages. The Greek writer Hegesias was nicknamed *Peisithanatos,* "Commender of Suicide," presumably because his views approximated those of Sophocles, who in *Oedipus at Colonus* observed that suicide was the next best thing to being a stillborn. Such a negative assessment of human existence permeates the thinking of the modern existentialist philosopher Albert Camus, who considered suicide the only real philosophical issue for contemporaries. Ironically thinkers who commend suicide so enthusiastically seldom carry it out.

When we pause long enough to think about the consequences of Qoheleth's decision to introduce his work with "I am Qoheleth," one thing stands out. This little bit of information merely highlights the extent to which the real author remains unknown. We can only speculate about his age, marital status, geographical location, and so much more.

Anonymity in the Bible

If the author of Ecclesiastes had followed the usual practice in his day, this discussion of a name would not have been necessary. After all, the other books in the Hebrew Bible were written anonymously. Over the centuries names came to be associated with some of them. Moses was said to have composed the first five books, Genesis through Deuteronomy, except for the account of his death, which later rabbis attributed either to God or to Joshua.

Several names are associated with the book of Psalms, most notably David, but the list also includes Moses, Solomon, Asaph, Heman, Ethan, and unspecified descendants of Korah. As patron of the sages, King Solomon is credited with most of the collections in the book of Proverbs, although two foreigners, Agur and Lemuel's mother, are also named as sources of brief sayings. Solomon's name is also linked with Song of Songs, the deuterocanonical Wisdom of Solomon, and other noncanonical works such as "The Odes of Solomon" and "Psalms of Solomon."[10] In rabbinic tradition, he is said to have written Song of Songs in his youth, Proverbs in his mature years, and Ecclesiastes in his dotage.

The prophetic collections identify the individuals believed to be responsible for their content, but the actual compilers of the oral presentations are not known. In the case of the last prophetic book, Malachi, the name actually is taken from the prediction that God would send "my messenger," *malaki,* to clear the way for divine presence (Mal 3:1). Even if Isaiah 40–55, which interpreters call Deutero-Isaiah, were literary from the beginning rather than oral, we do not know the identity of the brilliant poet who composed the comforting promises there.

According to an observation in Prov 25:1, a group of scribes known as Hezekiah's men copied a collection of sayings associated with Solomon. This brief hint of editorial activity at the royal court confirms scholarly supposition that texts believed to be sacred were subjected to periodic "updates." It became mandatory to revise specific predictions that failed to materialize, such as that in Jer 25:11–12 and 29:10, which Dan 9:1–27 reinterprets. A problem had arisen because Jeremiah's prediction that the exile would last seventy years was known to be false. This new calculation and similar theological adjustments indicate a living tradition behind the formation of a canon of scripture. By this means competing ideologies came to be represented in tangible ways, even if often creating tension and outright contradictions in sacred lore.

Just as failed prophecies required subsequent adjustments, changing social contexts and different circumstances called for words more appropriate to the new historical situation. Harsh denunciations of prophets who lived before the fall of Jerusalem and exile to Babylon were softened for a people who had endured the wrath of conquerors. Here and there someone even issued an invitation that seems calculated to arouse intellectual curiosity, as in Hos 14:10: "Whoever is wise will understand these words and the discerning will know them, for the paths of Yahweh are straight, and the righteous will walk in them but sinners will stumble on them."

Wisdom's Divine Source

The author of Ecclesiastes did not choose to let his teachings stand on their own. Instead he presented them as the insights of Qoheleth. Why did he break with established precedent? To state it differently, what did the author have to gain by stepping out of the shadows and claiming authorship of the work?

After all, he could not expect to receive royalties for his literary achievement the way modern authors and songwriters do. Nor could he hope to receive a prestigious fellowship, promotion to a tenured professorship, or appointment to a distinguished chair at a university. He could not anticipate a huge following, like those of pastors of megachurches, or the massive contributions that inevitably come to those who convince the populace they are serving God and not Mammon. Nothing like a Pulitzer Prize was awarded for contributions to ancient Israel's intellectual community. So why did Qoheleth claim authorship?

He surely knew that wisdom was thought to derive from God, its true source. In Mesopotamia, seven primordial wise teachers, called *apkallu (ummanu* in Sumerian) were believed to have mediated divine wisdom to mortals.[11] According to this belief that wisdom originated outside the human intellect, genuine knowledge was impossible apart from revelation.[12]

If all wisdom comes from God, it follows that human knowledge on its own is incomplete. That point can hardly be made more effectively than in the exquisite poem in the twenty-eighth chapter of the book of Job.[13] Against the backdrop of a description of God-like human achievement, specifically the discovery of precious ore deep within earth, the poet inquires about the place of wisdom, a far more valuable prize than mere jewels. This search, in contrast to seeking gold and lapis lazuli, yields no victorious shout. Instead seekers must be content with rumor, a secondhand report from mythic Abaddon and Death. These mysterious creatures fare no better than humans in matters of the intellect, for the intrinsic nature of understanding is its hidden quality, like God. This insight did not escape Ben Sira, and to emphasize its obscurity, he made a play on one of the Hebrew words by which wisdom was known. According to Ben Sira, wisdom is like her name, concealed from most people.

Then who has access to wisdom? The composer of Job 28 attributed that honor to God alone. God not only governs the universe, this poet said, but like a master teacher, he sharpens the divine intellect. How? By keen observation, putting what is seen into words, establishing hypotheses, and testing them for accuracy.

Exactly what God does with this knowledge depends on how one interprets the final verse in the poem: "And He said to Adam, 'Look, the fear of the Lord is wisdom and turning from evil is understanding.'" At issue is not merely the authenticity of this verse and the word *'adam.* Does the Hebrew word refer to primal man in the Garden of Eden, or does it indicate the human race in general?[14] Furthermore how can wisdom be both off limits to people and easily accessible? Equating wisdom with piety makes it available to everyone who worships the Lord, thus bringing the poem into line with a refrain in the book of Proverbs: "The fear of Yahweh is the beginning of knowledge" (Prov 1:7a and 9:10a)—and with the later theologian Anselm's theory of knowledge as faith seeking understanding.

With that statement readers are thrust into the middle of an ancient debate over access to wisdom. Was wisdom acquired by the astute use of eyes and ears, or was it a gift from on high? For some the proper avenue to knowledge was the study of nature and human beings. Insights about the best way to conduct one's daily affairs were gleaned from examining the behavior of insects, birds, and animals; through analogy this information was applied to humans in a way that promoted well-being.

For others, however, such human effort inevitably came up short. They believed that the divine intellect graciously made itself available to mortals. To promote this belief, they invented a myth of a mysterious persona and gave it feminine characteristics, like absolute character traits in Hebrew such as Righteousness and Truth, which, according to a psalm, kiss one another. The origin of this myth of personified wisdom appears to have been in Egypt, where the goddess *Maat* was thought to have embodied understanding. Even if that supposition is correct, Israelite versions of this fascinating figure go their own way.[15]

Personification of Wisdom

To some degree the earliest speculation in this vein is the most venturesome (Prov 8:22–31). Wisdom is called the first of God's creative acts, and therefore a witness to the origin of the universe. Because ancient Near Eastern creation stories are fundamentally about cosmogony,[16] this description of wisdom places her in primordial times before the formation of earth and sky. Moreover it exudes a sense of wonder as order is established by the creator, one that is best described as a dance of joy in the divine presence. Unfortunately a crucial word, *'amon,* leaves itself open to different interpretations. Was wisdom a master of the craft of building who advised the creator on how to construct the world? Was she a darling little one (a lover? a child?) who took pleasure in the human race and the environment that God provided for it? Or does the word *'amon,* refer to God as master builder?

The immediate sequel to this poem about personified wisdom emphasizes her life-giving qualities. She does some building of her own, erecting a house with seven pillars, perhaps a subtle allusion to the seven *apkallu* of hallowed memory. Once her house is in place, she prepares a banquet and invites guests to dine with her. Just as the creator vied with the forces of chaos, wisdom competed with her opposite, folly, who used her sexual allure as a potent weapon. Her invitation to forbidden sex has lethal consequences.

This account of personified wisdom in Prov 8:22–31 and 9:1–6 universalizes knowledge. That is not true of Ben Sira's elaboration of the imagery from the book of Proverbs. This intriguing text, Sir 24:1–29, is the culmination of multiple references to personified wisdom in the book. The summation combines biblical allusions with motifs from Egypt, especially the praise of her own virtues and achievements by the goddess Isis. The first stanza, 24:3–7, refers to wisdom's self-praise, apparently in heaven, for she is said to be speaking in the assembly of the Most High. She claims to have originated in God's mouth, like the divine creative word in Genesis 1, and to have fallen gently to earth like the mist in Gen 1:2. Both of these ideas are also at home in Egyptian myths of creation. Wisdom's throne is thought to be in a pillar of cloud, probably an allusion to Exod 13:21–22, and her dominion extends to all peoples, among whom she has sought a resting place in vain. Similarities with the Egyptian myth of Isis probably indicate intellectual contact between Jewish and Egyptian sages.

Stanza two (verses 8–13) recognizes wisdom's subservience to God, who orders her to take up residence in Jerusalem. In this setting, she boasts of having been created in the beginning. Curiously she takes on a priestly role in the holy tent, an obvious allusion to the tabernacle in the wilderness. Only here is wisdom brought into the realm of the temple as opposed to the royal palace and the classroom, whether in a building or more likely in the open air.[17]

The third stanza in this poem (verses 13–17) introduces images from nature, likening wisdom to trees and vines. The emphasis falls on stateliness and sources of perfumes and incense used in the ritual of the temple in Jerusalem.

The insatiable thirst for knowledge then gives rise to what follows. Like Prov 9:1–6, wisdom invites her listeners to eat their fill of her sweets, just as the young female lover in Song of Songs invites her beau to taste the pleasures of her body. Wisdom informs those who respond positively to her invitation that their hunger and thirst will be endless. Those who eat and drink will always want more.

Ben Sira's particularizing of the personification of wisdom does not stop with the location in Jerusalem and allusions to biblical tradition. Instead he took an additional step when identifying her with a written text, the torah of Moses. Even more brazenly, Ben Sira also identified his own teachings as divinely revealed. The shift from poetry to prose when equating wisdom and the torah is every bit as unexpected as the claim itself. So is the additional reference to four rivers flowing from the garden of Eden, plus the Jordan and the Nile, and to the limited knowledge of Adam, which, Ben Sira thought, will be replicated by Adam's last descendent.

At least one author objected to the idea that wisdom has taken up residence among mortals. According to 1 Enoch 42:1–2, she made the journey from heaven to earth and searched for a suitable resting place without succeeding in that quest. In the end she is said to have returned to her place of departure, leaving human beings to their own devices. By remaining silent about personified wisdom, Qoheleth exhibited similar courage, daring to differ with colleagues who engaged in speculation about her origin and presence among humans.

The highly charged eroticism associated with personified wisdom, which was subject to objection in some circles, but not where Song of Songs circulated, is domesticated in the deuterocanonical Wisdom of Solomon. The author of this first-century composition, which reeks of Greek influence while giving a reading of events in the book of Exodus similar to *midrash*,[18] linked wisdom with Solomon as a loving bride for whom he has prayed. Surprisingly this author also introduced a foreign concept: wisdom as a pure hypostasis, an emanation of divine attributes.

A total of twenty-one epithets linking her to God make wisdom an extension of the divine being (Wis Sol 7:22–23). The influence of Greek philosophy on this description of the divine emanation is easily recognized, as is the summary of the full range of science and philosophy that she is said to have taught Solomon (7:17–22). In doing so, the book claims, she merely passed on to her husband what she learned from the fashioner of all things.

Perhaps the most amazing observation about wisdom derives from the Stoic idea of emanation, the divine logos. The author used five metaphors to make this point: the breath of God's power, a pure emanation of divine glory, a reflection of eternal light, a spotless mirror of the working of God, and an image of his goodness (7:25–26). From here it is but a short leap to the logos as found in the prologue to the Gospel of John.

Qoheleth would have none of this speculation. He believed that knowledge is a human enterprise. No divine mediator assists in the intellectual quest.

Pride of Authorship

A possible explanation for Qoheleth's radical departure from biblical precedent is his exposure to what has been called the Greek pride of authorship. By the beginning of the second century B.C.E., and probably under Greek influence, Ben Sira released his teachings under his own name, and other intellectual giants, such as Philo of Alexandria and Josephus, soon followed. Ben Sira's motive for self-disclosure appears to have been directed toward attracting students to his school, although the self-references throughout the book demonstrate a well-developed ego.

Qoheleth's huge ego has been recognized by interpreters,[19] partly on the basis of the prominence of self-references in the description of royal achievements but also because of the many first-person verbs describing his thought processes. In 2:4–9, which boasts of Qoheleth's royal accomplishments, "for myself" (Hebrew *li*) occurs nine times, and the first-person indicator affixed to a verb appears eleven times. The cumulative effect is almost comedic, if not satiric.

Clusters such as this, however, can be found elsewhere in the Bible without arousing suspicion of a heightened ego in the authors. In Ruth 1:20–21 *li* occurs five times,[20] and a variant *bi* once, while the first-person pronoun is used once, the affixed verbal form once, and the objective suffix "me" once: "She said, 'Please, Yahweh, do not call me Naomi; call me Mara, for Shaddai has treated me very bitterly. I left full but Yahweh brought me back empty. Why should you call me Naomi and Yahweh has afflicted me and Shaddai has harmed me?'" Similarly Jonah 4:2–3 has three first-person suffixes on verbs and six first-person possessive pronouns.[21] ("Praying to Yahweh, he said: 'Yahweh, was not this what I said back home? Therefore I fled in haste toward Tarshish, for I knew . . . and now, Yahweh, please take my life from me, for my death is better than my life.'") Job's talkative interlocutor, Elihu, fills such self-reference to capacity. In Job 33:1–8 "my" appears nine times, the independent pronoun "I" twice; the first-person suffix is used on two verbs, the objective "me" occurs three times, and the verbal prefix "I" can be found once. In Job 36:2–4, the first-person preformative occurs on three verbs, while three possessives ("my") and one *li* ("for me") also occur. ("Wait a little while so I can make known that there are yet words for Eloah. I'll express my views widely, ascribe justice to my maker. For my words are certainly truthful; one with full knowledge is with you.")

Still Qoheleth's nine uses of the particle *li* to indicate personal advantage ("for myself alone") are different from the expression of misery by Naomi and Jonah, and Elihu's self-congratulatory remarks can be explained as a young man's desperate attempts to gain a hearing from older men, who were thought to have been wiser because of wider experience.

Even earlier texts from Egypt, Ugarit, and Mesopotamia have the beginnings of pride in scribal accomplishments.[22] On completing a text, scribes frequently penned colophons in which they identified themselves and stated that they have rendered the text accurately.[23] "The Babylonian Theodicy" contains an acrostic that lists the name of its author and identifies him as devout despite his unorthodox views, some of which were perilously close to blasphemy.[24] The scribe Ilimalku from Ugarit reveals much about his own personal circumstances and the gradual decline of the city Ugarit.[25] One can hardly read this material without sensing the scribe's own feeling of importance in chronicling this history.

From Egypt the "Teachings for Duauf" contrast the profession of a scribe with "blue-collar" jobs and point out that scribes have no bosses and achieve immortality through the reading of their names. A later scribe from Israel, Ben Sira, seems to have been familiar with this text. There is, however, a significant difference. For all his elitism, he recognized the crucial contribution these workers make to society. To assure its superiority, the scribal profession in Egypt and probably to some degree in Israel practiced "managed scarcity" somewhat like doctors and lawyers of bygone days.[26]

More important, scribes in Egypt believed that they attained immortality through the constant reading of their names. Because people read aloud in antiquity, the pronunciation of one's name could be heard by others within earshot. When an afterlife was thought to have been broadened to include ordinary individuals,[27] scribes began to seek prestige and power in this life through access to society's elite.

Royal Testaments and Grave Inscriptions

Perhaps Qoheleth's decision to identify himself as the author of the book had nothing to do with pride but everything to do with the afterlife. Egyptian royal testaments and autobiographical grave inscriptions identify the authors, give specifics about qualities that make individuals worthy of a future life of bliss, and complain about an early death.[28]

The brief account of Qoheleth's royal experiment echoes these royal testaments, and the prominence of death throughout the book[29] recalls the attitude toward death in the autobiographical inscriptions. Could Qoheleth have been familiar with these two types of literature from Egypt?

Not long after Qoheleth was active, testamentary literature became popular in Jewish circles.[30] Testaments are attributed to Adam, Moses, Solomon, Job, the three patriarchs (Abraham, Isaac, and Jacob), and the twelve patriarchs (Jacob's sons). In these instances, only Solomon among the individuals who present their last will and testament to posterity claimed to be a king, as was customary in Egypt.

In Greco-Roman circles testaments were so popular that school texts include *Grunius Coriccota,* a comic testament of a pig destined for the slaughterhouse. The text lists the various parts of the hog bequeathed to those who will consume them: bacon to one, tongue to another, feet to someone else, and so on.

Even if Qoheleth drew inspiration from royal inscriptions, he did not let them dominate his thought. The royal experiment ends at 2:12: "Then I turned to consider wisdom and maddening folly, for what can the person do who comes after the king? What he has already done." Ten chapters follow, and in them Qoheleth speaks as a subject, no longer as king. Moreover, Qoheleth's comments about death lack the distinctive feature of Egyptian autobiographical inscriptions, which are presented as postmortem declarations, like the Greek epitaph with which this book begins. In other words the authors address readers from the realm of the dead. Qoheleth adopted a wholly different rhetorical strategy.

Authorial Tease

There is some evidence that Qoheleth engaged in an authorial tease—somewhat like modern authors who distance themselves from what they have written. For instance Vladimir Nabokov warned readers of his controversial novel *Lolita* that he is not identical with the narrator of the story. The "I" of the narrative is a fictional character. Unlike Nabokov and others who do not wish to be confused with the narrator of stories they have written, Qoheleth seems to have inserted his persona in places other than the frequent self-references in verbal refrains. Rather than keeping himself at a distance, Qoheleth relished close contact with readers.

Having reached a low point that led him to hate life, Qoheleth asked this question: "For who can eat and enjoy life apart from me?" (2:25). Just as puzzling is his answer to his own question in 8:1: "Who is like the wise man, and who knows the interpretation of a matter? A man's wisdom lights up his countenance, and his strong face is illumined." Quite unexpectedly, he answered, "I do." The correct meaning, its *pesher,* was known to Qoheleth, he insisted, and the implication is that no one else has this knowledge. It is not surprising that both these texts have baffled interpreters, and not just because of their lack of clarity.

Qoheleth seems to have realized that successful writing often has the allusiveness of riddles. Not only does it offer clues that can unlock its mystery, but its obscurity also teases readers with surprising traps and linguistic ciphers. It may be true that people cannot bear to hear the truth, and teachers have to conceal it in coded language, as Picasso informs Lev in *The Gift of Asher Lev,* a novel by Chaim Potok. Friedrich Nietzsche once observed that "the deepest and inexhaustible books will probably always have something of the aphoristic and unexpected character of Pascal's *Pensées.*"[31] Others, such as Ludwig Wittgenstein, place the emphasis elsewhere. According to Wittgenstein, "What can be said at all can be said clearly, and whereof one cannot speak thereof one must be silent." In the same vein, he said: "The limits of my language mean the limits of my world."[32]

Apocalyptic Texts

The inclination to attribute literary works to legendary figures spread beyond testamentary literature. Apocalyptic texts such as the book of Daniel employ this device frequently; they purport to come from ancient heroes reaching as far back as the origin of humankind. The secret lore they disclose to an eager public is thought to be validated by its origin in the minds of people such as Enoch, who was believed to have been one of the Mesopotamian wise men from primordial times, *apkallu*.[33] These texts claim to be revelation from an angel who mediates divine truth. Human agents such as Ezra, Daniel, Elijah, or Adam merely pass along what they have received.[34] The New Testament apocalypse, Revelation, is attributed to John, the beloved disciple whose memory goes all the way back to the time of Jesus.[35]

Because of the historical scope of this material, it was necessary to identify the transmitters of such information. The fiction that the data were acquired during a journey in the heavens required that the speaker be someone who was believed to have a grasp of universal history. The rise and fall of nations, the destiny of individuals, and the eventual outcome of the struggle between good and evil were hidden from ordinary people. Only favored individuals, whose virtue earned them access to divine secrets, so it was believed, qualified as authors of apocalyptic literature.

Qoheleth gave little indication of having immersed himself in this kind of thinking. The nearest he came to it is the poetic description in 12:1–7 of the demise of old people and the backdrop of a darkness that resembles chaos, but the routine of funeral processions brought on by the event does not support an apocalyptic interpretation of this poignant account. The life of survivors goes on as usual, despite the similarities with prophetic descriptions of the day of Yahweh's judgement.[35]

Qoheleth's attitude toward access to divine secrets can be gleaned from the rejection of every claim to have information about the future: "Then I saw all God's work—that a person is not able to fathom the work that is done under the sun, on account of which he works to seek, but will not discover, and even if a wise man claims to know, he is not able to find it" (8:17). This categorical denial that anyone can discover what God is doing at any given moment seems to be a direct attack against the emerging influence of apocalyptic thought. In Qoheleth's view divine activity takes place behind a veil of secrecy, and that veil is lifted for no one.

The Lure of Sacred Writing

Then could the desire to have his teachings considered canonical explain Qoheleth's decision to identify himself as author? Not much is known about the canonization process, not even the approximate dates for the five divisions of the Torah, prophets, and the book of Psalms. Perhaps the Torah was believed to be final by the time of Ezra and Nehemiah, roughly the fourth century B.C.E. The prophetic canon must have been finalized before Chronicles was written about the same time as Ezra and Nehemiah. The book of Daniel, a prophetic reading of events, in some ways similar to Ezekiel, was placed in the third division, presumably because the second division was thought to be closed.

The third division, which is variously called Psalms, "the other writings," and the *hagiographa,* seems to have been open until New Testament times, when conflict between the followers of Jesus and traditional Judaism led to different views about scripture and its contents. Christians adopted a more comprehensive view of the canon, which allowed for the acceptance of the Septuagint as inspired, whereas Judaism limited the canon to the twenty-two books in the *Tanak*.[36]

Two things mitigate against the hypothesis that Qoheleth identified himself for the purpose of achieving canonical status for his teachings. First he quickly abandoned the fiction of Solomonic authorship. His reasons for doing so can be readily appreciated, for the disparity between his views and those presented as Solomon's in the book of Proverbs is huge. Second the self-identification is confusing, for it introduces the name *Qoheleth* along with the claim that he is a son of David, king in Jerusalem. No person named Qoheleth ever sat on the throne in Jerusalem.

Ethos

The most convincing reason for Qoheleth's self-identification is the result of his constant references to his personal experience. Qoheleth must surely have realized that these claims would mean nothing in a Hellenistic world without a validating identity with whom they could be associated. The issue is what Greek rhetoricians called "ethos." Teachings were believed to be true because the person behind them had integrity. A teacher's trustworthiness naturally extended to any observations about life.

Still this explanation for self-disclosure falters because the name *Qoheleth* hides more than it reveals. The name complicates matters in that its authorial deceit nullifies the reference to royal authorship and serves as a tease for readers of this extraordinary treatise. With it one encounters something akin to an author's ironic wink.[37] What, then, can we make of the many contradictions in the book? Did Qoheleth intentionally veil truth?

CHAPTER 2

Veiled Truth?

With the name *Qoheleth* raising more questions than it answers, a conscious rhetorical strategy of elusiveness may be at work. To be convincing, the author's deliberate personalizing of his insights required the exposure of his identity while their unorthodox nature demanded an element of subterfuge. For this reason the teacher laid claim to two altogether different identities. He said he was a ruler known to one and all, but he was also an unknown individual (at least to us), who called himself "Qoheleth."

His teachings are twice encoded in an inclusion that indicates a superlative. "'Utter futility,' they teach, 'utter futility. Everything is futile'" (1:2 and a shorter version in 12:8). In the same way that the Hebrew title of the exotic scroll Song of Songs and the expression "holy of holies" mean "the very best song" and "the holiest one of all," *habal habalim,* which I have translated as "utter futility," connotes the supreme emptiness. The "most" of nothing adds up to zero, and Qoheleth thought everything under the sun falls into that assessment of things. However one looks at it, the use of a superlative to signify nothing is hugely ironic.

Indeed, in one of the most perplexing observations in Ecclesiastes, a unit about the danger posed by (a particular kind of?) woman (7:26–29), it is said that Qoheleth's manner of finding the sum of things consisted of placing individual items alongside one another in the way an accountant does (literally, "one to one to find the total"). The text goes on to have Qoheleth confess personal failure in this endeavor despite sustained seeking: "That which I sought continually I did not find; one man in a thousand I found, but a woman in all these I did not find"(7:28). The abrupt shift from third to first person merely continues the simultaneous disclosure and concealment. Who speaks here? Someone other than Qoheleth initially, followed by personal observations from Qoheleth? And why the uncertainty?[1]

In the Bible speakers use language that hides their real intent for several reasons. Sometimes the nature of what they say places them in harm's way. Consequently they must maximize the deceit or pay the ultimate price of their lives. Perhaps the best example of this type of concealment is provided by the prophet Nathan, who had the dangerous task of pointing an accusing finger at David after the king's adulterous affair with Bathsheba and the royal mandate that resulted in the murder of her husband, Uriah, in an attempt to cover up David's abuse of power.[2]

Nathan's clever choice of a judicial parable enabled him to expose the king's wrongdoing while ostensibly describing an unnamed rich man's seizure of a poor person's pet lamb to feed his own guest. David's fury issued in condemnation of the offender, and only then did Nathan utter the incriminating words: "You are the man" (2 Sam 12:7).

A second example depends on royal compassion rather than anger. For raping Tamar, his half-sister, Amnon was slain by their brother Absalom. The father of all three, King David, banished Absalom for avenging Tamar's lost honor but grieved over his son's absence. Joab, the commander in chief of David's militia, devised a scheme to convince the king to rescind the banishment and return the favorite son to the royal court. Enlisting the help of a gifted actress[3] from the village of Tekoa, the hometown of the prophet Amos, Joab instructed her on what to say.

Pretending to be in mourning, she wove a heart-rending story about one of her two sons killing the other in a fight and the clan demanding that the surviving brother be put to death to avenge the murder, thus leaving her without offspring. A sympathetic David pardoned the imaginary killer and was deftly led to see that his treatment of Absalom had left a rift in the royal family.

The plan worked, just as Joab had hoped, but David resented being manipulated, and he suspected that Joab was behind the confrontation. Even after Absalom returned to Jerusalem, he was kept at some distance from his father, with dreadful consequences (2 Sam 14:1–24). That lack of personal contact resulted in an abortive attempt by Absalom to overthrow David, the reigning king.

A third example of veiled language involves one of David's advisers, who remained loyal to the king when Absalom sought to usurp the throne from his father. This counselor, Hushai, faced a difficult task when his colleague Ahithophel threw his considerable weight behind the rebel son. In those days, so the narrator says, Ahithophel's counsel was reputed to have been equivalent to inquiring into a divine oracle: "Now the advice of Ahithophel that he dispensed in those days was just as if one sought counsel from God" (2 Sam 16:23b).

Pretending to have turned against David also, Hushai used his inimitable eloquence to persuade Absalom to delay the attack on his father. Hushai spoke of summoning all Israel from the northern and southern extremes, falling on David like dew, and using ropes to drag a city (in which David had taken refuge) into a valley so that not a single piece of it could be found. More important, he used the first-person plural, "we," to assure Absalom that he could count on the one offering this advice to assist in its implementation.

The "grand" language touched Absalom so deeply that he chose to ignore Ahithophel's sound advice to act quickly before David had time to gather his troops and plan his defensive strategy. Hushai's hidden agenda and duplicitous language were far more than a rhetorical ruse. They saved his life and that of the king.

These three examples are exceptional in that they involve interaction with a ruler. Qoheleth recognized that those who serve kings may incur their wrath (8:2–4;

10:14), and he advised against fleeing in these circumstances, for the long arm of the militia could easily reach anyone who abandoned his post and went on the run. This bit of advice may be a set piece from an era when the southern kingdom of Judah had a local sovereign. In Qoheleth's time the supreme monarch lived in either Syria or Egypt, and Qoheleth's hearers had no close contact with him. Obviously Qoheleth's evasiveness was not generated by anxiety over inciting the fury of a ruler.

Internal Quotations

Is there a possible explanation for the way he seems to have grasped both horns of a dilemma? Several suggestions have been made to explain the opposing statement. One of the earliest and most persistent explanations is that Qoheleth cited the opinions of others with whom he took issue.[4] This way of explaining the different views in the book relies on a theory of genre, specifically that Ecclesiastes consists of a dialogue between a skeptic and a traditional sage. Emphasizing its dialogic nature, Theodore Perry inserted clarifying additions to identify different speakers in his translation of Qoheleth's sayings,[5] just as some interpreters posit them in Song of Songs as if it were a drama comprising speeches by two lovers.[6] In Song of Songs changes in the gender of speakers makes the dramatic interpretation plausible.

This theory of an imaginary opponent whose views are introduced only to be rejected has been subjected to extensive analysis.[7] The main problem with it is the absence of any linguistic markers for citations, leaving scholars with nothing but their own judgment about which statement among contradictory ones represents Qoheleth's own belief. That decision is not necessary in 8:17, where Qoheleth set his opinion over against that of someone else, for the syntax clearly indicates that Qoheleth questioned this confident sage's ability to fathom the wide range of activity taking place on earth. In short Qoheleth definitely knew how to distinguish his own view from that of a rival with whom he took issue.

Moreover he could easily have availed himself of traditional ways of indicating direct speech by another person. When a speaker is quoting someone else in Hebrew, the word *le'mor* ordinarily introduces it, as in Amos 7:10: "Then Amaziah the priest of Bethel sent to Israel's king Jeroboam, *saying:* 'Amos has conspired against you in the midst of Bethel; the land cannot bear all his words.'" Alternatively a formula for a direct quotation may be used, as in the immediate sequel to this verse: "For thus said Amos, 'Jeroboam will die by the sword and Israel will surely go into exile from its land'" (Amos 7:11).

Deconstruction of Ideas

A variant of the quotation hypothesis comes from contemporary literary theory. According to this interpretation, championed by Thomas Krüger in the influential Hermeneia commentary series, Qoheleth introduced an idea that he then proceeded to deconstruct.[8] The actual source of the problematic concept is unclear. It could have originated in his own mind, or it could have derived from someone else. In any event, according to this understanding of Qoheleth's teachings, original insights are held up for close inspection and their flaws exposed. In each instance the result is a revised interpretation that Qoheleth put forth as his reasoned conclusion. The sequence is thus one of orientation, disorientation, and reorientation.

This approach to the contradictions in Ecclesiastes applies both to opposing statements alongside one another and to differences that are located at some distance from each other. In this way earlier comments are said to be deconstructed in later chapters of the book, thus indicating Qoheleth's own development as a thinker.[9] In this view, for instance, his initial hatred of life eventually gave way to an enthusiastic endorsement of youthful pleasures. Qoheleth's final words, a grim description of old age and death, however, call into question such a positive reading of the book.

Editorial Additions

With the dawn of a critical approach to the Bible, the hypothesis of extensive quotations gave way to one about editorial activity.[10] Scholars thought they were able to detect sources underlying the present biblical text, especially in the first five books. Success in this endeavor led to its application to the rest of the Bible, with editorial glosses being isolated in prophetic books too. Julius Wellhausen's classic reaction to the juxtaposition of what he called "blood and roses" in the book of Amos illustrates the problem. Would a prophet whose message was overwhelmingly threatening have added the abrupt utopian ending ("In those days I will raise up the fallen booth of David; I will repair its breaches, raise up its ruins, rebuild it as formerly. . . . I will plant them on their land so they will never be uprooted from the land I have given them. Yahweh has spoken," 9:11–15)? Or would Hosea have envisioned the sudden reversal of divine intention for the Ephramite kingdom that makes chapter 2 so difficult to comprehend? On the assumption of a single author, how can anyone make sense of the promise of wholesale destruction in 2:1–13 and complete restoration in 2:14–23? What an odd combination. "I will slay her with thirst" and "I will speak tenderly to her." It seems much more likely that biblical texts were a living tradition, one that changed as historical circumstances did.

This evidence of editorial activity is paralleled in classic texts from the ancient Near East. Perhaps the best example is the Gilgamesh Epic, which Jeffrey Tigay has shown to have been extensively reworked over centuries.[11] In light of editorial activity in the Bible and in parallel sources, it is certainly possible that a work as controversial as Ecclesiastes would have been subjected to editorial glosses. That conclusion seems inevitable when one takes into account the two epilogues that refer to Qoheleth in the third person.

Once we have acknowledged the probability that Ecclesiastes has been subjected to editing, we confront a larger problem than that raised by the hypothesis of citations. What sets the editorial additions apart from their context? Early claims that nearly half the book comes from people other than Qoheleth have fallen by the wayside, and recent interpreters seldom list more than three or four glosses besides the epilogues and possible thematic statements.[12] The reasons for this sea change are more substantial than a conservative trend in contemporary scholarship.

At least four difficulties are said to beset a theory of editorial additions.[13] First there are linguistic links between the hypothetical glosses and Qoheleth's own views. That objection loses force when one recognizes that skilled editors can choose grammar, syntax, and vocabulary that replicate the linguistic use of the person they are trying to correct. Second the glosses also fail to remove contradictions. This criticism rests on an unprovable assumption that the editor intended to remove all disparities in the book and not just the most glaring ones. Third skepticism remains despite the glosses. This objection is persuasive only if one thinks the purpose of the editorial additions was to eradicate rather than tone down Qoheleth's fundamental intellectual approach to the world. Fourth the inconsistency lingers despite the supposed changes. Like the third objection, this argument works only if one believes that editors tried to make Qoheleth's teachings consistent. Ancient writers may have been more interested in presenting various sides of an issue than in consistency. The different views of creation in Genesis 1–2 demonstrate a preference for comprehensiveness. Scribes accustomed to such wide-ranging approaches to complex topics are probably the same people who would have added editorial comments to books such as Ecclesiastes.

Yes/But: A Stylistic Device

The influential commentary by Kurt Galling explains the contradictions as a stylistic device best signified by the expression *Zwar/Aber Aussage* ("Yes/but saying").[14] In other words Galling interpreted the opposing statements as Qoheleth's way of recognizing some truth in both of them. The physicist Niels Bohr once observed, "One of the favorite maxims of my father was the distinction between the two sorts of truths, profound truths recognized by the fact that the opposite is also a profound truth, in contrast to trivialities where opposites are obviously absurd."[15] For the moment two examples suffice. On the one hand, Qoheleth said that back-breaking labor is a waste of time because it does not bring lasting benefit. On the other hand, he conceded, hard work earns wages that enable people to survive. More perplexing are Qoheleth's comments about divine judgment, which amount to a denial that it exists and an affirmation that it takes place.

This rhetorical strategy amounts to a twofold response to activity. It assesses things both positively and negatively, reminding everyone that a simple "yes" or "no" does not adequately evaluate complex circumstances. While wisdom may be better than folly, because intelligence helps an individual avoid many of life's pitfalls, the same fate comes to one and all, canceling the supposed benefits of knowledge. In this way the initial "yes" is corrected by the "no" that follows. To state things differently, an adversative "but" follows the affirmation, and nothing is actually what it appears to be. Intelligence may be superior to weapons of war, but one evil person can bring devastation. Knowledge, Qoheleth recognized, can be put to destructive use.

Perhaps the most arresting instance of ambivalent advice concerns the place of pleasure in life. Qoheleth shifted to the imperative mode when urging young men to follow their desires but to keep in mind the fact that they will eventually be judged in the divine court. Qoheleth's language expresses the deep desires embedded within the subconscious as well as the ephemeral lust that the eyes bring to bear on decision making. Furthermore, by using this exact language about desires of the heart and following one's eyes, Qoheleth branded himself a sinner in the judgment of those for whom Num 15:39 was authoritative.

A Diary

Another explanation for the conflicting observations in Ecclesiastes has its basis in genre. What if the book consists of random statements gathered in a diary and compiled over a lifetime? As the years go by and historical circumstances change, one's attitudes are affected by any number of things. The countless entries in Blaise Pascal's *Pensées* are a case in point. Individuals who possess exceptional minds refuse to simplify complicated problems, and honesty compels those who are blessed with extraordinary intelligence to accept partial insights. The philosopher Alfred North Whitehead recognized this truth when writing: "There are no whole truths; all truths are half-truths. It is trying to treat them as whole truths that plays the devil."[16]

The elapse of time between observations goes a long way in explaining contradictory statements. The vast differences, both in terms of style and content, between the first part of Wolfgang von Goethe's *Faust* and the second part are to some degree influenced by the five decades separating their composition. Other reasons for these differences may have been primary, especially Goethe's desire to distinguish the Hebraic perspective on the problem of evil from the Hellenistic, but the poet's own intellectual development over the years is most certainly reflected in the differences between the two parts of the work.

Striving for Universality

Yet another reason for the contradictions in Ecclesiastes is the author's striving for universality.[17] The use of *ḳol* ("everything") in Qoheleth's assessment of reality as *hebel,* which I have provisionally translated by "futile," required him to consider things from various points of view. How could he judge work to be a waste of effort in the long run without recognizing that it had some temporary benefits? It therefore follows that opposing sentiments may be an indication that Qoheleth wanted to present a complete picture rather than emphasizing only one side of an issue.

We have already seen how he set individual items alongside the sum of the parts. The language is highly suggestive, for it refers to the task of calculating the total on the basis of all the single items that can be brought together. Despite his effort, however, Qoheleth admitted that he failed in this quest ("which I continually sought but did not discover," 7:28a). His failure was not total, for he claimed to have found only one thing, "that God made humans upright but they have sought out numerous contrivances" (7:29). The use of a word resembling that for the sum in verse 27 has been variously translated but seems to suggest "schemes" or "implements of aggression."

Complicating this interpretation of Qoheleth's thought is a partial corrective to the admission of failure in 7:27. He went on to say: "One man in a thousand I have found, but a woman in all these I have not found" (7:28b). A low opinion of mortals can be found elsewhere in the Bible—"Most perverse—the mind, and twisted is it, who can grasp it"? (Jer 17:9); "They are corrupt and abominable; no one does the good" (Ps 14:1b)—but the misogyny is unmatched. Does it accurately reflect Qoheleth's view?[18]

Such a harsh judgment does not harmonize with his encouragement to "enjoy life with the woman you love." For this reason, among others, several recent interpreters have taken the statement as a popular saying that Qoheleth cited because it was contrary to his own view. In other words he was unable to confirm the negative evaluation of women and the slightly more favorable one of men. What did he discover? That all human beings have changed from good to bad.

Uncertainty Owing to an Irrational Universe

What if Qoheleth were ambivalent in assessing things as either good or bad? In that case uncertainty would have given rise to tenuous conclusions and perhaps even to contrasting opinions on a given topic. Qoheleth does not appear to have lacked confidence in his ability to judge things, for he made absolutist statements again and again, including: "There is nothing new under the sun" (1:9b). Still he acknowledged limits imposed on the intellect by God, which necessitate humble recognition that some things will always remain a mystery (3:11), at least to human beings. Like Socrates, he could say "I know that I know nothing."

The main reason for the hidden aspects of reality is the absence of rationality in the universe. Because simple logic often fails, things are largely unpredictable. Qoheleth described events as they took place, whether random or organized. Not until Ben Sira did the Stoic idea of a rational universe, the divine logos, appear in a Hebraic work. According to this view, the world is perfectly balanced with positive reinforcement for good conduct and appropriate punishment for wicked behavior. Harmony, that is, prevails throughout the universe, which is governed by the divine intellect itself.[19]

For Qoheleth, however, the logical and therefore expected results of various activities did not always materialize. The race is not invariably won by the fastest runner, and the victory does not come to the stronger militia in every instance. Why? Chance is an uncontrollable factor in all circumstances. The fastest runner may stumble and fall, and the weaker foe may outmaneuver the stronger one. In short every human activity is subject to something that Qoheleth called *miqreh,* "accidental occurrence, chance, happenstance." Even the brilliant are victimized in this way, and their natural expectation of receiving food, wealth, and favor may be met with disappointment, according to 9:11: "Again I perceived under the sun that the race is not to the swift, nor the battle to the strong, nor yet bread to the wise, and riches to the astute, nor favor to the informed, for time and mischance meet them all."[20]

A Narrative Frame

Michael Fox has studied all the preceding explanations for the contradictions in Ecclesiastes and judged them to be inadequate. Therefore he has offered a fresh approach to the problem by redefining the book's genre.[21] In essence Fox thinks a narrator frames Qoheleth's teaching in a way that subjects them to the correction found in the so-called epilogues. He uses Joel Chandler Harris's *The Tales of Uncle Remus* as a modern example of a framing narrator who presents the views of each character as other than his own. More important, Fox appeals to ancient Near Eastern texts—"The Instruction of Kagemni," "The Prophecy of Neferti, "The Complaint of Ipuwer," "Anksheshonky," and "The Tale of an Eloquent Peasant"—in which a speaker is framed within an introductory and a concluding narrative. In this way unorthodox teachings are aired and the narrator is kept at a safe distance from them.

Moreover Fox thinks Qoheleth was reflecting on his past experience, which means that some of the teachings are twice removed from the final form of the book. That is, Qoheleth reflected on his earlier insights and the narrator, one step further removed from Qoheleth, subjected his radical views to the traditional norms of fearing God and keeping divine commandments. In this way Qoheleth's dangerous teachings are robbed of their appeal to young students.

This approach to the book has been endorsed by other critics,[22] largely because it allows them to avoid the theory of editorial additions. In the end, however, even Fox has to reckon with the probability of an editorial supplement, specifically the second epilogue.[23] Is there a better explanation for the contradictions than that of a narrative framework?

A Rhetorical Strategy Suggesting Hebel

I think there is. Qoheleth employed a rhetorical strategy that illustrates the utter futility of attaining definitive knowledge. He seems to have considered life's complexities beyond logical resolution. In his internal debate, he argued both sides passionately, for in the end he could not choose one over the other. Honesty compelled him to be inconsistent. Quite simply, he said, there is no profit, but wisdom benefits those who see the sun (7:11); everything is *hebel,* but some things bring pleasure; seeking wisdom is feeding on the wind, but wisdom is better than folly; wisdom illuminates a dark path, but a little folly weighs more than wisdom and honor; a similar fate comes to everyone, but God has set a time for judgment; pleasure accomplishes nothing, but life should be enjoyed during youth; toil is futile, but it provides wealth.

Like the author of a Babylonian text conveniently labeled "A Pessimistic Dialogue between a Master and a Slave,"[24] Qoheleth recognized that something positive and something negative could be said about most decisions an individual makes.

The Babylonian text makes this idea perfectly clear. Driving a chariot to the palace can be both exhilarating and dangerous; dining can be both intellectually stimulating, like Greek symposia, and conducive to indigestion; riding in the open country can yield wild game for the table, but it puts the hunter at risk; having children is a decision that brings much joy, but it also breaks up the family of one's parents; setting out on a path of unlawful conduct can produce wealth, but it may result in capital punishment; loving a woman gives pleasure, but it can be hazardous; sacrificing to one's god puts the deity in one's debt, but refusing to feed the gods will make them follow you around like a dog looking for a bone; lending grain to someone has the promise of profit, but collecting what is owed is a nightmare; becoming a philanthropist raises one's stature in others' eyes, but death cancels any benefit from generosity.

Because the arguments on each side of these activities seem to carry equal weight, the author's conclusion is almost inevitable. "What is good?" the poet asks, and has the master respond: "To have our necks broken and be thrown in the river." Why? Because no one can transcend the limits imposed on humans; that is, no one can reach the heavens or encompass the underworld.[25] Then what should be done? The first idea is to eliminate the source of dialogue, but the poet realizes that it will not work, for the master cannot survive three days on his own. So the obliging servant, the proverbial "yes man," is given the last word, and interpreters are divided about the true nature of the debate, whether comedy or satire.[26]

This ancient text fascinates me for reasons other than its literary power. As a sophomore in college, I debated the grand national champions of 1953 and 1954. The topic for 1954 was this: Resolved that the United States should institute a policy of free trade with China. (How hugely ironic that subject appears today in light of the disparity in exports between the two countries.) As every debater knows, one must be prepared to argue for either the affirmative or the negative with equal passion and with clarity regardless of personal views. Even as a novice, I realized that a simple "yes" or "no" was not an adequate response to such a complicated topic.

Qoheleth's contradictory observations may be the result of internal debate, one that is signaled by his repeated revelation that he considered the relative merits of a matter (literally, "I said to my heart").[27] It is difficult to imagine a more effective means of conveying the futility of existence than by contradicting one's own conclusions. Whether intentional or not, this rhetorical strategy highlights the absurdity and futility of everything under the sun.

Having examined several possible reasons for contradictions in Ecclesiastes and proposing that the opposing statements may be a conscious rhetorical strategy to express Qoheleth's internal debate, I have suggested that presenting opposite views in this way nicely illustrates the utter futility of existence itself. While my explanation for the presence of contradictions in some ways resembles the "yes/but" approach, it differs in that the emphasis falls on the unreliability of both alternatives, the "yes" and the "but." The reason: everything is *hebel.* I now turn to the task of determining the contextual meaning of Qoheleth's favorite word, *hebel,* as well as to the expressions *re'ut ruah* and *ra'yon ruah.* By using this vocabulary, does Qoheleth press the notion of concealment even further? Just how elusive does he think the essence of reality may be?

CHAPTER 3

Elusive Essence

Why did Qoheleth chose to place a veil over his teachings by reaching contradictory conclusions about so many things? Despite the various answers offered by various interpreters, the real reason for the many contradictions within the book seems most likely to be Qoheleth's decision to employ a rhetorical strategy that highlights the utter futility of all knowledge. He sought to convey the conviction that the intellect, like everything else, is *hebel,* a word used thirty-nine times in Ecclesiastes.[1] In this chapter I shall explore the rich nuances of this word in Qoheleth's discourse against the backdrop of its use in the rest of the Bible. *Hebel* has three basic senses: brevity, sickness, and insubstantiality.[2]

We do not need to read far in the canon before encountering the first use of the word. It belongs to the victim of a brother's jealousy, the ill-fated Abel in Gen 4:2–10. Angry at what he perceived to be an instance of divine partiality, the acceptance of a sacrifice brought by Abel and rejection of his own, Cain rose up against his brother and killed him. The text identifies Abel as a shepherd (*ro'eh*) and Cain as a worker (*'obed*) of the soil. Two features of this story resonate with linguistic practice in Ecclesiastes. The name *Abel* (*hebel*) is synonymous with transience. Its basic etymology is a breath or vapor, something as light as mist or smoke, the most ephemeral of things, the waste product of breathing. Furthermore Abel's occupation involved shepherding (*ro'eh*).

A Theme Word and a Refrain

Both *hebel* as "brevity" and the word that indicates shepherding (*re'ut* or a variant *ra'yon*) occur in Ecclesiastes. Perhaps the most convincing instance of transience in the book is found in 11:10: "Remove worry from your mind and banish harm from your body, for youth and black hair [a metaphor for dawn?] are fleeting." Ephemerality also appears to be the point in 9:9, where the expression "all the days of your brief life" occurs twice. It can be argued, however, that Qoheleth urged listeners to enjoy life with the women they love during all the empty or meaningless days God has bestowed on them. With that suggestion, we have moved beyond the sense of *hebel* in the tale of human origins.

Returning to the Hebrew noun for Abel's occupation, we note that Qoheleth employed a form of it in two refrains. The dominant one, *re'ut ruah,* occurs seven times, the variant twice. For now I leave the crucial words untranslated but note that the object of *re'ut* is the wind:

1:14 "I observed every work that is done under the sun; everything is *hebel* and *re'ut ruah.*"

2:11 "Then I turned to all my work that my hands had done, and to the wealth I labored to acquire; and everything was *hebel* and *re'ut ruah,* and there was no gain under the sun."

2:17 "So I hated life, for the work that was done under the sun was grievous to me because everything was *hebel and re'ut ruah.*"

2:26 "For to the one who pleases him he [God] gives wisdom, knowledge, and happiness but to the sinner he gives the bother of gathering and amassing to bestow on the one God favors. This also is *hebel* and *re'ut ruah.*"

4:4 "I saw all the toil and all skilful activity—that it was one person's envy of another. This, too, is *hebel* and *re'ut ruah.*"

4:6 "Better is a hand full of rest than two hands full of toil and *re'ut ruah.*"

6:9 "Better is the sight of the eyes than the roving of desire; all this is *hebel* and *re'ut ruah.*"

1:17 "So I determined to know wisdom and knowledge, madness and folly; I understood that all this is *ra'yon ruah.*"

4:16 "There was no end to all the people, to all who were before him, moreover, those who come later will not rejoice in him; surely this also is *hebel* and *ra'yon ruah.*"

In every instance but two, a combination occurs and *hebel* comes first with either *re'ut ruah* or *ra'yon* completing the thought. The exceptions, in 1:17 and 4:6, have the two expressions but lack the initial *hebel.* In a single case the verb for toiling (*'amal*) occurs with *ruah* as a description of human activity. "This is also a serious injustice; exactly as he came so shall he go, and what profit does he have that he toils for the wind?"

For Qoheleth economic surplus was fundamental when trying to evaluate life. The question "what does a person profit from all his toil at which he labors under the sun?" stands alongside the thematic refrain in 1:2 describing everything by the superlative of *hebel.* Qoheleth answered the question about the profit in 2:11, after declaring that everything was *hebel* and *re'ut ruah.* In short he concluded that "there was no profit under the sun." He contradicted that judgment, nevertheless, when insisting that knowledge is profitable because it bestows life on those who hold it (7:12) and that a field is an advantage under certain conditions, although just what these advantages are remains a matter of dispute (5:8).

Do the phrase *re'ut ruah* and its variant throw light on the meaning of *hebel* for Qoheleth? The combination refers to some kind of activity directed at the wind, either chasing after or feeding on something as insubstantial as the wind. The verb *ra'ah* can refer to each of these: the act of deriving nurture from something, the care of sheep that allows them to find adequate food, and the internal drive that makes someone strive for a goal.[3] The object of this activity, the wind, complicates matters. Did Qoheleth describe the futile attempt to herd the restless wind, the equally unsatisfactory effort to feed on air, or the mere desire that leads to striving after an invisible yet very present reality? Even more baffling is the fact that *ruah* also means "the spirit," a sense that does not seem apt in this phrase with the verb *ra'ah*.

Two texts outside Ecclesiastes muddy the waters. In Hos 12:2 we read that Ephraim did something to the wind involving the verb *ra'ah*. The parallel stich carries the image further by adding "and chases after the east wind." In synonymous parallelism the thought seems to be consistent, and one must translate the first participial phrase by "tends the wind." In other words Judah's rival, the northern state, is occupied with a futile task of shepherding wayward people.

A different sense of *ra'ah* appears to occur in Prov 15:14, which describes fools as feeding on folly. Here too, however, the parallel stich may permit a different reading of *ra'ah*, for it refers to the mind's pursuit of knowledge. In context the sequel can mean that fools strive for, or chase after, folly. Desire seems to lie at the center of the disputed verb. That meaning is confirmed by the Septuagint's translation in Ps 37:3 of the same verb by "desire." Whereas the Hebrew text has "Trust in Yahweh and do good; inhabit earth and seek faithfulness," the translator of the Hebrew into Greek apparently read the final word differently (*hamonah* instead of *'amunah*, "its bounty" rather than "its faithfulness").

In a few instances Qoheleth used *hebel* in ways that illuminate its special sense in his total argument. According to 2:21, an individual who has combined intellect with skill in amassing wealth must relinquish it into the hands of someone who has not earned the riches. Such circumstances constitute both *hebel* and a grievous evil, according to Qoheleth. Similarly in 6:2 he complained about an instance when a person receives vast riches as a divine gift but for some unstated reason was unable to consume any of them, leaving them to be enjoyed by a stranger. This situation struck Qoheleth as both *hebel* and a serious sickness.

Hebel *outside Ecclesiastes*

Just as in Qoheleth's discourse *hebel* must signify something akin to transience, sickness, and emptiness, it has the same breadth of meaning elsewhere in the Bible, beginning with the name of Abel and ending with the description of idols as devoid of substance.

A poignant pun in 2 Kgs 17:15 links the worshippers of idols with worthlessness (*hahebel>wayyehbalu*), and Deut 32:21b places *hebel* in parallelism with *lo' 'el* (not God), thereby suggesting that idols have no vitality: "They have stirred me to anger with 'not god,' provoked me with their idols." The powerlessness of idols is the subject of several texts (such as Jer 10:3, 8, 15; 14:22; 16:19 and Jonah 2:9), where *hebel* occurs. In Jer 16:19–20 an imaginary confession is placed in the mouths of foreign nations: "Our fathers inherited only a lie, an idol (*hebel*) lacking profit; do men make gods for themselves, and they are not God?"

Psalm 62:10 takes one further step toward divesting the noun of any content: "Surely humans are *hebel*, mortals, lies; in ascending scales, they are less than a single *hebel*." Isaiah 57:13 seems to make a similar point when insisting that the things that have been collected, presumably idols, will be unable to rescue those who cry out, and they will be carried off by the wind, snatched up by a breeze (*hebel*).

Qoheleth's Chief Complaints

Although Qoheleth pronounced everything *hebel*, he seems to have been particularly agitated over three things. They are work, the failure of a just reward for good behavior,[4] and the uncertainty associated with the inheritor of one's estate. Among the other things he mentioned, a few are obviously *hebel*, for example the birth of a stillborn, irksome insomnia, and fickle admirers. Others are less so, as in happiness and goodness, youth and the dawn of life. Still others are innocuous at best: verbosity, dreams, and the laughter of fools. The possibility that a single destiny awaits both humans and mortals seems immaterial, except that Qoheleth's point is to question the idea that mortals can anticipate some sort of life after death other than the gloomy concept of Sheol.[5] Above all divine arbitrariness and human ignorance about the future fall in the category of *hebel*, as does the insatiable appetite for more.

Is Hebel *a Universal Claim?*

Norbert Lohfink has argued that Qoheleth's claim that everything (*kol*) is *hebel* is restricted to what immediately precedes or follows the statement.[6] In that case not everything belongs to the category we have roughly defined as transience, sickness, and insubstantiality. The ubiquity of the comprehensive term *kol*, as well as the inclusions at the beginning and end of Qoheleth's teaching, suggest otherwise.[7] Furthermore, if life itself is *hebel* in his estimation, as in 2:17, that judgment is surely all-embracing. "Then I hated life, for the work that was done under the sun was grievous to me because everything was futile and shepherding the wind."

Therein lies a problem. If everything is *hebel*, a single term should apply to all thirty-nine uses of the word. No such equivalent exists in English, or in any other language, ancient or modern, so far as I know. Michael Fox has suggested "absurd" as the one descriptive term for all occurrences of *hebel* in Ecclesiastes,[8] but even he does not carry through with that narrow interpretation at 11:10, which he translates as follows: "And remove irritation from your heart and banish unpleasantness from your flesh, for youth and juvanescence are fleeting." It seems likely that Qoheleth used *hebel* in all three of the senses found elsewhere in the Bible, and translators must choose in each instance whether the best rendering is "transience" (brief, ephemeral), "sickness" (foul, unpleasant, evil), or "insubstantiality" (futile, absurd, empty). In my judgment the consistent use of a single word such as vanity (or absurdity) to translate *hebel* throughout the book impoverishes Qoheleth's language. For him the word was omnivalent, symbolic, and material; interpreters are left to decide where each of these alternatives applies.

Other words certainly exist in Hebrew to express emptiness and the lack of profit. The alternatives indicate something insubstantial like a vapor, which captures the meaning in some of Qoheleth's uses of *hebel*. They include *'ayin* ("nothing"), *riq* ("empty"), *shaw* ("unprofitable," "vanity"), and *tohu* ("nothingness," "unreality"). For some reason Qoheleth chose not to place any of these words in parallelism with *hebel* or to employ them alongside his favorite word.

Cognates of Hebel

Cognates of *hebel* are also found in the Bible, all describing something as transient and insubstantial. In Isa 64:5 it is said that the effect of sin is a withering away (*we-nabel*) like a leaf that is swept away by the wind. The little apocalypse, Isa 24–27, has an astonishing promise for an oppressed people, the rising of the dead: "Your dead will live, your corpses (*nebelati*) rise; you who dwell in the dust, wake up and sing; for your dew is the dew of light and earth will cause Rephaim to fall" (Isa 26:19). The mythic images involving the shades and the magical powers of the dew remain difficult to grasp.[9] Is this an image of earth giving birth to Rephaim?[10] Still the parallelism between the dead and *nebelati* implies something insubstantial. Finally Ps 102:27 asserts that even the heavens Yahweh made will perish, wearing out (*yiblu*) like a garment, but their maker will remain. The next verse goes on to contrast discarded clothes with the one whose years do not end. Interestingly Qoheleth contrasted the demise of humankind with the permanence of the earth (1:4).

The Origin of Qoheleth's Claim

Qoheleth's claim that everything is ephemeral, sick, or slightly more than nothing is an audacious one. Does it grow out of the Solomonic fiction? It is well known that kings in the ancient Near East were not reticent about touting their own accomplishments, and Solomon was reputed to have been the wisest of all. But even if true, that pedigree would hardly qualify him to make a sweeping assertion about everything, much of which he could not have seen, given his limited existence in space and time.

The Hellenistic period was a time when philosophers searched for the essence of things. For example Thales is known for claiming that everything comes down to four elements: earth, air, fire, and water. Qoheleth's initial poem about the cyclical rhythm of nature resonates with this focus on the fundamental structure of the world in which we live, for in it these four elements are primary. Monimus, another philosopher, is said to have described everything as a mist, a view that comes close to what Qoheleth thought.[11] The search for the essentials of life led to some fascinating observations by the sages.[12]

The Search for Essences

The most striking example of this search for the bare necessities occurs in Sirach. Like Qoheleth, Ben Sira provided conflicting responses. In Sir 29:21 he defined the principle things of life as water, bread, clothing, and a home to cover one's nakedness. In Sir 39:25–27, however, he expanded the list as follows: "The essentials of every human need are water, fire, iron, salt, the marrow of wheat, milk, honey, blood of the grape, oil, and clothing."

One way to understand the inconsistency is to recognize sociological advancement. In this scenario Ben Sira's thinking mirrors the cultural development from village life to an urban setting by the two rival states, Judah and Ephraim. A better approach is to recognize two distinct aims on Ben Sira's part as reflected in the larger contexts. The Spartan list of a mere four basic needs is set within a discussion of social responsibility to offer assistance to members of the community who fall on hard times. By contrast the expansive cataloging of life's fundamental needs functions as a theodicy, the defense of divine justice.

In the first instance, Ben Sira realized that, when confronted with widespread hunger, regardless of its particular expression, life can be sustained by bread and water for nurture and clothing and shelter for protection from the elements and from the shame of being seen naked. Everything else is disposable property and constitutes a fund into which one can reach to offer charitable assistance to the needy. Charity, he thought, is preferable to lending money to the poor not only because of the potential of loans to increase one's enemies but also because gifts to others in distress lay up a treasury in heaven on which one can later draw.

In the second instance, Ben Sira reflected on divine largesse, which he considered to be generous indeed. The first part of his remarks about life's necessities is indebted to a Stoic concept, the functional dualities of opposites in nature. Ben Sira's thoughts also reflect biblical lore about a promised land of milk and honey, as well as the lavish descriptions of Canaan as a place of abundant grain, oil, and wine. In addition his second list mentions fire, iron, and salt. Fire was essential for cooking and forging implements of agriculture and warfare. Iron was necessary to improve the quality of life through tools and weapons, while salt enhances flavor and is a preservative.

In both versions water takes precedence, perhaps because bread, the other ingredient that is absolutely essential for life, depends on it. Fire occupies the second position in the longer account because of its role in transforming grain into bread and the warmth it provides during cold weather. In neither list does meat appear, a noteworthy departure from Deut 32:13–14, which mentions honey, oil, curds, lamb, wheat, and wine. The absence of meat in Ben Sira's list comes closest to the actual daily diet in ancient Israel.

Although Qoheleth did not use the language about life's necessities, he did urge his male listeners, in language similar to the barmaid's in the Gilgamesh Epic, to eat bread and drink wine joyfully, to wear white, and to keep ample oil on the head, an absolute necessity in an arid climate.[13] Above all he mentioned something that is missing from all the other biblical lists: the love of a woman. He knew that mere survival was not enough, for life consists of more than satisfying the appetite and staying warm. Hence for him an emotional component complemented the other necessities.

Interest in the Universal

What if Qoheleth's language about everything being *hebel* is part of a philosophical search for the universal, the sum total of all existence? That quest certainly interested the Stoics, who ventured the opinion that the divine logos is the constituent of everything. Because it penetrated the entire universe, the logos was considered the structuring principle of all things. Accordingly they coined the sentence "He is the all," which Ben Sira quoted when contemplating the way opposites exist in the universe without canceling each other out.

Some late biblical texts attest a similar interest in the universal. Deutero-Isaiah's insistence that Yahweh made everything, stretching out the heavens alone and spreading out the earth without assistance from anyone, may be a reaction to the role of adviser attributed to personified wisdom in Prov 8:22–31. The expression, "the creator of everything" (*hakkol*) occurs twice in the book of Jeremiah (Jer 10:16 and 51:19). Sometimes the universal language is ambiguous; it may look back to the beginning of time but also include the present moment (compare Isa 45:7 and Ps 119:91). In these instances everything can refer to the created opposites, weal and woe, and to the divine word and integrity. Psalm 103:19 is more inclusive; it refers to heavenly beings and everything they do. More restrictive is the Chronicler's use of *hakkol* with reference to the complete offerings that were dedicated to the construction of the temple during Solomon's reign (1 Chron 29:14).

Qoheleth's use of *hakkol* shares this same ambiguity. Not every occurrence of the word indicates the totality of existence. Its threefold use in 3:20 refers to all living creatures; hence its applicability is universal only when referring to a specific object. The same is true of 6:6, where the universality of death is again the topic. As with his use of *hebel,* the language indicating everything must be examined case by case.

Does Qoheleth Vacillate about Everything Being Hebel?

Does anything suggest that Qoheleth changed his mind about everything being *hebel?* Some interpreters have reached this conclusion because of its gradual disappearance toward the end of the book,[14] but the evidence does not support the claim. While the majority of its uses occur in the first six chapters, *hebel* appears often after that as well. Chapter 11 even has two uses, and the inclusion in 12:8 increases that number to three. Clearly he did not abandon the view that everything is *hebel.*

Are there discrete units within Ecclesiastes that seem to operate outside the claim that everything is *hebel?* The poem in 1:4–11 about the cyclical character of nature and insatiable human drive for knowledge despite an inability to declare all that is known lacks the word *hebel*. It should not be overlooked, however, that the inclusion in 1:2 and thematic question about profit in 1:3 hover over it. The two collections of proverbial sayings in 7:1–14 and 10:1–20 stand out from the rest of the book, but even the first of these has "This also is *hebel*" (7:6) as a judgment about the laughter of fools. Furthermore the very first verse after this collection begins with Qoheleth's announcement that he has seen everything[15] in his brief or futile days and then goes on to specify his grievance. What is it? That good people perish in their righteousness and evil people prolong their days of villainy. The second collection has no reference to life's brevity, foulness, or insubstantiality, but its content is perfectly at home with Qoheleth's general observations about the utter incongruity between expectation and reality, what Michael Fox calls the absurd in an existential sense.

Qoheleth and Psalm 39

While Qoheleth's use of *hebel* is not unique, no other biblical writer made it thematic in the way he did. The closest anyone else came may be found in Psalm 39, a rich source for a study of intertextuality. Because the similarities between this psalm and Qoheleth are striking, a closer look is in order. Psalm 39 addresses the distinction between thoughts and speech, a problem also articulated in the narrative that introduces Job and the monstrous test consented to by Yahweh. By saying "In all this Job did not sin with his lips" (Job 2:10b), the omniscient narrator exonerated a scrupulous father from any spoken offense against Yahweh, leaving open the possibility of rebellious thoughts. It did not take readers long to provide what the narrator neglected to do; in the eyes of some early rabbis, Job was guilty of thinking unseemliness of Yahweh. In a delicious bit of irony, the narrator actually had Job harbor the fear that his children have gone astray and blessed[16] Elohim *in their thoughts* while in a sinful state. In Job's view sin's pernicious tentacles extended beyond the deed to the thought that later expressed itself in action. The poet who composed Psalm 39 determined to avoid both types of offense,[17] but in the end he abandoned his voluntary silence for speech that ultimately echoes Job's plea to be left alone to die: "I reject {life}; I would not live a long time; leave me alone, for my days are empty" (Job 7:16; compare Job 9:27; 10:20; and 14:6).

Warnings against loose speech abound in international wisdom.[18] The danger of being suspected of disloyalty to the ruling administration was real as was punishment for false accusation and lies in general within a kinship society. Teachers compared a spoken word to an arrow that, once released, could not be recalled. They also warned that a spoken word could be carried by a bird to unintended ears. In the imagination of teachers, the tongue's power over an individual resembled a ship's rudder. In each instance a tiny instrument wielded control over something many times its size. The teachers' realism gave rise to such gems as the description of a gossiper who could not resist the latest tasty morsel.

In their zeal, however, teachers sought to monitor even the thought that lay behind words and deeds. Sometimes they attributed irreligious reasoning to practical atheists, whom they labeled "fools."[19] At other times they adopted a pedagogy of uttering the unthinkable and thereby allowing untraditional views wider distribution in the same way some early rabbis employed the principle of uttering the impermissible and medieval philosophers introduced forbidden ideas into discourse as things to be rejected.[20] The introductory formula varied—"Do not say";[21] "Were it possible to say"; or "Heretics claim"—but the result was similar. Students widened their intellectual horizons by reflecting on ideas that society found suspect.

The poet whose angst is exposed in Psalm 39 chafed from the inescapable situation that this worldview created. Two realities impinged on him: the brevity of human existence and the heavy hand of Yahweh. The second of these, punishment for sin, rendered the first one intolerable. The poet's provisional solution, a silence that was tantamount to withdrawing from life, brought further agitation. His extraordinary request for relief was fueled by his understanding of the human condition as *hebel,*[22] an assessment that placed him in a camp alongside Qoheleth. Psalm 39:2–14:

    2. I resolved that I would guard my way
       From sinning with my tongue;
       I would keep a muzzle to my mouth
       while the wicked one was in my presence.

    3. I was completely silent;
       I refrained[23] from good
       but my pain intensified.

    4. My mind was hot within me;
       a fire raged in my thoughts.
       I spoke out.

    5. Yahweh, tell me my end
       and what is the measure of my life;
       I want to know how fleeting I am.

    6. Look, you have set my days at handbreadths,
       and my span is nothing in your sight;
       surely every person standing[24] is total emptiness.

    7. Surely one walks as an image;[25]
       surely they hustle about—a breath;[26]
       he amasses but does not know who will gather in.

    8. And now, Lord, what can I anticipate?
       My hope is in you.[27]

    9. From every rebellion deliver me;
       lay not on me the reproach of a fool.

   10. I had been silent, not opening my mouth,
       for *you* did it.[28]

   11. Remove your blow from me;
       I am dying from the rebuke of your hand.

12. With punishment for iniquity you chastise a person,
    and you consume his treasure like a moth.
    Surely everyone is a breath.
13. Yahweh, hear my prayer,
    and listen to my outbursts;
    do not ignore my tears,[29]
    for I am a resident alien with you,
    a sojourner like all my ancestors.[30]
14. Look away from me so that I can smile
    before I die and am not.

Psalm 39 is unique in that it begins with the verb *'amarti* ("I resolved"). In the Psalter the closest thing to it is Ps 82:6, which has "I had thought you were gods" to indicate previous disposition in the same way *'amarti* does in 39:2. The translation above is relatively straightforward except for verse 6. I take *nissab* to suggest fixity, like one standing erect, but it may be a musical notation like *sela* at the end of this verse and six verses later[31] or certainty about the human condition. The harsh tone and ambiguity of "for *you* did it" in the tenth verse prompted a later translator to render the clause in Greek less offensively: "for you made me." This slight change transformed an accusation into acknowledgment of Yahweh as personal creator. The occasion for the poet's charge of heavy-handedness on the part of the deity may be the silence referred to in verses 3–4a. Hence the pluperfect translation in verse 10 rather than an improbable present tense.

Structure

The structure of the poem is unclear, for clues point to different ways of dividing its individual units. First: three vocatives (two uses of the divine name the Tetragrammaton and a single use of Lord) suggest a tripartite prayer (5–7; 8–12; 13–14) that is introduced by verses 2–4. Second: the two refrains that conclude verses 6 and 12 and universalize the assessment of human existence as transience may indicate a two-part psalm with a final plea in verses 13–14. Whoever added the two instances of *sela* apparently viewed the poem as a composition comprising two units.

Both readings are predicated on the assumption that the poem was composed by a single author, but Otto Kaiser has reached an entirely different conclusion on the basis of theme alone.[32] The concentration on *hebel* in verses 5–7 and 12 have led him to postulate an older didactic poem that a redactor fashioned into a "school text" resembling Job 28, Qoh 3:1–8, Sir 24:1–22, and Wis Sol 2:1–9. By excising the first "all" and *nissab* in verse 6, as well as "for iniquity" six verses later, Kaiser attributes greater uniformity to an original poem than its present form exhibits. The four uses of "surely" in verses 6, 7, and 12 may reinforce his interpretation, if they are seen as isolating the short poem from its larger context.

Because the original poem that Kaiser has separated from the larger psalm lacks distinctive markers that point to a date, one could argue that it is a *late* insertion.[33] Its theme, life's transience, seems more at home in postexilic texts than in earlier ones. Viewing this unit about life's transience as a late insertion is subject to the objection that "I spoke out" requires something other than "and now." The expression "and now" ordinarily marks strong transition,[34] whereas "I spoke out" should be followed by something that explains why the poet abandoned an earlier resolve to remain quiet. As the psalm stands now, the poet moves from the awareness of personal *hebel* to the generalization that everyone's existence is *hebel* before asking: "What can *I* expect?" in a world that lacks real substance.

Content

Psalm 39 is a supplication for relief from an unspecified affliction that is interpreted as punishment for an infraction of divine rule. The prayer consists of three separate petitions (the last one reinforced by cohortatives [vv. 13–14]) and is introduced by an autobiographical snippet. Whereas the usual lament introduced by "How long" inquires about the duration of present suffering, this one asks about the number of days remaining before the grim reaper's scythe does its work.[35] In the absence of response, the psalmist determines to shorten those days by foregoing Yahweh's presence.

The exposure of the poet's inner feelings[36] echoes those of Jeremiah, who also chafed from conduct that he considered inappropriate for Yahweh. In both instances adopting a policy of silence resulted in mental agitation that overcame the resolve to keep quiet. Two things about this personal revelation in verses 1–4 conceal more than they reveal. Who is the evil one? Why did the poet abstain from good?

Apparently the "scoundrel" is nearby, but why was refraining from speech an effective response to the presence of a wicked one? We know that sages wrestled with this issue, for they preserved an answer in sayings juxtaposed to one another in Prov 26:4–5. Depending on the situation, one should either answer a fool to expose his stupidity or refuse to dignify a remark by responding. Was the poet afraid that he might say something that would encourage the wicked one, perhaps an expression of envy for prosperous evildoers like that laid bare in Ps 73:3–14?[37] Or does the opening verb in the sense of "resolve" point to cases such as Pss 14:1 and 53:2, where this verb is followed by "in my mind"? In other words is the psalmist afraid of voicing doubt that might strengthen practical atheists?

The second issue in the personal data that remains unclear is the statement that the poet refrained from good. One way of resolving the difficulty is to understand the expression as elliptical,[38] its meaning being "to do nothing" either good or bad. The verb would then have the sense of showing inactivity, as in Judg 18:9 and 1 Kgs 22:3.[39] If the poet neither spoke nor did anything, there was less possibility of giving offense, for both words and deeds are often ambiguous. Another approach to the problem is to interpret the response to the presence of a wicked person against the background of the sages' warning against helping sinners. Charity, in other words, must be closely monitored lest one strengthen those bent on wrongdoing.

Curiously the poet's good intentions only intensified the angst, creating a raging inferno within the mind and the seat of emotions. Humans, he learned, need something other than the instrument that effectively controls the mouths and behavior of domesticated animals. That discovery did not prevent a later teacher, Ben Sira, from using different symbolism in a prayer that a guard and a seal be placed on his mouth to prevent harmful speech (Sir 22:27–23:3). In addition, he requested that whips be set over his thoughts lest enemies exult over his misfortune.[40] Ben Sira's petition is immediately followed by a section in the Greek text identified as "discipline of the tongue" (Sir 23:7–15).

When the psalmist said he refrained from good, he obviously implied that he believed one capable of doing the good. That view was not universally shared, for a few thinkers considered goodness beyond the capacity of humans. In the reasoning of some, the mind is more devious than anything else (Jer 17:9a),[41] and consequently no one is able to do good—compare Ps 62:10, "Surely humans are *hebel,* mortals a lie; on scales for weighing, together they weigh more than a breath [*hebel*]" and Ps 116:11). Or is that opinion restricted to fools as in Ps 14:1? Apparently not, for this low view of humans is also attributed to Yahweh in the next two verses. Such hyperbole stands in tension with the mention of the righteous in verse 5, unless righteousness is judged to be less demanding than goodness. In that case goodness would be a habitus and righteousness a temporary achievement.

The first prayer that shatters the self-imposed silence seeks information that is hidden from most people: the precise time of their death. The poet chose his language carefully, opting for the Hebrew noun "end" that Amos used to refer to the disappearance of a nation. This desire to know one's ultimate destiny fueled an entire enterprise that promised secret knowledge about the future.[42] The psalmist bypassed these professionals and went directly to Yahweh. Others may have calculated human longevity as one hundred and twenty years[43] or as the more realistic seventy to eighty years, but the poet refused to enter into a mythic explanation for a human life span. Instead he shifted from duration to the quality of existence,[44] which he described as total emptiness, a mere image devoid of substance despite every hustle and bustle. Ironically he saw his own brief existence as nothing in Yahweh's presence, presumably because the deity is not subject to time's erosive power.

The second prayer alternates between trust and accusation. The poet's only hope lies in the Lord, but this taskmaster exacts a heavy toll on mere humans. The language of painful discipline dominates this section, but so does that of death-dealing punishment. No wonder the poet boldly accused the Lord even while explaining his earlier mutism. His emotions evoked the same extreme words, "for *you* did it," that the destruction of Jerusalem generated in the composer of Lam 1:21. Comparing

Yahweh to a destructive moth, the psalmist reduces existence to a single breath, a rare concrete sense of *hebel.*

The third prayer, or rather outburst, employs the language of disenfranchisement to describe the poet's powerlessness. The resident alien and the sojourner[45] were protected by provisions that Yahweh was believed to have established. The powerful reminder that Abraham and all Israel's ancestors were but pilgrims on a brief journey invokes special consideration, the hospitality extended to visitors. Nevertheless the poet abandoned all hope and requested that Yahweh hasten the end by looking away.

Affinities with Other Psalms

The four occurrences of "surely" in Psalm 39 are two less than the six in Psalm 62, where *hebel* is said to be the human essence in that an individual weighs less than a breath (Ps 62:10). In both psalms the exclamatory particle reinforces a low assessment of humankind, as if the judgment would not stand on its own. The psalmist who composed 144:4 compared people to a breath, but the weaker observation does not require any emphasis. Moreover, the initial statement in Ps 62:2 employs the same adjective that the poet uses in Ps 39:3 to characterize himself as silent. The sixth verse in Psalm 62, nearly identical with verse 1, has the imperative of the verb "to be silent" plus a reference to hope, as in Ps 39:8. Verses 2–5 and 6–9, the two literary units in Psalm 62 that *precede* the comment about human transience, are each set off by the musical notation *sela,* unlike its appearance in Psalm 39 *following* a refrain about humans as *hebel.*

The author of Psalm 90 chose a different way to express the brevity of human existence, comparing people to grass, which flourishes briefly and then dies. In his view the irrevocable decree that relegates humans to dust in verse 3 became more oppressive in light of the short span allotted to humans, especially when Yahweh's chastisement for offenses makes daily existence unbearable. The comparison of humans to a flower in Job 14:2 may be more elegant,[46] but flowers also wither and die. Both images, grass and flowers, are combined in Ps 103:15–17 and in Isa 40:6–8, which contrast their brief flourishing to Yahweh's steadfast love and word respectively. In Isa 40:6–8, the divine breath changes vitality into its opposite, like the desert winds. The word for breath is *ruah,* for *hebel* never applies to Yahweh but does describe idols.

Resemblances to Qoheleth

Whereas these texts move from human transience to divine immutability, Qoheleth emphasized the anthropological angst resulting from life's brevity, anxiety made worse by its unfairness. Etymologically the root *hebel* signifies "breath," breeze," or "vapor." This concrete use occurs in the Bible only occasionally, as in Isa 57:13 (// to *ruah*) and Pss 39:12; 62:10.[47] In context with *ruah, hebel* hovers in the background of

Jer 10:14–15 (= 51:17–18) but usually has a metaphorical sense, especially in polemic against the worship of idols and/or foreign gods.[48] Frequently *hebel* indicates futility (Job 9:29; Ps 94:11; Isa 30:7; 49:4; Lam 4:17), a meaning that Qoheleth used interchangeably with the sense of ephemerality. *Hebel* also has this latter nuance in Job 7:16; Pss 39:6; 78:33; and 144:4.

Affinities between Psalm 39 and Qoheleth go beyond a common theme, life as *hebel*. There are also some close syntactical relationships. Both authors refer to individuals who labor to accumulate things but cannot know who will gather them in. This particular problem expressed itself for Qoheleth in the context of inheritance (2:18–23). He complained that he had used both wit and energy to acquire goods only to pass them along to a stranger who might lack intelligence altogether.

By dividing consonants differently in Ps 39:7, the picture changes from walking as an image to walking in a shadow,[49] which occurred in Qoheleth. For him a shadow prefigured the emptiness of life rather than providing relief from the hot sun.

Thus far the affinities between Psalm 39 and Qoheleth have been striking. Three others, somewhat less persuasive, are worth considering. The psalmist worried about extinction with these words: "before I go and am no more." Two things in this phrase recall Qoheleth: the verb for dying, which Qoheleth used in its participial form,[50] and the negative particle denoting extinction.[51] The former is an abbreviated reference to going to be with dead ancestors, a euphemism for dying. The additional particle simply reflects the usual belief among Semites that a shadowy existence in Sheol was no real life. Hence the psalmist anticipated personal annihilation, at least on earth. The image of returning to dust is apt, for what distinguished a person no longer remains once the ravages of time have done their ruinous work. The third similarity between Psalm 39 and Qoheleth is the rare use of a verb for voluntary silence (Qoh 3:7; Ps 39:2).[52] Qoheleth did not move from his recognition of transience and rampant injustice to prayer. His response to the danger of loose speech is less extreme than the psalmist's although the occasion for guarding the tongue differs greatly. Qoheleth's justification for limited speaking is the distance separating *Elohim* from humans,[53] not the fear of a human enemy. For the psalmist, suffering led to a concept of *hebel* but did not generate a desire to enjoy life as it did for Qoheleth.[54]

Another significant difference is the way each thinker expressed inner resolve. The psalmist used "I said" alone, but Qoheleth added "in my thoughts" to verbs of speaking. This linguistic expression occurs most often in Qoheleth and Psalms, although it can be found elsewhere.[55] In Deut 29:18 three different verbs in the same semantic realm occur: "Everyone who exalts himself inwardly, thinking 'I shall be safe although I follow my rebellious mind.'" The usual verbs for speaking plus the reference to the mind can be nuanced variously as "resolved," "prayed," "thought," "mused," and imagined." Here are examples of each use.

Gen 8:21: "Yahweh resolved, 'I will never again destroy the earth because of humankind, for the human imagination is pernicious from youth'. . . ."
Gen 24:45: "Before I had finished praying, Rebekah approached. . . ."

1 Sam 27:1: "David thought, 'I shall now perish by Saul's hand.'"
Gen 17:17: "Abraham fell on his face; laughing, he mused, 'Can a child be born to one who is a hundred years old?'"
Deut 7:17: "If you imagine, 'These nations are more numerous than we; how can we dispossess them?'"

About two thirds of these expressions occur in Genesis, Deuteronomy, Psalms, and Qoheleth. Qoheleth's uses are noteworthy, given the brevity of the book when compared with the other three.

The unusual "I meditated with my mind" in Ps 77:6 introduces the idea of accompaniment, as if the mind joins the psalmist in the thought process. On the basis of the Egyptian concept of communing with one's *ba,* or soul, Michael Fox interprets Qoheleth's language about speaking with the heart as conversation between two separate and independent entities.[56] Fox does this despite a solitary use of "I spoke with my heart" in Qoh 1:16. Fox's reading of Qoheleth rests on the assumption that the usual prepositional *be* has the sense of accompaniment rather than expressing location. If Qoheleth had wished to indicate dialogue between him and the mind as the seat of cognition, he could have done so by exclusive use of the preposition "with" after verbs of speaking. That he did not do so suggests that he was not influenced by an Egyptian idiom when combining verbs of speech with the expression "with my heart."

Still, the personification of the heart, at least metaphorically, does take place in the Hebrew Bible. According to Prov 14:10, the heart possesses the power of perception, "knowing" its own bitterness, and Ps 27:8 attributes speech to it ("My heart says to you, 'Seek my face'"). In both instances the cognitive aspect seems to give way to the emotive, and one cannot rule out a purely symbolic understanding of this language.

The contexts containing the language about speaking with the heart are overwhelmingly negative. To many moderns the fool is perhaps the most sympathetic one who engages in this practice: "The fool reasons: 'There is no god'" (Pss 14:1; 53:1). "The fool boasts: 'I cannot be moved. . . . God has forgotten; he hides his face [and] never looks; . . . You will not inquire'" (Ps 10:6, 11, 13). The fiction of an omniscient narrator permits readers to grasp the innermost thoughts of others, especially when the intention is devious. Even a tendency to see oneself in the best light is exposed in Esth 6:6: "Haman thought; 'To whom would the king want to do a kindness more than to me?'"

A temporary suspension of justice encourages the wicked to presume an inactive deity: "Those who say, 'Yahweh will do neither good nor evil'" (Zeph 1:12). In the interest of humility, the newly freed Israelites are warned to give credit to Yahweh: "Do not boast: 'My strength and might acquired this wealth for me'" (Deut 8:17). The most extreme instance of *hubris* in the Bible evokes this disparaging comment: "You thought: 'I will ascend to heaven above El's stars, set up my throne, sit in the mount of assembly in the abode of Saphon, mount the back of a cloud, [and] be like Elyon'" (Isa 14:13–14). Nations too are reminded that they are subject to Yahweh:

"Who say: 'I am, and there is none besides me'" (Isa 47:10); "Who think; 'Who will bring me down to earth?'" (Obad 3).

A positive use of this expression is rare, such as Yahweh's determination to show a favorable face despite the inherent flaw in human nature. In Jer 5:24 the negative introduction does not rule out an attempt in a positive direction: "They do not say: 'Let us fear Yahweh our God who gives rain. . . .'" One characteristic of the good person who makes a cameo appearance in Psalm 15 is the inner acknowledgment of truth in verse 2. The rare use of a participle in this expression implies that truthfulness is habitual, just as a similar one in Obad 3 suggests an arrogant state of mind.

Qoheleth used the expression under discussion eight times. In 2:1, 15; 3:17, 18 it takes the form "I said in my heart," changing to "I spoke (*dabar*) with my heart" in the second of two occurrences in 2:15. In 1:16 it has a different preposition, "with," standing alone. In 9:1 the verb "to give" is followed by the preposition "to," yielding: "For all this *I committed to my mind*. . . ."[57] Similarly 8:16 has "When *I set my mind* to know wisdom. . . ." As was true of Gen 27:41, in which Esau contemplated murder, the expression is not rigid, for there a subject falls between the verb and "in his heart." Qoheleth varied the preposition, using the prefix "in" as well as freestanding "with" and "to." He also prefaced the expression with a direct object following a causative or emphatic "for." In Qoheleth's case the expression is self-revelatory, its autobiographical form differing from the others, which are instances of imaginary mind reading.[58]

At best, the preceding exercise in intertextuality[59] demonstrates that Qoheleth was not alone in viewing existence as *hebel* and that others took note of the lack of justice where reward for labor was concerned. Above all a close reading of Psalm 39 shows that at least one independent thinker who was in some ways like Qoheleth risked an intimacy with Yahweh that exposed his weakness and temerity. The psalmist journeyed from voluntary to obligatory silence, in between these hoping in vain[60] to be granted the status of sojourner. In the end he opted for nonexistence, but it freed him from chastisement.[61]

Qoheleth searched for the essence of reality and discovered its elusive nature, which he summed up in a single word, *hebel,* and an accompanying phrase indicating something futile with the wind as its object. Was Qoheleth's manner of gathering information about his world just as deceptive as reality itself?

CHAPTER 4

Ocular Deception

In his view of reality as altogether elusive and his emphasis on the futility—even absurdity, to the point of foulness (*hebel*)—of the chase or the invisible food (the two meanings of *re'ut ruah*) could Qoheleth's sight have been obscured, his vision blurred, by uncontrollable factors? I shall now explore the possibility that his eyes deceived him. At issue is the trustworthiness of conclusions based on sight.

The Primacy of Sight

The verb *ra'ah* ("to see") is one of Qoheleth's favorites.[1] It occurs more than forty times and has at least three meanings. In most instances the primary sense is that of catching sight of something (such as the sun, work, injustice, or profit). In some cases the verb suggests more than looking upon something but actually participating in it, hence "experiencing" or "enjoying" life, the good, of wealth. Occasionally, *ra'ah* has the wider nuance of "perceiving" or "recognizing," as in 9:11, where Qoheleth perceived that chance frustrates normal expectations about winners and losers. Similarly in 4:7 he recognized the futility of hoarding wealth, especially when the hoarder has no heir.

Moreover in rare cases Qoheleth claimed to observe far more than the eye is capable of capturing. In 2:24 he credited the deity with endowing humans with the capacity to enjoy life. In 7:29 he invited readers to see what he had figured out: that God made human beings "just," but they have searched for many contrivances. The meaning of the rare word that I have translated as "contrivances" seems to indicate clever inventions that Qoheleth thought damaged the innate character of people.[2]

In all his talk about seeing, Qoheleth did not neglect the eye itself. In fact, along with the first occurrence of the verb *ra'ah* comes an assessment that the eye is never satisfied with seeing (1:8). Because knowledge is acquired by sight and sound, Qoheleth gave voice to the endless thirst for knowledge. In his estimation neither eye nor ear is ever filled to capacity, much less running over with surfeit.

Even when basking in the royal fiction of satisfying every desire, he recognized the powerful role of the eye in generating the perception of both "want" and "need": "I withheld nothing my eyes asked for" (2:10a). The eyes are not the sole agents of desire, for the mind also participates in the human drive to accumulate more and more. Hence, Qoheleth added, "I did not deny my mind [*leb,* 'heart'] any joy."

Therein lies a problem. Desire is less stable than sight. So Qoheleth observed that the sight of the eyes is better than wandering desire (6:9). With this observation he added a second agent of desire: the *nephesh* ("throat," "appetite"). The image is captivating: the *nephesh* functions like feet, moving from place to place while the eyes remain fixed at one spot. Perhaps Qoheleth thought of the limits imposed on the eyes by one's range of vision. In contrast the *nephesh* has no restriction on its desires and can roam freely.[3]

Like eyes and *nephesh,* the mind is always restless (2:22). Whether from fulfilled desire, which brings anxiety over the possibility of losing it, or from unfulfilled desire, the mind becomes the seat of worry (2:23) both by day and by night. This too, according to Qoheleth, is futile. The reason is, of course, the impossibility of stilling the restlessness despite Qoheleth's admonition to the young: "Remove care from your mind and banish sorrow from your flesh" (11:10a). Why? "Because youth and black hair are short-lived" (10:10b).

In 6:9 the arresting image of desire wandering hither and yon like the provocateur in the prologue to the book of Job brings the homonyms *ra'ah* and *ra'ah* into close proximity. It is as if Qoheleth thought the act of seeing resembles a chase, in this case, of something insubstantial like air. Alternatively he compared seeing to feeding on wind. Neither pursuit nor dining on thin air brings rest to the hungry eyes, mind, or throat.

According to Qoheleth, the mind (*leb*) is not just restless for more. It is actually corrupt, filled with evil approaching madness (9:3). The doubling of the noun for cognition in this verse leaves no room for exonerating the organ of thought. It actively strives (2:22), expresses itself in hasty vows and prayer (5:1),[4] and tries to discern wisdom (8:16). Whereas the eye and ear are never full, the mind is satiated (*male',* "to be full").[5] The haunting sequel to this statement about a mind overflowing with *ra'* ("sadness" or "evil") captures life's existential moment with a simple phrase ("and afterwards to the dead").

The "heart" is frequently the *object* of something in Qoheleth's discourse. Most notably he spoke to it, turned to it, set it a task, laid a thought on it. Or the living take something to heart, that is, ponder it. The mind is also subject to harm from unbridled speech (7:21), for words really do hurt in the same way sticks and stones do, Shakespeare notwithstanding. Some things (for example a bribe) bring destruction, because the mind loses its ability to render an impartial judgment (7:7).

The Minimal Role of Hearing

It appears that Qoheleth accepted the adage "seeing is believing." He did not place comparable emphasis on hearing, the other avenue to knowledge. That is why the comment in the first epilogue about Qoheleth as listener seems at odds with his teachings—if, that is, the verb does not specify the act of weighing traditional sayings in an intellectual sense.[6]

Rarely did Qoheleth even mention hearing, and never did he say he learned something by listening. Besides observing that the ear never tires of listening, he cautioned against paying close attention to the chatter of slaves, who may curse their owner when they think it safe to do so (7:21). He also narrated a tale of missed opportunity, a village's failure to hear the advice of a poor but wise man (7:17).[7] The closest Qoheleth came to extoling listening is found in a comparative saying: "It is better to listen to the rebuke of a wise person than to hear the praise of fools" (7:5).

In this regard he is a long way from the Egyptian sage Ptahhotep, who inserted a long statement about hearing near the end of his instruction.[8] For him the hearer was the model student. In fact the two words, *hearing* and *obeying,* are virtually synonymous. A similar semantic occurrence can be found in Deuteronomy,[9] with its frequent emphasis on obedience, and in Proverbs, where the narrating voice, presumably that of a parent, admonishes the son to hear.[10] Similarly personified wisdom urges the young to pay heed to her teachings.[11]

Then when Ben Sira gave specific advice to his students, he told them to look around until they found intelligent people and to listen carefully to them. Hearing was apparently the best way to acquire knowledge in an era when even reading was aloud rather than silent.

The obvious reason is that an oral culture continued to dominate education despite a surge in scribal activity.[12] Several factors contributed to the primacy of hearing over reading, the most important of which was the cost of manuscripts. Only wealthy families could afford to own scrolls. Moreover there was little demand for written materials because of a low rate of literacy, and little in an agrarian society encouraged young men, or women for that matter, to go through the rigors of learning to read and write more than at an elementary level. Most literary activity probably took place in scribal guilds, and these elites practiced managed scarcity for economic reasons.[13]

An Oral Culture

A close examination of the literature produced by the sages in Judah (and Israel) reveals an astonishing fact. The wise rarely used the verb "to write." For example Job expressed the wish that the charges levied against him be written on stone, incised with lead inlay, like the Behistun Rock Inscription that records the exploits of the Persian king Darius (Job 19:23–24). What Job longed for is exceptional, a permanent testimony of his innocence that would be visible to everyone.

The verb "to write" occurs also in the first epilogue in Ecclesiastes. Here it is said that Qoheleth "sought to find pleasant sayings" and "reliable words were faithfully written" (12:10).[14] Remarkably the epilogist did not credit Qoheleth with the actual writing. A similar situation exists where the prophets are concerned. For the most part, they seem to have spoken their oracles to live audiences. With the passing of time, some of their collected words were recorded for posterity.[15] Some interpreters think Ezekiel marks a transition from the oral to the written stage,[16] and the later author of Isaiah 40–55 wrote a message of hope to an exiled people in Babylon.[17]

Even though King Solomon was believed to have been wiser than anyone else in the East and in Egypt, he is not said to have written anything. Instead 1 Kgs 5:9–14 uses the verb for speaking when reporting on his vast contributions to proverbial lore, all of which concern nature (trees, beasts, birds, creeping things, and fish), unlike the sayings attributed to him in the book of Proverbs. Even there royal sponsorship is all that is claimed, either for Solomon or for Hezekiah, a king of the eighth century who endured the ignominy of being shut up like a bird in a cage, according to an inscription of Sennacherib of Assyria.[18] The crucial word in Prov 25:1 is "copied," and those who are said to have done the transmitting are called "Hezekiah's men," about whom nothing is known.

In Prov 30:1, the sayings of Agur are introduced in a manner similar to prophetic books—and not merely in the initial "the words of Agur" (compare Jer 1:1; Amos 1:1). Two other peculiar features of this verse echo prophecy, probably intentionally. They are the word that can mean either an oracle or indicate a gentilic, the Massaite, and the formula "oracle of X," in this case followed by "the man" rather than the deity (compare Nah 1:1, Hab 1:1, and Mal 1:1 for the former, Joel 2:12, Amos 2:16, Obad 1:4, and Nah 3:5 for the latter).[19]

The other brief proverbial collection by a foreigner, Prov 31:1–9, also begins in the way Agur's sayings do: "The words pertaining to Lemuel, king of Massa, which his mother taught him" (Prov 31:1). The queen's advice to the prince is spoken directly, as one would expect, rather than conveyed in writing. Her rhetoric emphasizes action and speech, conduct that does not inhibit the prince's role as champion of the weak, and talk that lends a voice to those who need assistance from someone in power.[20]

The biblical requirement that there be two witnesses to confirm a testimony before a court of justice is tacit acknowledgment of the unreliability of witnesses. A late story, preserved in the Apocrypha, about Susanna, a virtuous and beautiful woman who was accused of adultery by two lecherous judges, implies that even the testimony of two witnesses was not a safeguard against miscarriage of justice.[21] Modern jurisprudence has frequently demonstrated the inaccuracy of witnesses to a crime. Either their eyes deceive them, or their memory is faulty. In test after test, witnesses of a staged scene do not agree on what they have just seen.

If the eye cannot be trusted, what does that suggest about Qoheleth's emphasis on personal observation? At least it places a question mark over his sweeping claims. "Everything" did not lie within the scope of his vision; yet he said he had seen everything (7:15) even though he mentioned only two things in this immediate context. As we have seen, universalizing begins to surface in Deutero-Isaiah, additions to the book of Jeremiah, and in Chronicles, reaching its zenith in Sirach's replication of the Stoic motto about the unity of all things ("He is the all").[22]

People do often use the expression "Now I've seen everything," when coming up against bizarre behavior. Is that all Qoheleth conveyed with his observations about everything under the sun? In view of the fact that the poem about nature's rhythm in 1:4–11 alludes to earth, wind, fire, and water, precisely the four elements of the universe according to the Greek philosopher Thales, something more than exaggeration is at work here. The search for a totalizing unity that occupied Stoic philosophers seems to have invaded the thought of a few biblical authors.[23]

What Was There for Qoheleth To See?

Qoheleth's constant appeal to personal observation invites speculation about the kind of world he experienced, his historical context.[24] So does the possibility that he was familiar with current philosophy. He left little information that historians can use to locate him in a specific time and place. A few things seem to point to the Judean province, while his syntax and grammar resemble that of the latest books in the Hebrew Bible and postbiblical (rabbinic) Hebrew, with its strong Aramaic influence.

The following features of Ecclesiastes fit better in Israel than in the other locations that have been suggested as its place of origin: almond tree, cisterns, the pulley used for drawing water from deep wells, meteorological factors such as the clouds returning after rain, and certain peculiarities of language that belong to late Hebrew.

Some things can definitely be said about the historical context of the book, but they are less specific than one would wish. From incidental comments throughout the book, readers catch a glimpse of the intellectual scene; the religious, economic, and political reality; and the institution of the family.

The Intellectual Scene

Incidental references to a flourishing intellectual community, the search for the interpretation of a thing, its *pesher,* offset a comment about the tedium accompanying rigorous scholarly pursuit.[25] The activity resembles that at Qumran; it had not yet developed into sophisticated hermeneutic involving rabbinic *peshat* and *derash*.[26] A confident "in your face" style of debate represents epistemological agnosticism about competing absolutist claims but stops short of stifling intellectual curiosity the way Ben Sira did when coming up against intellectual hubris. This sort of conflict characterizes an open society with competing value systems, one with a high appreciation for refined rhetoric and compositional skill. According to the first epilogue, ordinary people have been brought into the scope of Qoheleth's instruction.

There are also indications that Qoheleth was engaged in an effort to convey philosophy with a language that is minimally suited for such a task.[27] At least he practiced second-order thinking, a way of reflecting on the process of thinking itself. For example he used *miqreh* ("chance") to indicate human destiny, *heshbon* as the bottom line in an economic balance sheet, and the temporal extension of *'olam* to refer to eternity.

In this matter he resembles certain thinkers in the Hellenistic world, just as his characterization of everything as *hebel* reminds one of Monimus, who called the visible world mist or smoke. And the poem in 3:2–8, which mentions twenty-eight polarities, echoes the Stoic division of the universe into balanced opposites.[28] Stoics also endeavored to arrive at universal truths in the way Qoheleth tried to embrace the totality of existence in what he taught.

The Religious Context

A robust religious community struggled to stay above water despite a loss of certainty about traditional affirmations. For some, death had become an acute problem because of an emerging ego, a rise in individualism. The age-old question about survival beyond the grave became profoundly existential once the exalted sense of an extended family dimmed. Life suddenly lost its meaning, and Qoheleth refused to offer comfort in the form of divine presence in the way the composer of Ps 73:23–26 did.[29] It reads: "But I am continually with you; you hold me by my right hand. You lead me by your counsel, and afterward you receive me (in honor). Whom have I in heaven (but you), and besides you I desire nothing on earth. My flesh and my heart may waste away; God is my rock and portion forever." The most Qoheleth dared to say takes the interrogative mode: "Who knows?" The answer that really functions as a negation: "Nobody knows."[30]

Even in skeptical societies, religion is not completely obliterated. Official acts of piety persisted. Funerals, always open to crass commercialism (as in modern society) as well as undeserved eulogies, retained their hold on the populace. Professional mourners went about their tasks and were matched by singers of merrier tunes. Caution tempered prayer and sacred vows lest the deity be angered, and the cult failed to bring holiness near.[31] Fear is the natural consequence, and along with it an epistemological agnosticism. Still Qoheleth thought God is generous almost to a fault, if the number of occurrences of the verb "to give" with Elohim as subject indicate his genuine feelings.[32] The problem is, however, that these gifts are not distributed according to a principle of worth. Furthermore they rest outside human control in a deterministic universe,[33] which means that human destiny lies in a distant deity's hands. Such a situation contrasts with the worldview of early wisdom, according to which virtuous conduct went a long way toward assuring a life of health and prosperity.

The Economy

Qoheleth lived in a time of economic prosperity, but as in the West today, the affluence of a few came at the expense of the middle class and even the poor. Fortunes were quickly made and just as quickly lost; the high risk included the potential for enormous wealth.[34] Talented individuals, along with the unscrupulous, accumulated vast wealth, often at the expense of enjoyment. The ambitious worked long hours and spent restless nights worrying about losing possessions to thieves or having them squandered by inept or greedy employees. Investments in mercantile enterprises on the high seas offered a risky alternative to pastoral and agricultural endeavors, which were also subject to the whim of nature. Watching for the right moment to venture forth in either alternative threatened the entire activity, as did dependence on magic, whether by spells or a divining rod (11:1–8).

A moneyed economy brought new problems, not the least of which was the disposition of wealth at one's death. Unwritten laws and custom dictated that the firstborn son would inherit the family's land, but these had been circumvented by bureaucratic seizure of estates or by loss through enforced debt. The interest on borrowing money or seed was astronomical, and a single season of low yield could place farmers in jeopardy, often leading to the sale of their children into servitude.[35] In such a situation, it was legitimate to ponder questions such as: "To whom will my wealth go at my death, and will that person be worthy of it?"

Judging from the conduct of the rich described in much of the Bible, wealth has the potential to destroy the soul. This sociological and theological insight appears with absolute clarity in a brief prayer on the lips of a foreigner named Agur. His fervent request was that he not be given too much—lest he forget his status as creature, existence *coram deo,* before the heart of God—or too little, lest he be forced to steal and by doing so sully the sacred name (Prov 30:8–9). In praying and in identifying himself personally with God ("my God"), Agur did something that Qoheleth never did.

Fortunes come, and fortunes go. Anxiety about having a profit at the end of the day seems to have prevailed in Qoheleth's time, but to no avail. The constant rise and fall resulted in a literary convention about princes going on foot while former slaves rode on horses. In this kind of world, there was no stability.

In some ways Qoheleth's world was typical, with pockets of wealth and pockets of poverty. He mentioned vessels of gold and silver; expensive perfumes, clothes, oil, and wine; and royal opulence. There were slaves, concubines, and wretched victims of oppression without a defender. Laborers toiled at catching fish and fowl, repairing walls, wielding axes, patching leaky roofs, grinding grain, guarding estates, sowing seeds, harvesting crops, and many other activities.

The Political Reality

A multitiered bureaucracy watched over Qoheleth's world. A foreign sovereign sat at the top, and under his vigilance powerful appointees spent their waking hours raising revenue for the royal treasury by collecting taxes from subjects and secretly funneling as much as possible into their personal accounts.[36] An Orwellian "Big Brother" was a constant presence, making it dangerous to utter rebellious thoughts. The Persian system of provinces, each with royal representatives known as the "eyes" of the king, guaranteed that citizens would remember their status as subjects of a foreign ruler. Nevertheless the ancient royal ideology, according to which kings were expected to champion the causes of widows, orphans, and the needy, retained its appeal, a least to the marginalized.[37] Qoheleth recognized that a king was a profit for a field (5:8), by which he may have meant that a semblance of stability is assured by royal force. Still this tacit acknowledgment of some benefit from royalty is miles away from the Greek notion of "philosopher kings."

The Family

In this society the family bore a heavy burden. Gone was the Davidic dynasty with its propaganda about Jerusalem as a holy city, and with its demise the weakened status of the cult was evident. The family went a long way toward filling the void left by both, and the status of women appears to have been elevated, if the personification of wisdom and the praise of the good wife in Prov 31:10–31 represent societal views.

Within the inner circle of the family, we hear about both joy and sorrow. Welcome births attest to divine activity and human ignorance about gestation, while stillborns indicate that the deity's involvement did not always guarantee safe delivery of a fetus. Flies ruined costly perfumes; miserliness generated bitterness; illness prevented enjoyment of wealth; and the aging process portended a dark future. Further afield brigands attacked travelers; snakes bit their charmers; rocks fell on workers; and the less-agile or careless fell into pits or ravines.

A greater danger awaited foolish young people. The femme fatale was reputed to represent the embodiment of evil. Instead of encouraging the young to reject women completely, however, Qoheleth urged each of them to enjoy life with the woman he loved. We never hear the voice of the young; it is as if children were to be seen but not heard.[38] Their silence was typical in the ancient world; in wisdom texts only the Egyptian Instruction of Ani has a son break this code of silence.[39]

Qoheleth's rhetoric makes it difficult to ascertain the extent of individualism within the intimacy of the family. He had drunk deeply from the cup of egocentricity, if his confident self-references are indicative of his inner attitude. Only once did he overcome this egoism long enough to advocate solidarity, but even then selfishness ruled (4:9–12). He was interested only in what a companion can do to help him.

Some Surprises

This summary of Qoheleth's historical context yields a few surprises. There is no evidence of urban complexity despite three references to the city Jerusalem; no mention of ethnic groups or cultural clashes such as those discussed in the books of Ezra and Nehemiah; a complete silence about two important religious institutions, prophets and priests; similar silence about the worship of idols; nothing about mediators between a distant deity and humans, not even angels and personified wisdom; and no indication that apocalyptic thinking had become rampant.

Silence about Idols

Some of these omissions are extraordinary. Both biblical and deuterocanonical literature attack idolatry mercilessly. For example Ps 115:5–7 expresses this biting sarcasm:

"They have mouths but cannot speak, eyes but cannot see. They have ears but cannot hear, noses but cannot smell. They have hands but cannot feel, feet but cannot walk. No sound rises from their throats" (compare Jer 10:14–15 and Bel and the Dragon).[40] The explanation for the worship of idols given in Wisdom of Solomon explains its powerful grip on the people. A grieving father made an image of his dead son and knelt before it in deep reverence. A patriotic citizen fashioned a likeness of a distant ruler and paid it the deepest respect. A talented artist created an image with such beauty that it surely deserved to be worshipped. The scorn displayed here is mild when compared to sarcastic mockery elsewhere about the inability of idols to protect themselves against thieves, menstrual women, fire, and bird droppings.[41]

Lack of Interest in Prophets and Priests

Qoheleth's failure to mention prophets probably reflects their declining status, owing to the close relationship between prophets and royalty, both pro and con; the difficulty of distinguishing an authentic word of Yahweh from a bogus one;[42] and the shift from mediating an oracle in the deity's name to interpreting words delivered by earlier prophets. The result of this disappearance of a mediated word by human messengers was a heightening of expectation that a prophet such as Moses would soon appear or that Elijah would return.

The role of priests had changed drastically with the destruction of the cult center in 586 B.C.E. The dedication of a new temple in 516 did little to restore priestly status, for the new construction brought tears to the eyes of those who remembered the splendor of Solomon's architectural achievement and compared the new house of worship to that grand memory. Competing factions within the priesthood vied for the few perks of the profession, and the rival cultic centers in nearby Samaria and Alexandria created constant conflict. Nevertheless, by the beginning of the second century B.C.E., the impact of the officiating High Priest Simon brought only praise from Ben Sira, leaving this sage in a state of awe. Still the jockeying for power and prestige by purchasing the office of high priest soon tainted the profession.

No Angelic Mediation

Although Qoheleth said nothing about angels who mediate the divine word to humans, others were less reticent. They reported that angels entered the daily lives of good people such as Tobit[43] and Ezra (of Second Esdras), bringing restoration to the former and defending God's actions, or inactivity, in the face of Ezra's agonizing struggle to understand a cruel world. These heavenly beings were identified by name, and they functioned as tour guides for a few special people who were taken on heavenly journeys. None of the recognizable signs of apocalypticism is detectable in Qoheleth's teaching.

This survey of Qoheleth's immediate environment reveals little that enables us to locate him in a particular place and time. The strongest evidence is linguistic, and it suggests that he belonged to a period when Aramaic had made huge inroads into the Hebrew language. This conclusion is strengthened by the growing influence of Hellenism.[44] The brief fragments of the book that were discovered at Qumran have been given a date around 140 B.C.E.[45] All this points to a date in the fourth or third century for Qoheleth's activity. Most interpreters opt for about 250 B.C.E.[46]

Like no other biblical author, Qoheleth put his personal stamp on his teachings. They stand or fall, as it were, with his reputation for honest and accurate interpretation of what he observed. His legacy, however, has been brought into question by the frame narrative. Did the author of the second epilogue believe Qoheleth was an iconoclast, a teacher whose words were dangerous? His teachings, however, include the hidden assumptions that are entirely traditional. Do these cultural givens exonerate him from the charge of endangering the young, like Socrates, and legitimate his observations even if he did succumb to ocular deception?

CHAPTER 5

Surreptitious Givens

If Qoheleth's eyes did occasionally deceive him, his conclusions cannot always be trusted. Like everyone else, he was encased in a suit of armor that he did not choose and of which he was probably unaware. His ancestors "clothed" him with their own worldview, which as a child he put on without a moment's thought. In a sense his parents armed him day after day so that their ideas became his. That is how every society works. If in later years he blazed trails like the pioneers in the United States who headed west, he still remained in many respects a child of his time.

Culture's Sway

Everyone is shaped by societal norms and customs, even those individuals who openly resist them.[1] Hidden controls take various forms: the language of discourse by which we give voice to our most intricate thoughts, the myths we fabricate as the script in which we read the drama of our lives and the truths by which we live, the groups to which we belong and those we choose to avoid; the deep-seated and at times unrecognizable motives that make us act in a given manner, the level of access to the world's goods and desired pleasures, the expected compensation for action and feared consequences of inaction, and much more.

This enculturation to a large extent makes us who we are. There is no such thing as a self-made man or woman. These controls govern both thought and action. Some of the forces shaping our lives are overt, but most are covert. They sneak up on us and assume a clandestine character. Even our way of perceiving is to some extent affected by what we expect to see, and that in turn is passed on by our descendants.[2] Anyone who doubts this assessment need only listen to speech patterns in different regions of the United States and observe the actions of people in the Bible Belt and others in California or Manhattan.

In some ways Qoheleth resembles a modern scientist who supplements findings in the laboratory with personal religious views. The researcher may follow rigid rules of scientific investigation, reaching verifiable conclusions in every case. Her findings are completely dictated by the same method that an atheistic scientist uses. If their investigations are carried out in an objective manner, both should reach the same conclusion.

Outside the laboratory, she may believe in God as creator, judge, and sustainer of life. Nothing in her research ever demonstrates the accuracy of these assumptions. And nothing discredits it. By definition God is invisible. Hidden too are divine footprints. Nevertheless she prays fervently to the unknowable and molds her life according to a pattern derived from what she perceives to be revelation.

Furthermore, in areas susceptible to scientific inquiry, she allows its findings to speak authoritatively, even when they concern the evolution of human beings, the age of the universe, and natural law. Where science can speak, she lets it do so; but she also believes in a reality that transcends space and time, if only because it enables her to express gratitude for the beauty of the universe and goodness in some people.

Qoheleth has been called the first empirical thinker in the Bible.[3] This judgment needs to be qualified to the degree by which hidden assumptions compromised a purely objective inquiry and quite possibly in the matter of trailblazing.[4] I take them up in reverse order.

The Beginnings of Empirical Thinking

Assuming that Qoheleth's method was empirical, was he the first canonical thinker to practice it? Two anecdotes preserved in the book of Proverbs suggest that others deserve recognition for basing their insights on personal observation rather than relying on revelation. The first is in Prov 24:30–34: "I passed by the field of a lazy man, by the vineyard of a stupid person. And, look, thorns had gone up all over it; weeds covered it completely; its stone enclosure lay in ruins. I looked and thought about it; I observed and learned a lesson. A little sleep, a little slumber, a little embracing of the hands in bed, and your poverty[5] will come apace, your want, like a man with a shield."

This moral tale presents a lesson acquired solely through careful observation. The unknown sage deduced a "truth" from what is evident to the naked eye. For all we know, he may be entirely wrong about the reason for the deterioration of the vineyard. Sickness, or even death, may have prevented the owner from caring for his property. So we come to one of the problems encountered by all who depend on their eyes alone for interpreting reality. Motives lie beneath the surface.

This sage's approach is exactly like Qoheleth's. Both men looked and reflected on what they saw. Even their language is similar in one respect; both followed up their observation with deep thought that they expressed in this way: "I looked and *took it to heart.*" There are differences, to be sure, but they are attributable to the demands of parallelism, to which Qoheleth was less bound.[6] The sage used two verbs for seeing, *hazah* and *ra'ah,* whereas Qoheleth employed the latter alone. The unnamed sage was also more explicit about the result of sight, saying, "I learned a lesson."

The other example of an empirical method of inquiry in the book of Proverbs deals with a temptation confronting young men, and those not so young, in every generation: the strong attraction of illicit sex. Adopting a standard motif of the time—a goddess gazing out a window[7]—this moralist painted a grim picture of a youth's fatal decision.

The plot is simple, the story's ramifications complex. A parental figure—possibly a mother given the location from which the unfolding scene is observed—describes a seduction and its consequence. A young man wandered in the direction of an adulterous woman, whether consciously or not we are not told. A married woman looking for a night of sexual pleasure confronted him and used a combination of eloquence and its arousal of desire to lure the unsuspecting victim into a trap that cost him dearly.

The woman addressed all his concerns. Her husband had gone on a long trip; she had prepared everything for optimal enjoyment; there was no ritual impairment to her having sex; and she was eager to share her bed with him. She resembles the personification of a wanton described as a foil to personified wisdom in Proverbs 9. There the seductress used a persuasive argument designed to appeal to a young man's love of the forbidden. Her words get right to the point: "Stolen water is sweet and bread eaten furtively is pleasant."

Neither seductress, however, mentioned a lesson that had played itself out so frequently that it had become proverbial. What is that? Simply that a cuckolded husband will exact heavy revenge that no payment of money can ward off (Prov 6:34–35). That lesson was known to the person peering through the window. Accordingly the episode concludes with a comment about the young man's inability to grasp the gravity of the situation: "He does not know that his *nephesh* is (at stake)." He is a fool undergoing punishment, like an ox on the way to be slaughtered or a bird walking into a trap. The word I have translated "punishment" (*musar*) is identical with that rendered as "lesson" in the previous anecdote.[8]

The doomed youth is said to lack sense; the same idiom is used in Prov 24:30b ("devoid of heart"). He is identified as a boy (*na'ar,* a Hebrew word that covers a broad range of years). By contrast the owner of the overgrown vineyard is presumably an adult. Typical of youth, the lad was on the move. In the other anecdote, the observer was passing by. The same verb occurs in both episodes, as does the verb meaning "to embrace," but the lazy owner hugged his inactive hands, and the seductress was clinging to the young man. Likewise, in the initial colon each anecdote uses a verb for seeing other than *ra'ah,* the one Qoheleth prefers (*shakaph* and *hazah*) and then follows with a form of *ra'ah.* Both examples end with haunting images: death's inner chambers and a warrior's shield, symbolic of the thief's invulnerability and thus the helplessness of the one being robbed.

Was Qoheleth Really an Empirical Thinker?

Like these unknown teachers, Qoheleth also based many insights on personal experience, which he gleaned for everything it offered—as with Ruth in Boaz's grain fields. In doing so Qoheleth practiced empirical investigations into reality. But only up to a point. Much of what he said belongs to cultural assumptions for which no proof existed. Most of these ideas that supplement his empirical observations relate to the deity, but not all of them.

Perhaps the most astonishing assertion Qoheleth made is anthropological rather than theological. He insisted that there is no righteous person on earth who does good and does not sin (7:20). Christian readers who have been burdened with the concept of a fall and the doctrine of original sin may not find his assertion out of line, but even they would have to admit that such a statement cannot be proven. True, Qoheleth may have failed to see anyone who in his judgment qualified for the label "good," but he surely made a claim he could not support with conclusive evidence, for virtue is not transparent to onlookers.

In this respect Qoheleth was quite traditional. Human failure is a frequent theme in the Hebrew Bible, often fueled by the desire to exonerate Yahweh from the charge of treating the chosen people unfairly. Perhaps the most extreme articulation of this low view of human nature was placed in a prophet's mouth. Not surprisingly the one chosen for this unflattering observation was Jeremiah, who also voiced a similarly uncharitable view of the God he faithfully served: "The heart is more corrupt than everything else; it is perverse; who can comprehend it?" (Jer 17:9). According to Jeremiah, the mind is sick beyond healing. If the claim were true, we could not trust this or any other statement by a human being. The whole unit of Jer 17:5–11 juxtaposes deceitful minds and theological dogma with exquisite irony.[9] The brunt of the text is that humans cannot be trusted but God can. Trusted to do what? The answer is presented as divine speech: "I Yahweh search the mind, test the conscience, to repay every person according to deeds and actions" (Jer 17:10). Yahweh's failure to follow through on this promise is ubiquitous, however, almost matching the theme about human failure. It is even voiced by the patriarch Abraham, who dared to ask: "Shall not the judge of the whole earth do what is right?" (Gen 18:25).[10]

Psalm 14 states that Yahweh looks down from heaven on mortals to see a thoughtful person, one who seeks Elohim. (The verbs for observing are precisely those describing the encounter between the young man and the adulteress.) What does Yahweh see? "That everyone has turned away, altogether putrid, no one does good; not even one" (Ps 14:3). This view of mortals was so popular that a duplicate of Psalm 14 was preserved as Psalm 53, with the change of Yahweh to Elohim in accord with the section of the Psalter that has the divine name Elohim in preference to Yahweh.[11]

To justify their view of Elohim as just, Job's friends subscribed to the jaundiced understanding of human nature. Elpihaz stated it bluntly: neither heavenly creatures nor heaven itself are innocent in God's sight; "how much less, one abominable and foul, man who drinks iniquity like water" (Job 15:15–16).[12] In a society where these views dominated, Qoheleth's characterization of mortals as guilty should come as no surprise.

Assumptions about God

Just as Qoheleth accepted certain views about humans that were rampant in society, he also took over reigning assumptions about God. In this respect, as in others, Qoheleth was selective. Of the three major concepts—creator, judge, and redeemer—he chose only the first two. And even the first, God as creator, scarcely resembles what is said elsewhere in the canon. There the emphasis falls on cosmogony, the ordering of the cosmos as a stable entity capable of sustaining life. In ancient imagery, this divine act consisted of at least two things.

Creator and Judge

The first task was to defeat the forces of chaos.[13] Creation therefore entailed a battle. The enemy varied with the culture involved: Tiamat and her consort, Kingu, in the Mesopotamian account; Apophis in Egypt; Baal and Mot in Canaan; Tehom, Rahab, and Tannin in Israel. The champions differed too: Marduk, Re, El, and Yahweh. The conflict reflected nature's rhythm: in Mesopotamia the arrival of the rainy seasons with their accompanying flood waters, which formed new land from alluvial silt; the struggle between day and night in Egypt; the threat of drought in Canaan; and general chaos in Israel.

The manner of the creative deed also varied, with three modes competing for priority. The struggle between the forces of order and chaos was by far the most widespread, but the surviving literature from all over the ancient Near East also has remnants of the alternative ways for forming the world. One was sexual, and the other consisted of divine fiat. In Mesopotamia the union of Apsu and Tiamat, who symbolize fresh water and salt water, resulted in the birth of other gods representing elements of nature.[14] The Egyptian story sometimes consists of masturbation, and the Canaanite version focuses on sexual congress and the building of a palace for Baal, which has been taken as a sort of creation myth, a stabilizing of the world. In Enuma elish, the Mesopotamian story of creation, Marduk commands a garment into existence to demonstrate his worthiness to champion the gods; in the Egyptian Memphite theology creation is by divine command;[15] and in the biblical version of the priestly account, Elohim speaks the elements of the cosmos into existence, except for preexisting matter called Tohu, the Hebrew equivalent of Tiamat, and Bohu. The divine command transformed the existing darkness and restless waters into a viable cosmos.

Once a world came into being, it had to be made livable. That meant overcoming the chaotic waters underground. The earth was thought to have been anchored by the sinking of pylons into the ocean below, and a metal-like firmament prevented the waters above from wreaking havoc. Occasional earthquakes were all that remained of the forces that had to be contained, as if they heeded a divine rebuke: "This far you may come, and no farther."

None of the elaborate cosmogonic activity shows up in Qoheleth's teachings. If he viewed the deity as creator, the emphasis fell on divine activity involving the lives of humans. For example an enigmatic verse seems to touch on the act of creation, at least as it impacts on humans: "He has made everything beautiful in its time; he has also placed *h 'lm* in their mind, yet so that human beings cannot discover the work of Elohim from beginning to end (3:11). Or: "Everything he does is appropriate for its time. . . ."[16]

I have left the crucial word untranslated. As the Masoretes pointed out, it indicates temporality, our modern sense of eternity. For Qoheleth the word would have implied a long time into the future, not endless time. Assigned different vowels, it refers to the hidden, secrets beyond discovery by the naked eye but known to Elohim, according to 12:14 where the verbal root has this unmistakable meaning: "For God will bring every action into judgment, the hidden, whether good or evil." The same use occurs in Job 28:11: "He dams up the sources of streams so that hidden things can be brought to light."[17] We must remember that the Hebrew text lacked vowels in Qoheleth's time, and their absence accounts for the ambiguity of *h 'lm*.

The context supports both interpretations. For some interpreters the heavy emphasis on a time for everything in the tight unit 3:2–8 requires a temporal meaning for the untranslated word.[18] In addition the temporal phrase at the end of the verse seems to confirm this reading. In my view 3:9 shifts away from the idea of a set time for all things, substituting the notion of profit from toil. The following verse continues the theme of human activity, which is deemed a loathsome business imposed by Elohim either as affliction or as tedium. Verse 11 then clarifies that divine gift.

On a temporal reading of *h 'lm,* Qoheleth said that Elohim causes everything to take place precisely at the right time, for he has put a sense of eternity in the human mind. Nevertheless God has made it impossible for the recipients of this dubious gift ever to discover its essence or to find its scope.

On my reading Qoheleth's point was that Elohim has made all things beautiful in their time, that is, appropriate. Still whatever the creator put in the human mind lies beyond reach. Consequently it remains forever hidden. In Qoheleth's view divine activity is not subject to human scrutiny. Like the deity, it is a mystery. On both readings the emphasis falls on secrecy.

If Qoheleth really referred to creation in the usual sense, he divested it of virtually every identifying feature. Even his choice of language distances him from the priestly narrative in Gen 1:1–2:4a. Instead of the elevated verb *bara'*, which is always restricted to divine activity,[19] he used the ordinary word for making or doing something. In the Genesis account the verb *'asah* is used seven times, however, the same number of times as *bara'*, so the narrative implies that both the "making" and the "creating" were perfect. In the ancient world, seven symbolized perfection.

Bara' introduces the creative process in Gen 1:1, indicates the creation of the powerful sea monsters in Gen 1:21, designates the creation of *'adam* emphatically through three occurrences of the verb in Gen 1:27, and is used at the conclusion, once with reference to all that has been created (Gen 2:3) and once in an infinitive clause with a temporal meaning: "when they were created" (Gen 2:4).[20] The verb *'asah* occurs to indicate the making of the firmament (Gen 1:17), the sun and moon (Gen 1:17), the wild beasts, cattle, and creeping things (Gen 1:25), the summation of God's work (Gen 1:31), the cessation of work (two times in Gen 2:2), and a final summation (Gen 2:3).

One significant difference between Qoheleth's observation and the priestly version is the descriptive adjective applied to everything. For Qoheleth it is "beautiful," but Gen 1:1–2:4a drones away with the word "good." In the end an adverb modifies this oft-used word, asserting the exceptional goodness of everything God has made: "And God saw everything he had made, and it was *very* good" (Gen 1:31).

In 7:13 Qoheleth took issue with that assessment of things: "Look at God's work, for who can straighten what he has twisted?"[21] That idea led Qoheleth to reflect on another cultural assumption: that Yahweh creates weal and woe, life and death.[22] The desire to have everything under Yahweh's control is understandable so long as he is thought to be favorably inclined. It is comforting to believe that the one you worship has complete sovereignty over events.

This belief was also a way of asserting the dominance of one's special deity over alternative gods, as in Psalm 82, where Eloah pronounces a death sentence on them for failing to champion the cause of the powerless. Ironically even Eloah must be encouraged to rise up and act as defender of those on the margins of society—the poor, the orphan, the widow, the foreigner. It follows that possessing supreme power does not always guarantee the expected results.[23]

Nevertheless the conviction that Yahweh dispensed both good and bad was not limited to any one strand of biblical literature. It is found in Deut 32:39—"See then that I, I am he, and there is no god besides me. I kill, and I enliven; I have wounded, and I will heal, and no one can deliver from my hand"—and in Isa 45:7—"I form light and create darkness, make well-being and create woe; I Yahweh do all these things." Notably the verb *bara'* occurs in this verse only where undesirable things are mentioned. Even the prologue to the book of Job presents the same idea. Here Job responded to his wife as follows: "You are talking like one of the foolish women. We accept good from God and we accept harm." I have translated the response as a statement. It may be a question without the usual marker for the interrogative: "Should we accept (only) the good from God and not accept the bad?" (Job 2:10). The same idea appears in Job's first reaction to the loss of everything, including his sons and daughters: "Naked I came from my mother's womb, and naked I shall return there.[24] Yahweh has given, and Yahweh has taken. Blessed be Yahweh's name." (1:21).

In this vein Qoheleth observed that Elohim sends good days and bad days. How should one respond? Qoheleth advised enjoyment of the good times and reflection during evil times. The pondering of reasons for the bad things is to no avail, he warned, for the deepest thinking anyone is capable of doing will not point to blame on God's part (7:14).

Now if both good and evil derive from Elohim, are human beings not responsible for any calamity they experience? Qoheleth refused to let them off the hook that easily. According to 7:29, God made humans upright but they have distorted their true nature. Has Qoheleth forgotten that he said that everything the deity does endures, or stated differently, that the twisted cannot be straightened?

Did the Yahwistic story of creation and fall in Gen 2:4b–3:24 influence Qoheleth, as some interpreters think? If so, Qoheleth came nowhere near describing the fall—or the creation for that matter—in intimate detail the way the Yahwist did. We may say that the Yahwist tickled the fantasy while Qoheleth left everything to the imagination, or in the language of Erich Auerbach, the Yahwist provided background and Qoheleth was content to give foreground.[25]

Did Qoheleth ever indicate that "creator" is a workable noun in his vocabulary? That brings us to 12:1, every bit as controversial as 3:11: "Remember your *bore'eyka* in the days of your youth before the evil days come and years arrive of which you will say, 'I have no pleasure in them.'" Once again, I have left the crucial word untranslated. Why? First because it is plural and unique. Its unusual form has been explained as a plural of majesty, but that explanation has failed to convince many interpreters. Second the idea of creator seems intrusive in this context. The obvious reason is that Qoheleth could have chosen a perfectly clear word, "your maker." Why would he use one that only obscures things? Qoheleth had just urged young people in the strongest language to enjoy their brief youth, with a cautionary codicil, however, that God will judge them. A shift to God as creator seems particularly jarring.

Early rabbis were troubled by this strange word. Consider this response: "Know whence you came (*b'rk,* your source), whither you are going (*bwrk,* your grave), and before whom you are destined to give an accounting (*bwr'yk,* your creator)" (Abot 3:1). This saying, attributed to Akabya ben Mahalel (first century c.e.), was explained by the illustrious Aqiba in the following manner. The unusual word has three resonances. The first alludes to Prov 5:15–19, where a wife is likened to a cistern and the husband is told to drink only from his own cistern. The second picks up on a similar Hebrew word for a grave, and the third one echoes a word for creator.[26]

In context, the three allusions within a single word make sense. The wife is the source of pleasure to which the young men are called, the grave stands for the moment of death toward which all inevitably march, and the creator has made both possible.[27] If this verse really alludes to the third of these, it differs from the other apparent references to divine activity. Qoheleth seemed more interested in the way Elohim controls events. Causation, indeed determinism, best describes what Qoheleth thought about the deity's role in the world. Qoheleth failed to mention a single aspect of cosmogony. The contrast with the book of Job could not be greater, for the author of that poetic masterpiece described the cosmological and meteorological aspects of God's creative work at great length.[28]

Both authors agreed, however, that the deity is intimately involved in the birth of humans. For Qoheleth birth was a grand mystery beyond comprehension, but he was certain that God's activity lies behind the livening of a fetus. The author of the book of Job was less reserved if nevertheless amazed at the process. He compared it to a weaver who integrates different strands into a desirable pattern, a cheese maker who mixes the proper ingredients and oversees their coagulation, and a worker in clay who mixes water and clay, shapes the mix until it takes form, and lays it out to dry in the sun or fires it in a kiln.[29]

Divine Generosity

Neither "creator" nor "judge" was Qoheleth's favorite word with God in mind. Perhaps a verb best indicates the way Qoheleth thought about Elohim. That verb is "to give." He used it often with God as subject. Unfortunately just what God bestows on individuals is not always welcome. Near the beginning of Ecclesiastes, Qoheleth said that Elohim has given an unhappy business to humans (1:13). That is not all. Qoheleth attached an infinitive to this declaration about divine generosity. Its meaning is disputed. Either mortals are destined to occupy themselves with irksome business or they afflict themselves with an unwelcome activity.

Qoheleth returned to this theme in 3:10: "I have seen the sorry business that God has given mortals to occupy themselves with." Because Qoheleth believed that anything Elohim did lasts forever, he assumed that it could not be changed. The result of this dubious gift, in his view, was fear before the deity; the purpose lying behind Elohim's activity was the wish to instill awe, reverence, even dread (3:14).

With this comment, Qoheleth moved away from the reigning concept of the "fear of Yahweh" in Job 28:28: "The fear of Yahweh is wisdom; turning from evil is understanding."[30] Similarly Prov 1:7a sums up the widespread view that the fear of Yahweh is the beginning, or first principle, of knowledge. For Qoheleth, fear of God was unrelated to the educational process.

If respect for the deity were rewarded, one should withhold objection; but adoration of God does not bring divine favor. Even though Qoheleth appears to have subscribed to the traditional view that things go well for those who fear God (8:12–13), he admitted that exceptions occur (8:14). In making this important but realistic exception, he did something that Job's three friends were not willing to do. They reasoned from Job's extreme calamity that he had to be guilty of some terrible offense against the deity.[31] For Qoheleth the scales of justice were both blind and unreliable, and that left him with a jaded perspective: "I said: 'All this is absurd.'"

Then did Qoheleth think Elohim was indifferent to human worth? Had the teacher reached the conclusion that Job's friends had arrived at, specifically that human conduct does not affect the deity in the least because of his majesty?[32] Not really, for Qoheleth observed that obedience is more acceptable than the sacrifice of fools (4:17) and that the person who fears God will escape the clutches of the femme fatale (7:26). Excessive piety like Job's, as well as extreme wickedness, are strategies that bring divine wrath, Qoheleth thought. For this reason one ought to avoid either extreme and by doing so move forward unmolested (7:18).

It is obvious that Qoheleth did little more than dance around the concepts of creator and judge applying to God. Did he do the same for the third divine epithet that pervades scripture? The notion of redeemer, celebrated beautifully in the story of the exodus from Egyptian bondage, was for centuries kept out of sapiential literature. The authors of the collections in the book of Proverbs firmly believed that Yahweh was an intimate of those who feared him, but in their surviving teachings they never moved beyond this individualism to the belief that Yahweh was actively at work as redeemer of a chosen people.

Redeemer?

In a moment of desperation Job dared to think of a personal redeemer.[33] Then he backed off when reality chased fantasy out the window (Job 19:25). Not until the second century sage Ben Sira did this widening of the role of deity enter wisdom literature. If divine determinism (6:10; 9:1) fixes human choices for good or ill and if Elohim sends both good and bad days, how can mortals be held responsible for their actions? And if the idea of Elohim as judge is thereby called into question, how much more foreign to Qoheleth's discourse is the comforting belief in providence. Perhaps the most that can be said concerns the divine disposition. Qoheleth made the astonishing statement that God has already approved the enjoyment of those who have the ability to eat and drink.

Most intriguing of all is Qoheleth's obscure remark that God seeks the pursued (3:15). What in the world did he mean by this? Ben Sira made a similar observation: "Do not say, "Who can have power over me? For the Lord is searching for the past" (Sir 5:3). The sentence can also mean "For the Lord searches for the persecuted."[34] The first reading warns against thinking that Yahweh is too busy to bother with the tiny matter of punishing sinners. The emphasis would then fall on a holiness that is wholly transcendental. The second reading stresses something quite different: divine compassion. Qoheleth's remark approximates the first option: God is so preoccupied with the coming and going of events in their proper time that human well-being commands little attention.

If a virtuous life does not catch the deity's attention, what does? Qoheleth thought rash speech, even in prayer, could be an irritant. So could the failure to fulfill a sacred vow. From Ugaritic literature—in which all kinds of misfortune struck Karitu, who made a solemn promise in a time of dire need and subsequently forgot to carry through on it[35]—it is clear that Qoheleth took up a touchy topic, one that is all too familiar in the canon. The deity's response, however, may be considered mild. Punishment does not extend beyond personal property (5:1–6).

In this rare discussion of aspects of worship, Qoheleth referred to a messenger before whom a sinner pleads that an error of judgment has brought them face to face. Who is this mysterious figure? Some interpreters think the messenger is a priest sent to collect the promised payment for depositing in the temple's treasury.[36] Two additional possibilities come to mind. In his distress Job imagined that three figures might come to his aid: an advocate, a redeemer, and a witness. To these Elihu added a fourth, a messenger, probably sent from heaven, who will come to the defense of a repentant sinner, even one facing the divine accuser (Job 33:23). Egyptian texts point to another possibility. Death is called a messenger, but no amount of protest can deter this angel from its assigned task.[37] The adversarial role of the messenger in Qoheleth's remark favors the first or third interpretation: a priest or death.

In one way Qoheleth's thought is entirely orthodox. At death the life breath returns to its source. Behind this graphic image of the *ruah* departing when a human being expires and rising to enter the divine *nephesh* (throat) lies the story from Genesis about Yahweh breathing life into the first human. Dust is expendable, as it were, but the animating breath is precious beyond measure.

An empire consisting of provinces overseen by administrators, who in turn were watched by the supreme monarch, seems to have influenced Qoheleth's view of divine sovereignty. Carried to extreme, this unflattering presentation of lordship suggests that Elohim sees the injustices that plague the weak but does nothing to correct them. Providential care does not belong to Qoheleth's understanding of God.

Of one thing Qoheleth was certain. Elohim controls the duration of human life. Others may have speculated about the optimum years one can expect—whether 120 years as in the Ballad of Heroes discovered at Emar or a modest 70, possibly even 80, as in Ps 90:10—but Qoheleth did no such thing. He seems to have been content to dwell on the brevity, absurdity, and emptiness of whatever time God grants an individual.

I began this discussion by posing a question about the accuracy of the claim that Qoheleth practiced an empirical approach to reality. The extensive analysis of his views about God demonstrates how far-reaching were the presuppositions for which no evidence existed. In fact Qoheleth was aware that God's footprints left no sign in the sand. He went to great lengths to emphasize the secretive nature of divine activity: "I have seen all God's work, that a person cannot find the work that is done under the sun although he labors to search for it but cannot find it; and even if a wise man claims to know, he cannot discover it" (8:17).[38] Three negations of the verb for finding something and two auxiliary verbs expressing the inability to do something make Qoheleth's words maximally emphatic.

How then could Qoheleth say so much about divine activity? He may have followed an empirical approach where visible reality is concerned, but he had much to say about matters of faith. Various ideas about God had crept into his worldview. They may be unorthodox for the most part, but they were still central to his thought. In some ways these surreptitious givens are some of the most fascinating aspects of his teachings.

CHAPTER 6

Victorious Time

A weary traveler, wandering alone in a dense forest, hears heavy footsteps in the distance and quickens his pace, fearing that a ferocious beast will devour him. As the frightening sounds come closer and closer, he runs frantically and falls headlong into he knows not what. Fortunately his luck has not run out yet, for his hands grasp a vine and he holds on for dear life. Under his dangling feet, he sees an abyss awaiting him. As he clings desperately to the vine, he watches two rats, one white and the other black, chewing away at it. To quench his growing thirst, he sips dew that has collected on the leaves of the vine. Before long, the rats chew through the vine; it snaps and sends the doomed traveler into the abyss.

This allegory of time, going back to the early theologian Augustine and retold by Fyodor Dostoyevsky in *The Brothers Karamazov,* graphically depicts the human dilemma. We are sojourners in a dangerous land, and against our will we have been suspended over our final resting place while day and night eat away at our lifeline, the time we have been allotted on earth by genetic disposition, choice, and pure luck or lack of it. Still, even in dire straits, we manage to find moments of pleasure before plunging into utter darkness.

The Temporal Expression "Under the Sun"

Qoheleth's consciousness of time's ravages found expression again and again. He chose the great marker of time's passage, the sun, to highlight his total message.[1] For him the phrase "under the sun" and a variant, "under heaven," characterized human existence: life takes place on earth beneath the bright reminder that the thread is quickly running out (compare Job 7:6). The words "under the sun" occur twenty-nine times, "under heaven" three times. In addition Qoheleth was not averse to using the simple word *earth* to designate the place of human activity (as in 5:1; 8:14; and 11:2).

Others coined the expression "under the sun" long before Qoheleth. In the Gilgamesh Epic we read: "Only the gods [live] forever under the sun. As for mankind numbered are their days; whatever they achieve is but the wind."[2] The phrase "under the sun" is attested in a twelfth-century Elamite document and in Phoenician inscriptions from the sixth and fifth centuries B.C.E.[3] Qoheleth's use extends from 1:3 to 10:5, with only chapter 7 not represented in this block of material. The variant, "under heaven," is restricted to the first three chapters. Both expressions are missing from the last two chapters of the book. In chapters eleven and twelve "on earth" appears in the only place where "under the sun" might have been used (11:2). A mere eighteen verses in this section derive from Qoheleth. In them, however, the sun is ever present as a source of pleasure and a marker of time, along with the dark of night. To them are added morning and evening (11:6), in reverse order from the frequent references to them in Genesis 1 ("And there was evening and there was morning, the first [second, third, fourth, fifth, sixth] day.") Additionally Qoheleth mentioned youth and old age as notable periods in life.

The phrase "under the sun" accurately indicates most human activity in a world before the invention of electric lights extended the hours of both work and play. With darkness came the cessation of work and the retreat into first caves, then tents, and later houses, all with dim lighting. In this world the transition from day to night was easily discernible. It was also an invitation to rest weary bodies from the day's toil.

Qoheleth's near obsession with time is hardly surprising, for earlier sages made much of action at the right moment. So did he, but with one difference. Whereas they believed it possible to seize the right time to act, Qoheleth despaired of doing so, with one possible exception. In 10:17 he pronounced a land happy when kings are mature and princes eat at the proper time and show restraint. Even here, however, he gave utterance to an ideal, one that may not be attainable.

In 8:5–6 he wrestled with the incongruity between the traditional belief that the wise know time and procedure (*mishpat*)[4] and the fact that harm falls unexpectedly and is therefore beyond human control. He elaborated on this idea further in 9:12 by comparing the fate of humans to that of fish caught in a net and birds snared in a trap. The dominant idea is the unexpected nature of the calamity.[5]

The vexing problem of evil is brought under the umbrella of time's circular movement in 3:1. The coexistence of good and evil and the absence of any rhyme or reason to their disposition led Qoheleth, or a glossator, to insist that God will act as judge in due time. On what basis did he reach this strange conclusion? That there is a time for every matter as stated in 3:1. If that assertion is correct, then there must surely be a time to judge—just as there must be one for refraining from judging.[6]

There Is a Time for Everything

With that observation, we have come to the famous poem about a time for everything under the sky. It is probably the only thing many people know about the book of Ecclesiastes other than the mistranslated refrain "vanity of vanities; everything is vanity." This brief poem has been made into a popular song, "Turn, Turn, Turn," and is often read at funerals, especially those for people who have been prematurely snatched from the land of the living.[7]

> For everything there is a season,
> And a time for every matter under the heavens.
> A time to give birth and a time to die,

A time to plant and a time to pull up what has been planted.
A time to kill and a time to heal.
A time to dismantle and a time to build.
A time to weep and a time to laugh,
A time of mourning and a time of dancing.
A time to throw stones away and a time to gather stones,
A time to embrace and a time to refrain from embracing.
A time to search and a time to count as lost,
A time to keep and a time to throw away.
A time to rip and a time to sew,
A time to be quiet and a time to talk.
A time to love and a time to hate,
A time of war and a time of peace.

(3:1–8)

The poem proper, verses 2–8, consists of fourteen antitheses, polarities that symbolize completion as well as perfection. For ancient Hebrews, seven was the symbol of perfection; twice seven was even better if that is possible. The syntax (the temporal noun *'et* followed by infinitives with a preposition *lamed* prefixed) is broken in the second colon of the sixth pair by infinitives without *lamed* and in the last colon of the poem, where nouns appear. The *lamed* with the infinitives is also missing after the second *'et* in the first colon of verse 5. The effect of the symmetry is mesmerizing, like the ticking of a clock.[8]

Reminiscent of catalogs that were popular in the ancient world for educating scribes,[9] the poem covers a wide range of activities, beginning with birth and ending with peace. The first paired opposite usually matches the third, and the second corresponds to the fourth. This arrangement of things has a chiastic effect, an *abb'a* form that is made emphatic by the last four pairs: love/hate/war/peace. The sequence in the first three opposites is striking: being born//planting, dying//uprooting, killing//dismantling, healing//building, weeping//mourning, laughing//dancing.

The opening antitheses, birth and death, lie outside human control.[10] All the others take place between these critical points. In the first pair of opposites, the scene shifts from the human to the plant world.[11] The choice of vocabulary occasionally indicates an interest in echoing a sound, as in verse 4, where *reḵod* ("to dance") occurs rather than *semaḥ* ("to rejoice") and imitates *sepod* ("to mourn"). Similarly *libnot* ("to build") in verse 3 sounds much like *libḵot* ("to weep") in the next verse.[12]

Catalogs were particularly useful in teaching information about nature, language, and geography.[13] Among other things, they aided students in remembering the names of rivers and constellations, the types of insects and animals, the location of cities and countries, and the correct translations of foreign words. Catalogs were also vital to various professions. The practice of medicine depended on the knowledge of specific diseases and their treatments; the interpretation of dreams required information about different "signs"; and the same applied to priestly divination.[14] In addition catalogs of virtues and vices were helpful in ethical instruction.[15]

Kinship with Stoic Philosophy

Bringing similar items together in a single list was a convenient way to teach both writing and knowledge about the world. On a more sophisticated level, catalogs helped philosophers come to terms with the structure of the universe. Stoic philosophers proposed that the universe consisted of opposites that balanced each other, bringing stability to all things. On one side there was evil in various forms, but on the other side an equal number of good things were in evidence. Nature was believed to be in perfect harmony. People were therefore given a lesson in how to bring tranquility into their own lives, balancing the impulses through the proper use of the intellect.

The affinities between Stoic philosophy and this poem have led to the hypothesis that Qoheleth used a brief text of foreign extraction to express his own thoughts.[16] The suggestion should not be ruled out without further ado, for popular Greek philosophy penetrated the thoughts of the Jewish intelligentsia at an early time,[17] possibly even by the third century B.C.E.. In the beginning of the second century B.C.E., Ben Sira appears to have quoted the Stoic confession—"He is the all" (Sir 43:27)—and even described the structure of the universe as made up of antitheses. "All things exist in pairs, one opposite the other, and he made nothing that was incomplete. Each thing strengthens the good parts of the other; who can get enough of seeing God's glory?" (Sir 42:24–25).[18]

The kind of thinking that can lead to the conclusion that all things exist in pairs was not lost to Israel's poets and storytellers. Binary thinking seems innate, as shown by its frequent occurrence in world literature. There are blessings and curses, friends and enemies, human and nonhuman, male and female, white and black, sick and healthy, large and small, rich and poor, and so forth. Israel's deity was believed to have created both weal and woe, hence to have universal sway over the lives of worshippers. The poem in 3:2–8 does not go beyond this simple recognition of antitheses and therefore may be from Qoheleth himself.

Was the Poem Exhaustive?

Not everything in ordinary existence has found expression here. The most obvious missing subject, apart from sex, is eating and sleeping. I say "apart from sex" cautiously, for this powerful drive may be subsumed under the category "embrace," or even under "love." Not satisfied with these possibilities, rabbis responsible for Midrash Rabbah on Qoheleth interpreted the images of gathering stones and casting stones as being sexually active and as continence.[19] This view is partly based on the fact that the images are in parallelism with embracing and its lack. Two difficulties with this interpretation are immediately apparent. The verb for "embrace" can mean casual greeting by friends, and a sexual reading of gathering and casting stones would make this line the only metaphor in the poem. That is possible but less likely if other explanations of the images can be found.

Three unlikely suggestions have been offered: the counting of sheep, the keeping of a record of commercial transactions, and a bundle of the living.[20] The first implies that illiterate shepherds kept a tally of sheep in their care by the number of pebbles placed in a bag, easily adding or taking away a pebble when an animal was acquired or lost. Merchants could have kept a record of sales and expenses in the same way. The biblical idea of a bundle of the living, with pebbles representing those still alive, has also been suggested as a possible background of the image about gathering and collecting stones. It is hard to believe that anyone thought Yahweh, the keeper of the bundle of the living, needed such an aid to memory.

In my view a more probable explanation comes from agriculture. The gathering of stones is for the purpose of clearing a field for cultivation. The stones were piled up in terraces to prevent erosion and to collect vital rain through its slow absorption into the soil. The casting of stones occurred during warfare to make the fields of the enemies temporarily useless (2 Kgs 3:19, 25).

The absence of eating and sleeping in this catalog shows that it was not intended to be exhaustive. It probably has an illustrative purpose, like so much more that Qoheleth said. He was also silent about another important dimension of daily life in the ancient world: worship. Unlike eating and sleeping, however, there was no acceptable antithesis for reverence.

The Element of Chance

In Qoheleth's mind, there may have been a time for everything, but one tiny factor made it impossible to discover the right moment for a given act. That little element of surprise was chance (*miqreh*), a totally unexpected happening that made a mockery of plans. It has been said that the way to make God laugh is to make plans. Chance occurs with the same irony as the thwarting of the best-laid plans. Anatole France once said that "chance is the pseudonym of God when he did not want to sign."

Moreover this element of surprise even touches us at our most vulnerable moment. A single fate strikes humans and beasts, making no distinction between beings who bear the divine image, according to the priestly account of creation, and the animals that are thought to be subservient to humans. Nor does virtue factor into the play of fate, which strikes the unsuspecting in a wholly arbitrary manner (9:1–5). The linking of time, mischance, (*pega'*) and fate is a natural one (9:11), regardless of the activity they intrude on. Most distressingly for the wise, this combination renders their only negotiable ware null and void. No amount of intelligence or wisdom can prevent chance from ruining their lives. Its dancing partners are chosen indiscriminately.

This negative view of *miqreh* is not intrinsic to the noun and consequently provides a clue about Qoheleth's attitude to life. A different use of the notion of chance occurs in the story about Ruth. A young Moabite woman, vulnerable on all three counts,[21] Ruth ventured into the grain fields in the Judean hills to glean the spilled barley for herself and her impoverished mother-in-law. The narrative states that "by chance" she chose the field of Boaz, a kinsman of Elimelech, her deceased father-in-law (Ruth 2:3). In this context the noun comes close to conveying the lofty idea of divine providence. From the perspective of the narrator, Ruth's choice of a field was more than luck, as the development of the story demonstrates. This decision on her part gives substance to the theological statement that Yahweh had visited his people to give them food (Ruth 1:6). Bethlehem had once again become a house of bread,[22] and Yahweh was believed to be smiling as before.

Death: The End Point of Everything Alive

There may be a time for everything, but Qoheleth's clear association of time and death is sobering. He seems to have been ever aware of death's ominous presence; it has even been said that the book has the scent of a tomb.[23] In days when the dead were not embalmed, the stench must have been palpable, hence the practice of burying the dead without delay.

Qoheleth's near obsession with death was not unique in the ancient Near East. The Gilgamesh Epic recorded the adventures of the king of Uruk and his friend Enkidu, who went in search of eternal life. Hardly had they begun the quest when Gilgamesh and Enkidu angered the gods and Enkidu paid the ultimate price.[24] Gilgamesh observed the decomposition of his friend's body, pondered the effect of death, and then set off on a journey to the island on which Utnapishtim (Ziusudra in the Sumerian version), the survivor of the flood, lives with his wife, both having been granted eternal life.

The persistent Gilgamesh finally reached his destination and obtained a leaf from the tree of life, but only after succumbing to sleep as a perpetual reminder of his mortality. With leaf in hand, Gilgamesh set out for home. On the way he stopped at an oasis and laid his precious prize aside long enough for a refreshing swim. To his horror a snake devoured the leaf, shed its skin,[25] and slithered away.

Both this story about the loss of immortality and that preserved in Genesis blame a snake for the human dilemma. Behind both accounts lies the popular belief that snakes rejuvenate themselves periodically, a deduction from the fact that they shed their skins. The biblical account apportions blame among all three characters, Adam, Eve, and the serpent. Their reaction to the divine inquisition is a classic example of passing the buck. The man blamed God and the woman, who in turn blamed the serpent. As last in line, it had no one to blame.

There is an episode in the Danel Epic from Ugarit that touches on the human desire to live forever. In it Danel gave his son Aqhat a magnificent warrior's bow that the goddess Anat desired to obtain for herself. Her first ploy was to offer herself to Aqhat in exchange for the bow, but her record at marriage failed to impress him. Her second move was to offer him eternal life. Spurning both offers, Aqhat made a fatal mistake by mocking her prowess as a warrior. In doing so, however, he reminded her that glaze will be poured on his head like that of all other mortals: "Further life—how can mortal attain it? / How can mortal attain life enduring? / Glaze will be poured [on] my head, / Plaster upon my pate; / And I'll die as everyone dies, / I too shall assuredly die" (*ANET*, 151).

In short he insisted that death is inevitable. The possession of such a bow was not enough to save Aqhat from the fury of a goddess spurned at love and mocked as a weak female.[26]

The biblical recognition of human mortality is not limited to the story about Adam and Eve, who failed to take advantage of the tree of life in the garden but focused attention on another tree that was specifically placed off limits by their maker. Their missed opportunity was the result of disobedience, in contrast to the Mesopotamian Adapa, who failed to become immortal by obeying the advice of a god. After being told by the god of wisdom to refuse food in the presence of other gods, he did so only to be informed that he has spurned the offer of living forever like the gods.[27]

The contrast between the deities in the two stories is not great. The biblical myth describes a maker who, fearing that his creatures will become like him, withholds that grand prize and expels them from the garden and all access to the life-giving tree. The other story depicts a deceptive god of wisdom who prevents more kindly gods, at least in this story, from bestowing immortality on a favored human being. In each myth the fault is not wholly a human one.

Two incidents from the life of David illustrate the awareness of human mortality in the Bible. The first involves the consequences of David's adulterous affair with Bathsheba. After compounding adultery with the mandate that sealed the fate of her husband at the hands of Ammonite soldiers, David learned from the prophet Nathan that his sin would cost him and the mother the life of the son born of the union with Bathsheba. The humbled king prayed for the child's life for seven days but to no avail. Later, defying custom, David bathed and ate instead of denying himself as a mourner. When asked to explain his strange behavior, he said: "While the child was alive I fasted and wept, for I thought, 'Who knows? Yahweh may have mercy and the child will live? But now he is dead. Why should I fast? Can I bring him back again? I shall go to him, but he will not return to me'" (2 Sam 12:22–23).[28]

Nothing in this episode indicates that the narrator recognizes how unfavorably it reflects on Yahweh. The belief in divine justice is not supported by the imposition of a death sentence on the child of the sinner. That inequity, at least by modern standards, did not dampen the popularity of the concept of transgenerational guilt (to the third and fourth generations), as stated in the confessional statement in Exod 34:6–7.[29]

The second incident took place late in David's reign. His son Absalom had been exiled from the king's presence, and the head of David's army devised a plan to bring the prince home again. Part of the speech by the astute woman from Tekoa who was entrusted with this task is as follows: "For we must all die; (we are) like water that is poured earthward that cannot be gathered up" (2 Sam 14:14a). The Hebrew grammar is emphatic, like death itself.

Like the authors of these texts in which death figures prominently as an issue to be pondered, Qoheleth did not view death as a cause for despair. Still he did not distinguish between a good death (an oxymoron?) and a bad death, as in some modern discussions. Ben Sira did nevertheless acknowledge that circumstances affect the way people view death. Individuals who are afflicted by disease and have meager resources look on death as welcome, whereas those who enjoy good health and ample resources do not put out a welcome mat for death's heavy feet (Sir 41:1–4). In Ben Sira's view, no one should fear the eternal decree, for it represents the good pleasure of the Most High. That is not Qoheleth's sentiment, but he would have agreed with Ben Sira that it does no good to argue about future life in the grave, whether its duration is ten, a hundred, or a thousand years.

Qoheleth's Description of Old Age and Death

The passing of time and its debilitating effect on the body was not hidden from Qoheleth. His description of old age as the prelude to eternity in 12:1–7 has a haunting effect.[30] The poem's powerful imagery combines scenes from a ruined estate, a threatening storm, nature's resurgence, and brokenness where it really matters. Metaphor, allegory, and literal description coalesce into complex images; together they give the impression of a unified whole. The three refrains enhance that feeling and place time at the center of thought: "before . . . before . . . before" (*'ad 'asher lo'*, verses 1, 2, and 6):

> And remember your wife[31] in the days of your youth,
> before the evil days come and the years approach
> of which you will say, "I have no pleasure in them."
> Before the sun is darkened and the light—and the moon and the stars—[32]
> And the clouds return after the rain.
> When the keepers of the house tremble and
> valiant men are stooped,
> And the grinding women cease because they are few,
> And those who look through the windows are dimmed;
> And the doors on the street are closed,
> When the sound of the grinding is muted,
> And one rises at the sound of the bird,
> And all daughters of song are brought low.
> Also they are afraid of heights,
> And terrors are in the path,
> And the almond blooms, the locust burdens itself,
> The caperberry is useless;
> For mankind goes to his eternal home,

And the mourners go about the street.
Before the silver cord is torn,
And the golden bowl is shattered,
And the jar by the fountain is broken,
And the pulley at the cistern is ruined.
And the dust returns to the earth as it was,
And the life breath returns to God who gave it.

The poem begins by contrasting youth and old age,[33] urging the young to remember their sources of pleasure in the brief span of time prior to the unwelcome process of aging. The two periods are aptly represented by days and years respectively, and the latter are even called evil.

If the images that follow are literal, they refer to the dimming of sight in the aged, the weakened state of slaves and their owners, stooped shoulders, diminished domestic workers, closed commerce, sleeplessness, poor tonal quality, heightened danger, signs of spring in nature, deaths, funerals, and the deterioration of things essential for life. A figurative interpretation emphasizes the collapse of a house in a storm, the rejuvenating impact of the rain on nature, and old age and death. The actual death is symbolized by the breaking of a lamp from which pours its source of light,[34] and the shattering of the vessel used to acquire water from a deep well.

An allegorical interpretation is found in rabbinic literature, but it applies to only a few verses. For example the keepers of the house are hands (or knees that hold up the body); its valiant men are the back; the grinders are teeth; the women who look through the windows are the eyes; the daughters of song are the vocal cords; the blossoming almond is white hair; and the useless caperberry is sexual desire.

The pictures of old age and existence in Sheol as darkness contrast mightily with the sweetness of light during youth. The interplay of human and nonhuman images stresses the intimate association of humankind with nature. The link lasts forever, for crumbling dust returns to the earth from which it came.[35] Spring has ended, and a permanent winter begins. The first two instances of "before" are followed by descriptions of the onset of old age, while the third one precedes the symbolic representations of death and the separation of life breath from dust. This topic is anticipated by the solemn allusion to human destiny: the journey to an eternal home.

The description of the tomb as an eternal home is attested elsewhere. A Palmyrene inscription from the end of the second century B.C.E. refers to "the house of eternity, that grave which Zabdeateh built," and Egyptians called the grave an eternal house, according to Diodorus Siculus.[36] A Punic inscription has the expression "a chamber of the eternal home." The idea of the grave as forever goes along with a denial of life after death other than some diminished form, conveniently called "shades."

The rich images combine with a lack of specific reference in so many cases to produce confusion, an appropriate feeling to imitate the onset of old age and the opening of the door for the death angel. The ambiguity begins with the word I have translated "wife" and continues in the apparent superfluous mention of light after sun and moon are said to have lost their luster. The distinction between the source of light for the two great lamps, sun and moon, in Gen 1:3 and 14–19 is duplicated in Qoheleth's "sun and the light—the moon and the stars."

Qoheleth's Random Thoughts about Death

Now if the images pertaining to old age and death are less than crystal clear, how much more obfuscating is what Qoheleth said about endless time and inhabitants of the eternal house. Perhaps his most surprising remark is that an evil woman is actually more bitter than death (7:26).[37] In light of his views about life, it is difficult to fathom that he believed anything could be worse than death. This saying about death is neutralized, however, by another: "Better is the day of death than of birth" (7:1b). The reasoning behind this axiom is clarified by Ben Sira's observation that happiness is only assured at death: "Count no one happy until his death" (Sir 11:28a). In other words a reputation is not permanently established until death, as some Roman moralists believed. Qoheleth's comment is set within that context, for 7:1a reads: "A good name is better than fine ointment." The alliteration within a chiasm is exquisite: *tob shem mishshemen tob.*

Some things that Qoheleth said about the dead can be confirmed. For instance they take nothing with them (5:15). As everyone knows, the funeral shroud has no pockets. Qoheleth's remark was directed against an acquisitive society bent on amassing a fortune. Moreover that the days of darkness will be many (11:8) is an obvious conclusion from observing local cemeteries. That the dead are quickly forgotten, though regrettable, is also obvious (1:11; 2:16).

The rest of Qoheleth's comments about the departed are mere guesses. By using the rhetorical question, "Who knows?" when pondering the exact destiny of humans and beasts (3:21), he admitted it. Still, he thought those in Sheol have lost their sight (3:22), mental capacity (9:5), participation in what goes on under the sun (9:6), and the possibility of receiving any reward (9:5). In 9:10 he summed up their bleak existence as devoid of work, thought, or knowledge in the place to which they are going. The participle *holek* ("going") underlines the fact that the journey has already begun, and the pronoun "you" personalizes it.

Resistance to Death as the End

Not everyone in ancient Israel was so reticent about the future. The legends about notables who cheated death stirred the imagination,[38] and strong feelings about intimacy between worshipper and deity fueled it. Yahweh's "taking" of Enoch and Elijah is widened to include others in Pss 49:8, 16 and 73:24, possibly also in Isa 53:8. The language of the stories about Enoch and Elijah employs understatement in Enoch and overstatement in Elijah. Of Enoch it is simply said, "He was not," and an explanatory statement adds, "For God took him." The account of Elijah's departure uses repetition to create an air of anticipation which the explosive finale does not disappoint. A chariot borne along by a whirlwind evokes a shout from an awestruck Elisha: "My Father! My Father! The chariot of Israel and its horses" (2 Kgs 2:12). An equivalent of the particle of nonexistence that applied to Enoch concludes the story about Elijah: "He [Elisha] saw him no more."

The subject addressed in Psalm 49 is life's fleeting character, a major theme for Qoheleth, although he did not call death a personal shepherd as in Ps 49:15. Both thinkers, however, compared humans with animals as equally perishable. The psalmist took pains to deny that anyone can escape death as did Enoch and Elijah (Ps 49:6–13), but then imagined that he might be an exception: "Surely God will ransom me from Sheol's grasp, for he will receive me" (Ps 49:16). The contrast between the fool's inability to take anything across the great divide[39] and being received by God provides a fine play on the two meanings of the verb *laqah* ("to take," "to receive").

The other psalm discusses the problem of the apparent success of scoundrels. It reaches a resolution only after a mind-stretching struggle, one that allowed the psalmist to transform the creed "Surely God is good to the upright, God to those whose hearts are pure" into a simple "But for me, God's drawing near is good to me" (Ps 73:1, 28). The heart, a thematic word that occurs six times here,[40] joins the three uses of the exclamatory "surely" in expressing the intensity of devotion to God. A powerful sense of nearness to God is reinforced by an awareness that God takes his hand and offers sound advice like that in Isa 30:20–21: "Yahweh will give you bread of adversity and water of affliction, but your Teacher will no longer be hidden, for your eyes will behold your Teacher, and your ears will hear a word from behind: 'This is the path; walk in it,' when you veer either to the right or to the left."

As in Job 19:26, the word *after* shows how tentatively the ancients talked about postmortem happenings. For Job the peeling of his skin signals death, revealing his momentary hope of a different ending as a pipe dream. The psalmist's afterwords can be interpreted either way, as postmortem hope or as deliverance from extreme danger in the present existence. The combined words *glory, forever, rock,* and *portion* lead me to believe the psalmist thought about a survival of the relationship with God after death. For him, death cannot blot out a love for God.[41]

If Ps 49:16 is open to doubt as to its future reference and Ps 73:24 only obliquely mentions death prior to Yahweh's receiving the worshipper into glory, Isa 53:8 explicitly refers to the servant's demise.[42] Both the grave and death are specified in verses 9 and 12. The verb "taken away" may mean that he died, or it may have a weightier sense, that of being received by Yahweh. The metaphorical language and the difficulty of determining whether the servant is an individual or all Israel complicate matters. If the servant were an individual, the text echoes *laqah* in Pss 49:16 and 73:24.

Thus far I have restricted my discussion to texts influenced by the language about the taking of Enoch and Elijah. Two other canonical texts touch on the idea of resurrection. In Isa 26:19 we read: "Your dead will live, their corpses will rise; Inhabitants of the dust, awake and exult! For your dew is radiant, And the earth will give birth to the shades." The verse seems out of context, but if it glosses verse 24: "They are dead, cannot live; shades never rise, surely you visited them and demolished them, and memory of them is destroyed." It does so in the spirit of Isa 25:8, the anticipated swallowing of death by a victorious Yahweh: "He will destroy death forever; my lord Yahweh will wipe away the tears from every face?"

The ambiguity disappears in Dan 12:2: "At that time your people will be delivered, all those found written in the book. Many who sleep in the land of dust will awake, some to everlasting life and others to continual reproach and contempt. The wise will shine like the radiance of the firmament; and those who lead many to righteousness, like stars forever and ever" (Dan 12:1b–3). Several things stand out here. The time of deliverance is pushed forward into a remote future; only those whose names are written in a heavenly book are rescued; and the bodily resurrection is limited to the exceptionally good and bad. From this small beginning, it is a long way to the full blown hope of the resurrection as found in 2 Macc 7:1–42, an early martyrology about a mother's seven sons who are hideously tortured and put to death. For the author of this story, the resurrection of the dying sons was beyond doubt.[43] The Alexandrian author of Wisdom of Solomon adopted a different approach to the injustices of ordinary existence, leaning in the direction of the Greek belief in an immortal soul.[44]

Against this groundswell of efforts to view the afterlife in a favorable light, Qoheleth did not stand alone. He was joined by the author of the book of Job and by Ben Sira. For these three, nature alone endures while humans are subjected to a shadowly existence in Sheol. In the end time is victorious.

Time was central in Qoheleth's thinking. For him everything had its own place in the calendar of events within the structure of the universe. Unfortunately no one was smart enough to recognize the proper moment for an action. The reason was chance. This unpredictable factor was supreme, rendering humans subject to whim. Sovereign too was death, the temporal end point that is set in motion at the beginning point, birth. Although some thinkers did their best to remove the sting of death by positing a bright future in another life, Qoheleth refused to join them. Did he try to make up for this loss by draining the cup of life to the last drop? He did advise to eat, drink, and enjoy life.

CHAPTER 7

Tasty Nectar

The sun's rising and setting was a daily reminder that time is sovereign, in the long run triumphing over everything. Still the sun rises and sets as usual, and the dead no longer witness its splendor or bow in subjection to time's supremacy. In the brief span of existence under the sun, what should one do? Like many other intellectuals in his day and in the centuries since then, Qoheleth searched for an adequate response to that question. His answer is a predictable one: "Enjoy yourself if you have the ability to do so."[1]

How did he arrive at this conclusion? He adopted the persona of a fictional king who uses his vast resources to surround himself with the things that bring pleasure. We know them well because of their wide appeal; so did the ancients. Qoheleth mentioned special accomplishments in a chosen endeavor: the construction of splendid houses, carefully designed vineyards and gardens, skillful horticulture, effective irrigation systems, the acquisition of others to do menial labor, herds, silver and gold, entertainers, and something mysterious, at least to later readers of this inventory of pleasure.[2] Astonishingly, however, these diversions did not bring happiness. Satisfying every conceivable desire merely wrung from Qoheleth a sad confession that "everything was empty, feeding on wind, and unprofitable under the sun" (2:11b).

What then of intellectual pursuits? Do they bring lasting joy? Qoheleth recognized that wisdom has a little value, like light as opposed to darkness, but that advantage is obliterated by the common destiny awaiting both wise and fool. "Why, then," he asked, "have I been so very knowledgeable?" His answer: "This is absurd." Why? Because nobody will remember the genius, or the dunce, for that matter.[3]

The thought of sharing a common destiny with fools prompted Qoheleth to make a stunning admission: "Therefore I hated life." Surrounded by his remarkable achievements and basking in a surfeit of pleasure, he loathed the things that made it possible—in his case, work and intelligence. Why? He was troubled by the fact that someone else would inherit his wealth, an unknown person who might not be worthy of it. Pondering this possibility brought Qoheleth much vexation and many sleepless nights. He therefore looked for a way to salvage life under the sun. Eating, drinking, and experiencing pleasure seemed to him an avenue to forgetfulness. Under their power, life's disappointments paled, at least momentarily. He voiced this theme seven times in the book.

I

There is nothing better[4] for a person than to eat, drink, and let himself enjoy good things with his wages;[5] I have also seen that this is from God's hand. For who can eat and who can have enjoyment apart from me? For God gives wisdom, knowledge, and joy to the individual who pleases him, but to the one who displeases him God gives the bother of gathering and collecting to give to another who pleases God. This is absurd and shepherding the wind. (2:24–26)

At least three things stand out in these initial remarks from Qoheleth about the triad of eating, drinking, and enjoyment. First the pleasure that one experiences in work and from earnings is said to lie outside human control. In this bold claim, Qoheleth challenged the traditional belief that the acquisition of knowledge, coupled with the fear of God, would guarantee success in attaining life's good things more often than not.[6] Qoheleth reached the shocking conclusion that God alone held the key that opened the door to pleasure.

Second Qoheleth carried the royal fiction to ridiculous extremes, according to the reading in the Masoretic text. All pleasure, it claims, is made possible by the king. Alternatively it states that no one can enjoy life as much as a ruler who has unlimited resources. If one changes the text to read "apart from him" instead of "apart from me,"[7] as stated in the previous verse, Qoheleth asserted that pleasure resides solely in divine control.

Third Qoheleth turned moral reasoning on its head. Leading a virtuous life, he said, does not always result in the enjoyment of life's good things, nor does "sowing wild oats" exempt one from reaping a bountiful harvest of pleasure. In Qoheleth's vocabulary the usual words for good people and bad people, *tob* and *hote'*, have lost their moral content and simply denote lucky and unlucky people. For him the designation of sinner had regained its original sense of "errant," like a sharpshooter missing the mark.[8]

If for Qoheleth enjoyment lay outside one's control, was limited to royalty, and had nothing to do with the way people conduct their lives, there is not the slightest hint of euphoria in the praise of pleasure. My translation of verse 24 has been influenced by the similar expression in 3:22, where a preposition of comparison (*min*) occurs. This reading takes enjoyment to be a relative advantage rather than an absolute good. A literal translation of the text in 2:24 is different: "There is nothing good in a human who eats and drinks. . . ." This expression corresponds to 3:12, which also has a preposition *beth* meaning "with" or "in" instead of a *min*. ("There is nothing good in them" [*bam* rather than in a man, *ba'adam,* as in 2:24]). This reading emphasizes the sinful nature of humans, a common theme in the Bible.

Regardless of the translation of verse 24, the meaning is reasonably clear. Qoheleth suggested that hatred of life need not rob one of pleasure. Something else, however, prevented Qoheleth from getting excited about the prospect of enjoying life: his belief that the ability to find pleasure is controlled by an arbitrary deity who does not take moral desert into consideration.[9] Thus Qoheleth posed a dilemma: If right living does not lead to enjoyment, what does? Human beings, he thought, are mere pawns in a divine game of chess, disposable and helpless. No wonder Qoheleth considered the whole situation absurd, indeed without purpose. Whether or not an individual actually finds enjoyment is subject to someone else's whim.

Qoheleth was enough of a realist to recognize that unseen factors can render one incapable of enjoying food, drink, and other things that bring a measure of satisfaction. He did not spell these out the way Ben Sira did when distinguishing between a welcome and an unwelcome death. This later sage noted that poor health and diminished resources radically affect a person's ability to derive satisfaction from food, drink, and other pleasures. Although Qoheleth left out the specifics, he carried the idea further than his successor. In Qoheleth's view God arbitrarily grants the ability to enjoy life to some and just as arbitrarily withholds it from others. This uncertainty about one's chances of enjoying a good meal sets Qoheleth apart from symposiatic literature as it developed in the Greek and Roman world. Moreover Qoheleth nowhere suggested that a robust intellectual discussion was part of the anticipated food and drink.

2

> I know that there is nothing good in them except to rejoice and to do good in their lifetime. And also every person who eats, drinks, and experiences good in all his labor—that is a gift of God. (3:12–13)

While the first recommendation of pleasure is introduced by a particle of nonexistence, Qoheleth's second one begins with a verb of cognition, which then gives way to the same particle that occurs earlier.

Perhaps the thing that stands out most in this version of Qoheleth's teaching about enjoyment is the inclusion of a moral component. Enjoyment is coupled with doing good—if the adjective *tob* carries its usual weight. If it does not, then Qoheleth simply varied the language of 2:24. Instead of saying "experience pleasure," he said, "do, that is, have pleasure."

A similar ambivalence surrounds his use of the word for accomplishment, which replaces the less pleasant expression for arduous labor in verse 13. With reference to God, *ma'aseh* ("work") often has a sense of mystery,[10] denoting divine activity that humans cannot comprehend. Qoheleth appears to have implied that one ought to derive some satisfaction from the things that occupy the mind and body during waking hours.

A striking correspondence occurs here as well. A divine gift is equated with the portion that is allotted to humans. Enjoyment is both a gift of God and a portion belonging to mortals. In Qoheleth's mind, there could be no talk of having the whole pie. A small slice is all that will be granted. It may leave one wishing for more, as did the first couple in the book of Genesis, but to no avail. Other canonical thinkers had explored at some length the problem of mortals desiring more than the deity permitted, both inside the garden and outside it, where in their view the curse on the land was always at play.[11]

The context of this remark about enjoyment emphasizes human failure to make effective use of a permanent gift, a desire either to obtain immortality or to uncover the deep mysteries of existence. In addition the context stresses the permanence of divine activity and its ultimate purpose—to instill awe and reverence in mortals. Not even the tiniest increment can be added to the portion bestowed on humans, or taken away. Of that much Qoheleth was certain.

3

And I have seen that there is nothing better than that a person enjoy his accomplishment, for it is his portion, because who can bring him to see what will take place after him? (3:22)

In Qoheleth's third observation about enjoyment a verb of seeing replaces that of cognition in the second one. Indeed seeing is thematic here. Moreover an equation of one's personal achievement and portion in life is also made. The objective reason Qoheleth offered for this recommendation is the inability to see into the future. Human ignorance about what will take place, either in one's own life or more probably after one's death—that is a basis for seizing the present moment. If Qoheleth's reference is to events after death, he was troubled for trivial reasons. If the temporal reference is during an individual's lifetime, his point is banal. Of course no one knows what will happen in the future.

4

This is what I myself have seen to be good, *that is appropriate,* namely to eat and drink and look on good things in all the possessions for which one toils under the sun the few days of life that God has given, for that is one's portion: Also every person to whom God gives riches and possessions and whom God empowers to eat some of it and to have a portion and to rejoice in one's toil: this is a gift of God. For he will not long remember the days of his life, because God keeps him occupied with the joy of his heart. (5:17–19; English, 5:18–20)

This fourth observation about enjoyment adds an aesthetic dimension. Until now, the only occurrence of the word *yapheh* has been in 3:11, where it characterizes the created order as either beautiful or appropriate. Still that lofty description of the cosmos is set within a sober analytic statement emphasizing human inability to profit from a mysterious divine gift. Now Qoheleth personally vouched for something that he considered almost perfect. Qoheleth seems to have been suggesting more than that of the Greek expressions *kalon philon* and *agathon hoti kalon,* which imply perfection.[12] Qoheleth's idea of limits pervades this entire unit about pleasure. Individuals, it says, have only a brief time in which to find pleasure; they are permitted to enjoy a mere portion of what they have earned; and they possess short memories.

Each of these limitations is given a theological rationale. Above all the life span is controlled by God although the Bible is inconsistent on the exact years allotted to humans. The desire to know one's life span exposes the same anxiety that gave rise to classics such as the Gilgamesh Epic.[13] Like moderns, the ancients asked why death is inevitable for humans. In a perfect order, they ought to enjoy the same benefits as the gods.[14] Obviously life under the sun is no perfect order. Just as God has imposed a limit on the days a person gets to live, he has restricted the benefits one participates in during that short stay under the sun. Worse still, individuals spend their waking hours accumulating wealth but then discover that their possessions are not at their disposal. Instead God controls access to the goods, enabling some to find pleasure but withholding it from others. Moreover there is no rational explanation for the divine choice. Subject to the Almighty's whims, human beings can do nothing to change their destiny for good.[15] Even the fortunate ones gain access to a mere portion of their own property.

In such circumstances the memory ought to be fully active, stimulated by a sense of wrongdoing in high places. That is not Qoheleth's conclusion. He thought the memory loses its power, as with someone who has no recollection of conduct during a drunken binge[16] or someone stricken with dementia.

Qoheleth did not indicate the vantage point from which the individual's memory loses its grip on reality. Did Qoheleth mean that people forget themselves and their misery while searching for pleasure? Nothing in Ecclesiastes ever indicates that Qoheleth was able to rise above self-absorption. His "me first" attitude lingers even in the sole reflection about the advantages of broadening one's horizons to include others. In that he is hardly different from the sages in general, for their primary interest was in improving their lot through education and the right conduct it inspired.

Perhaps Qoheleth thought of memory at the end of life when looking back over the sum total of existence and assessing the balance in it between good and bad. The short memory, Qoheleth thought, is directly attributable to God. Just what Qoheleth believed the deity does to affect the memory in this way is not clear. The uncertainty lies in the participle *ma'aneh,* which may be translated in three different ways: keeps him occupied, answers, and afflicts.[17]

The first of these suggests that the active quest for pleasure forces other concerns to the periphery, so dominant is the thought of following one's deepest desires. The second translation implies that revelation occurs precisely when people respond positively to the good things provided by the creator. Joy, therefore, adds ecstasy to ordinary existence, and that joy arrives only through thinking about one's mortality and the perfection of the divine ordering of things with joy at the center.[18] The third translation underscores the arbitrary way God treats humans, withholding eternal life and subjecting them to endless toil only occasionally relieved by pleasure.

It may not be necessary to choose one of these possibilities.[19] Qoheleth was surely aware of all three nuances of the verb *'anah.* He may have chosen it to guide hearers into thinking about the influence of mortality on conduct. Thinking about death can encourage deep reflection on the things that add a dimension to life beyond the ordinary.[20] Joy is surely something that is akin to the sublime. At the same time thinking about death reminds one of the many injustices that make life intolerable, especially when their source is divine.

Another word in Qoheleth's third observation about what is good has a similar ambiguity to the participle *ma'aneh.* That is the word *'amal,* which in his usage indicates back-breaking labor as well as the monetary result of that work.[21] Qoheleth may have urged workers to take pleasure in their toil, or he may have encouraged them to enjoy the fruit of their labor.

If the first of these two ideas is taken as the correct reading, it represents a shift away from the understanding of burdensome work as a curse placed on humans for disobeying the divine prohibition against eating the fruit of the tree in the center of the garden. Presumably, in the mind of the author, prior to that transgression tending the garden was not associated with having to coax the necessities of life out of inhospitable soil.

From personal experience I can attest that hard labor need not cripple the spirit. During my junior and senior years in high school, I worked in a cotton mill for forty-eight hours a week in addition to attending class every day. First as one who oiled looms and took rolls of cloth off them and later as a weaver, I learned to think about class assignments and pleasant things while performing exhausting duties. Farmers in ancient Israel may also have turned their hard labor into something less vexing than it would have been otherwise. "Whistle while you work" is no idle observation.

Admittedly that is not how the author of the Teachings for Duauf in ancient Egypt viewed the various professions in his day. His description of vocations other than that of a scribe leaves the impression that there was nothing desirable about any work other than intellectual endeavors. Ben Sira concurred, although he recognized the valuable contribution manual laborers make to society.[22]

The second of the possibilities above is self-explanatory. The proceeds from one's toil provide enjoyment whether they are the products of the farm or take the form of tangible wealth. Food brings pleasure, especially when shared with loved ones. And money answers everything, according to Qoheleth's thought-provoking comment in 10:19.

5

So I praised pleasure in that there is nothing for a man under the sun but to eat, drink, and rejoice, for it will stay with him in his wages the days of his life that God gives him under the sun. (8:15)

What is new in Qoheleth's fifth comment about pleasure? Two things advance beyond a mere observation about the "good and appropriate." Qoheleth no longer *described* the good; instead he offered an enthusiastic endorsement. Moreover he now thought the effects of enjoyment are not just a momentary sensation.

Does the context of this comment shed light on the new element? Qoheleth mentioned a problem that seems always to have plagued the judicial system. Justice is delayed, and this failure on the part of prosecutors encourages wrongdoers to carry out their nefarious deeds without fear of punishment. For Qoheleth this failure also indicted God, the ultimate judge.[23]

Later Jewish intellectuals addressed this problem in different ways. The author of Wisdom of Solomon offered a theological defense of divine long-suffering, which he attributed to a merciful sovereign.[24] In a perceptive, if somewhat selective reading of the Egyptian enslavement of the ancient people who, according to the story, later escaped and settled in the land of Canaan, he emphasized the manifold nature of God's compassion. According to this author, not only did God show extraordinary patience, giving the Egyptians sufficient time to repent, but God also tempered punishment, treating them more leniently than their crimes deserved.[25]

The Testament of Abraham takes a different approach.[26] It relates that an angel escorted Abraham on a journey through the heavens, from which vantage point the patriarch observed sinners in the act. Furious that God did not punish each evildoer immediately, he prayed for that result and God obliged him. The same thing happened again and again, until finally God warned Abraham that the entire human race would soon be wiped out. A bit late for many, Abraham realized the need for divine patience in the face of wickedness. What irony! It seems that the author thought the incident of the flood taught God a valuable lesson: the continuation of the human species depends on divine patience.[27]

In Qoheleth's view a delay in punishing the wicked makes them eager to do more evil. Their minds are saturated with thoughts of illicit conduct, filled to the brim with exciting possibilities. Qoheleth exaggerated for maximal effect, mentioning a hundred offenses without the sinner suffering the expected consequences of a shortened life. Still he insisted that evildoers will not go unpunished. Conversely good people will be rewarded for their devotion to God.[28]

The longevity of sinners, denied on principle by earlier sages, is here acknowledged. Qoheleth described the wicked as prolonging their days like (or in) a shadow. Biblical explanations for the flourishing of the wicked sometimes seem not to have been thought through, as when the long reign of the reviled King Manasseh is said to have resulted from divine foreknowledge. That is God knew that the king would eventually repent of his misdeeds. This illustration of divine patience inspired a later author to compose a prayer of penitence and attribute it to Manasseh.[29] More important, made possible by that patience, an ominous silence hovered over the enormous suffering of his victims.[30]

Qoheleth's second complaint concerns miscarriage of justice in yet another way. Decent people reap the harvest appropriate to sinners, and evil people receive the things that should go to the righteous. In these instances justice is truly blind—and not in a good sense. Normal expectations are reversed,[31] and the usual encouragements for ethical behavior vanish. No wonder Qoheleth framed this idea with his favorite word, which probably has the sense of absurdity in this instance. He began with an existing reality ("There is an absurdity") and ended with a personal assessment of things ("I thought, 'Surely this also is absurd'").

Given the negative tone of the total context, Qoheleth's assurance that all is well seems out of place. If he is right that punishment for sin is frequently postponed with undesirable results and that reward for good deeds is not forthcoming, all is not well. And if he is also right that inappropriate responses to deeds, either good or bad, are the norm, how could Qoheleth say that he knows things will turn out well despite present appearances? The obvious response to the Pollyanna attitude would be to relax in full knowledge that traditional orthodoxy is safe despite apparent evidence to the contrary. That view can hardly be anything less than tongue-in-cheek if it actually came from Qoheleth.

6

Go, eat your bread in joy and drink your wine in a pleasant spirit, for God has already approved your action. Always let your clothes be white, don't lack oil on your head, experience life with the woman you love all the days of your brief life that he has given you under the sun—all your empty days—for that is your portion in life and in your wages for which you toil under the sun. (9:7–9)

What prompted this significant linguistic shift from description and reported praise to imperatives? In the first place Qoheleth once more came up against divine mystery. He recognized that human deeds reside in God's hands. What he did not know is the divine demeanor. Does God love or hate?[32] That is the question. He did know, however, that the same destiny awaits everybody, regardless of their deeds. At this point Qoheleth got specific, lest anyone misunderstand. It makes no difference whether one is righteous or wicked, pure or impure, meticulous about sacrifice or neglecting the ritual, a good person or a transgressor, an oath taker or one who refuses religious swearing. All die, but before that their minds can be malicious and even mad. Then they join the dead. The sentence breaks off like life itself ("and afterwards to the dead").

For now though, the living possess something that is denied the dead. To illustrate this point, Qoheleth quoted a proverb: "A living dog is better than a dead lion." Its original application is unknown, but it may have been a response by a former widow to counter charges that she had made a poor choice in a second marriage.[33] Once again Qoheleth's observation may be tongue-in-cheek, especially when it reduces human knowledge to the unpleasant concept of mortality. How is awareness that one is going to die any advantage at all?[34]

While the dead know nothing, one may question Qoheleth's assertion that the memory of them is also erased. If the genitive is subjective instead of objective, their memory, that is, the verb "forgotten" seems inappropriate. Their memory, like all their attributes, has perished. Qoheleth's additional point is irrefutable. Powerful emotions such as love and zeal are silenced at death. Furthermore the deceased are no longer players in the game of life. Their particular portion has fallen to someone else.

This, then, is the context of Qoheleth's sixth comment about pleasure. It takes the form of an imperative, like conventional instructions in Egyptian wisdom and the sections in the book of Proverbs that resemble them (Prov 17:22–22:32).[35] The instructional form is more suited to young students, but nothing in Qoheleth's teachings thus far has suggested that he addressed youth rather than sophisticated adults. That information first appears in the second epilogue and appears to contradict the first epilogue, which states that Qoheleth taught the people, presumably adults.

Before now he simply referred to eating and drinking. Here he specified bread and wine. Also new is the assurance that such simple enjoyment has received a stamp of approval from God. What follows is close to the advice offered to Gilgamesh and Enkidu by a woman named Siduri at a tavern. It concerns light clothes, plenty of oil for the head, and the joys of a beloved.

The unusual Hebrew word that designates the beloved has troubled interpreters.[36] Why did Qoheleth not use the normal word for wife? If he was addressing young boys who had yet to marry, the expression makes sense. "The woman whom you love" was yet to be determined. For the moment, she was not a wife.

In view of the grim prospects awaiting everyone, Qoheleth's encouragement to act decisively is understandable. Live to the full, he said, for in Sheol you will be a shadow of your former self, lacking work, reason, knowledge, and wisdom.

It is notable that Qoheleth laced this admonition with a sobering reminder of life's emptiness and brevity. He used *hebel* twice, once with reference to the total experience on earth and once with the temporal expression for its duration. Twice too he used the form of *'amal,* once to indicate work and the other time to signify wages from labor.

This brief imperative defines *heleq,* one's portion from God. It consists of a simple repast, one that ought to be characterized by happiness. To that end Qoheleth used two clarifications: the relevant words are "joy" and a "positive attitude." To eat one's bread with joy and to drink wine in a jovial spirit redeems a day of toil and momentarily suppresses thoughts of one's impending departure from the stage of history.

7

Surely light is sweet and it is good for the eyes to look on the sun. However many years there are, let a man rejoice and remember the dark days, for they will be numerous. All that comes is empty. Rejoice, young man, in your youth, let your mind be happy in your youthful days, and walk in the ways of your mind and in the sight of your eyes, but know that God will bring you into judgment because of all those things. Remove care from your thoughts and banish pain from your body, for youth and black hair are fleeting. (11:7–10)

The form of Qoheleth's last word about enjoyment continues the imperative that first appeared in the sixth saying, but he mixed it with the jussive ("let him. . ."). In this final statement nothing is said about Qoheleth's constant staple, food and drink. Here the emphasis falls on the warmth of sunlight,[37] which is especially sweet to someone in advanced years with a poor circulatory system and thin blood, one who now reflects on what brought pleasure in earlier days.

The mood of this observation is hardly celebratory despite the encouragement to rejoice. The reason for the restraint is the brevity of youth and the long duration of the approaching dark days. Worse still, judgment for one's deeds awaits. There is irony in the juxtaposition of encouragement to follow your desires, knowing that you are simply heaping up offenses for which you will be held accountable. Even Qoheleth's language is calculated to emphasize the seriousness of the transgression, for it echoes the expression for willful sin in Num 15:39 (compare Sir 5:2).[38] It is as if he said: "Have fun playing with cobras, but keep in mind, 'they bite.'"

There is something almost pathetic in the admonition to rid one's mind of worry after being told about a day of judgment and to erase pain from the body, as if that were possible. If the reference to dawn symbolizes youth, it paves the way for some exquisite metaphors of the concluding poem about old age and death.

Although I have followed the usual practice in seeing verses 7 and 8 as part of this unit, there is sufficient reason to exclude them. The statement at the end of verse 8, that everything in the future is empty (*hebel*) typically sums up what has preceded.[39] Presumably Qoheleth referred to the coming existence in Sheol rather than to days of misery in one's lifetime.

When we examine the seven units in which Qoheleth tried to find something to excite the imagination in an absurd world, one thing stands out amid all the rest. The verb for enjoying life (*samah*) is not reinforced by other verbs with roughly the same sense.[40] Instead Qoheleth limited himself to the negative "nothing is better than" and the positive "be happy, rejoice." While being constantly reminded of life's brevity, emptiness, and absurdity, it is difficult to be happy.

Would other reinforcements have lightened the mood? He easily could have used *gil* ("to be glad unto rejoicing, to exult"), *ranan* ("to sing"), and *'alaz* ("to exult").[41] Elsewhere all three occur either in parallelism or in conjunction with *samah*:

"Sing, daughter Zion, shout Israel; rejoice and exult with your whole heart, daughter Jerusalem" (Zeph 3:14).
"Is not food cut off before our eyes, joy and gladness from the house of our God?" (Joel 1:16).
"Do not rejoice, O Israel! Do not exult like other nations. . ." (Hos 9:1).
"Let those who desire my vindication shout for joy and be glad" (Ps 35:27).
"Although you rejoice, although you exult, plunderers of my heritage. . ." (Jer 50:11).

These three verbs cover a wide range of emotion, from the ringing cry of victory over enemies to exuberant praise of Yahweh. To them could be added *ru'ah* ("to shout for joy") and *shir* ("to sing"), as in Job 38:7: "When together the morning stars sang out and all the heavenly beings shouted for joy." In short Qoheleth's lean vocabulary for rejoicing makes one wonder where his heart really was.

The imminent threat of dying can make us do strange things. An episode preserved in the book of Isaiah provides a vivid illustration. The approach of the Assyrian army of Sargon in 711 B.C.E. is said to have prompted Judean citizens to slaughter their sheep and oxen, to eat and drink merrily while offering this encouragement to one and all: "Let us eat and drink, for tomorrow we die" (Isa 22:13).

Because of life's brevity, for Qoheleth too death was fast approaching. In its shadow he could find no redeeming feature. The tasty nectar to which only a few had access was no valid basis for singing.

Qoheleth's observations about enjoyment end abruptly, leaving a dark cloud hanging over everything. Death, no longer a distant threat, has become present reality. At this moment Qoheleth's voice is stilled and others take up the narration. In their judgment the teachings of this strange teacher were inherently flawed.

CHAPTER 8

Flawed Genius

If some people are unable, for whatever reason, to heed Qoheleth's advice to enjoy life and if death threatens to cut short the pleasure others find, is there a serious flaw in his fundamental teaching? The epilogues in 12:9–14 appear to suggest exactly that. They comprise two triads of verses (12:9–11 and 12:12–14) that give important information about the speaker and either offer a summary of his insights or suggest an alternative teaching to what has appeared before.[1]

A Guide to Readers

Apparently someone thought readers of the body of the book would need guidance in some matters: Who was Qoheleth? Whom did he teach? What was his method of working? What was the effect of his teaching? Did he go too far? Did he leave out anything significant?

Who Was Qoheleth?

This first question is easily answered. He was a wise man, a *hakam*. This word, which functions both as a noun and an adjective, often simply refers to a person who possessed expertise in any number of crafts or who was especially astute.[2] Sometimes, however, *hakam* indicates professional status in a guild, as here. Both uses, the singular form in 12:9 and the plural in 12:11, refer to Qoheleth's membership in an elite class of sages.[3] Identifying him as part of this exclusive group suggests that people should listen to what he has to say.

We should note that this biographical comment is silent about the earlier claim of kingship, and it does not repeat the Solomonic fiction. Instead it merely associates the author with sages whose sayings were treasured and therefore preserved in writing, such as those in the book of Proverbs.

Whom Did Qoheleth Teach?

This second question provokes a surprising response. Rather than young boys, the expected answer, given the usual student body in the ancient Near East[4] and presumably in Israel, the word *ha'am* appears. Qoheleth taught the people, it states, as if to say that he resembled a peripatetic philosopher in Greek society. That is, his teachings were aimed at ordinary adults rather than children.[5] We see here a democratizing tendency in education.

What Was His Method of Working?

How did he go about his innovative endeavor? Like all effective instructors, he listened carefully to others, engaged in rigorous research, arranged arguments for maximum effect, and hunted for the most appealing vocabulary that did not require him to sacrifice the truth.[6] A combination of logos, ethos, and pathos may be implied.[7]

He valued rational thinking, backed by his own integrity of character and motivated by strong conviction that gave his word a mesmerizing effect of emptiness, like the universe itself. This last point is a deduction based on the necessity to put a positive spin on his teachings.

What Was the Effect of His Teaching?

Truth is painful at times, and what Qoheleth taught was especially disturbing. That is why the comparison of his teachings to nails and goads was felt to be necessary. Just as goads inflict pain on domestic animals, Qoheleth's words bring dismay. Still the goads work to make oxen behave in a desired way, and are therefore beneficial at least to humans. Moreover Qoheleth's insights into the nature of reality are believed to be reliable, like securely planted nails that will not give way under heavy pressure.

As we have seen, the obscure point about collections deriving from one shepherd is capable of at least three interpretations. It may be a metaphor for the divine source of such collections; in the ancient Near East the epithet shepherd often refers to a deity,[8] just as it does in the Bible.[9] Against this reading, however, is the probability that biblical wise men reached their conclusions on their own without disclosure of hidden secrets from God.[10] The expression "one shepherd" may indicate Solomonic authorship; yet this interpretation also seems unlikely because of the wide divergence of Qoheleth's teachings from those attributed to Solomon in the book of Proverbs. The most likely meaning of the phrase about a shepherd takes 'ehad ("one") to indicate "any."[11] The point would be that goads used by any shepherd were a necessary evil. Similarly Qoheleth's words stung the hearer while embodying useful information. It was disturbing to be reminded that all human achievements amount to a huge zero and that God is indifferent to goodness.[12]

What then was the firmly planted nail? Was it the knowledge that everything under the sun was *hebel* or that we should eat, drink, and be merry? Perhaps the metaphor should not be pressed beyond the mere assertion that Qoheleth's words were at the same time painful and useful.

There seems to be no doubt that the point was taken to mean something akin to the perennial town-gown conflict. That seems to be the purpose of the sharp warning in 12:12: "Beyond these, my son, be warned: the making of many scrolls has no end, and much learning is weariness to the flesh."[13]

Did Qoheleth Go Too Far?

We need not restrict ourselves to ancient Greece to witness the fear of untraditional teachings, although the death sentence imposed on Socrates shows how far even a highly cultured society will go to protect the innocent from what is thought to be dangerous. In the ecclesial community, the treatment of Galileo centuries ago and its modern corollary, the demonizing of Darwin, reveal the tenacity of a refusal to let the intellect roam freely in the quest for truth. So does the contemporary hue and cry over sex education for children.

Sadly some parts of the Bible sanction this limiting of intellectual pursuits, most notably Ben Sira's warning against investigating areas that have not been commanded: "Do not seek what is too difficult for you nor investigate things beyond your power. Ponder what has been commanded, because the hidden is not your concern. Do not meddle in matters beyond your ken, for more than you can understand has been shown you. Conceit has led many astray. Wrong thinking has impaired their judgment" (Sir 3:21–24).

We do not know what kind of speculation Ben Sira disliked, but several possibilities come to mind. He may have viewed probing of questions such as those in the book of Job dangerous and unproductive. Alternatively he may have considered speculation about the end times and astral influences a waste of time and energy.[14] The context suggests yet another possibility: he may have thought that the mere pursuit of the unknown led to intellectual pride. Whatever his reasons, Ben Sira veered from the position of the unknown composer of Prov 25:2, who wrote that "God's glory is to conceal things, but the glory of kings is to search them out." Once the exploration of the unknown was pronounced off limits to young thinkers, it was a tiny step to the stifling of intellectual pursuits altogether. That is precisely the attitude that the author of Second Esdras, also called Fourth Ezra, highlighted.[15] Remarkably this resistance to asking difficult questions is attributed to the angel Uriel, who had become the divine spokesman.[16]

The angel's argument rests on the undeniable fact that the human intellect often comes up against things that are destined to remain hidden and that a similar limitation prevents people from accomplishing everything they set out to do. The limits that Uriel mentioned involve simple things that we encounter every day as well as things outside the spatial and temporal realms: "Go, weigh for me the weight of fire, or measure for me a blast of wind, or call back for me the day that is past. . . . How many dwellings are in the heart of the sea, or how many streams are at the source of the deep, or how many streams are above the firmament, or which are the exits of Hades, or which are the entrances of paradise?" (2 Esd 4:5, 7).[17]

In short the angel discouraged Ezra from probing deeply into the ways by which God governs the world. Neither the delay in implementing justice nor the specific time frame for setting things right is, according to Uriel, a legitimate subject of investigation. Ezra was expected to trust God even in the face of apparent neglect of the covenanted people.

Such suppressing of intellectual curiosity inevitably leads to suspicion of doubt, which comes to expression in Wisdom of Solomon: "Because he is found by those who do not put him to the test, and manifests himself to those who do not distrust him" (Wis 1:2). Complete trust is expected regardless of circumstances. To question the divine ways, which implies an element of doubt, is said to make one incapable of understanding sacred mysteries. The author of the Epistle of James applied this idea to explain why prayer sometimes fails: "But ask in faith, never doubting, for the one who doubts is like a wave of the sea, driven and tossed by the wind, for the doubter, being double-minded and unstable in every way, must not expect to receive anything from the Lord" (Jas 1:6–8).

Something else stands out in Qoheleth's disclaimer about the fruit of intellectual endeavors. Suddenly the audience shifts from the people (ha'am) to young boys, the probable students addressed in Prov 1–9 by a teacher who may also have been their real parent. The references to both mother and father make it likely that the setting is the family, even if "my son" means "my student." In light of the fact that scribal schools consisted largely of children of the teacher, the instructions and sayings may be perfectly at home there. Understandably the strong verb "be warned" in this context carries a serious message that students ignore at their peril.[18]

Neither point in the warning has anything really new. Scribes both far and near busily occupied themselves with the task of producing literature. The written word took several forms and appeared in different media: cuneiform writing (wedge-shaped symbols), primarily on clay tablets in Mesopotamia and at Ugarit; hieroglyphics and demotic writing (cursive) on papyrus in Egypt; and alphabetic Hebrew and Aramaic in Israel on leather and occasionally on copper and stone. The extensive library at Qumran in the vicinity of the Dead Sea provides definitive evidence of the truth in the claim that the production of written texts was endless.

Curiously the brief anecdote in 4:13–16 about a ruler who came from poverty or imprisonment to the throne, reminiscent of the fictional story of Joseph's rise to a seat of authority, uses both the verb for being advised or warned (hizzaher) and the expression 'en qes ("there was no end to"). In that context, however, hakam has the usual sense of expertise—in this case at statecraft—which neither poverty nor imprisonment had dulled. It is even more surprising that youth is not viewed as an impediment to wise rule, and advanced years do not automatically guarantee wisdom. This attitude toward the young is closer to Greek thought than to Hebraic.

The effect of cutting off debate is to render opponents silent. The victory, however, is Pyrrhic. That is the force of the summation in verse 13a: "End of the matter; everything has been heard."[19] What a bold claim. Precious little in Qoheleth's teaching reads like a closed book. Matters are left tentative, issues unresolved, as if challenging hearers and readers to carry the argument further. True, Qoheleth made absolutist claims about everything being *hebel,* but he often examined competing perceptions without tipping his hand about his preference. For him there was no end, for each answer opened up another question, or two.

Has everything been heard? What wise man or woman would dare make such an assertion? And if "heard" has the sense of "obeying" as is frequently the case, the sentence is surely an exaggeration. Qoheleth has not made disciples of everyone, and there is little evidence that his views have ruled the day.[20] Quite the contrary, for the author of Wisdom of Solomon raised a powerful protest over the expression of carpe diem that characterizes Qoheleth's teaching. This sharp polemic against living for the moment shows how easy it is to misrepresent an opponent's view. Nowhere did Qoheleth voice such crass violence in the cause of self-indulgence as that articulated in Wis 2:10–12: "Let us oppress the righteous poor man; let us not spare the poor widow, or regard the gray hairs of the aged. But let our might be our law of right, for what is weak proves itself to be useless." Enjoyment for Qoheleth was made possible, if at all, by hard work and divine favor. It had nothing to do with oppressing defenseless members of society.

From the perspective of whoever wrote the imperative "Fear God and keep his commandments"—and claimed that these two activities were the sum total of humanity[21]—we may deduce that at least one person believed Qoheleth had wandered far beyond the essential knowledge about how one should behave. Instead of probing the secrets of the world around us, we should, so this individual believed, concentrate on religious duty.[22]

It is not as if Qoheleth neglected the first of these. Avoiding anything that would anger God was, he thought, in one's best interest. Fearing God was thus an absolute necessity. Moreover the expression "fear God" seems to have carried a basic sense of dread. In Qoheleth's view fearing God resembles the awe inherent to experiencing the numinous, a simultaneous attraction to and revulsion of the holy that Rudolf Otto named "mysterium tremendum et fascinans."[23] The prophet Isaiah illustrated the feeling exactly when reacting to an experience of holiness: "Woe is me, I am lost . . . for my eyes have seen the King, the Lord of hosts" (Isa 6:5).

Did Qoheleth Leave Out Anything Significant?

The second imperative, "keep his commandments," goes beyond anything that Qoheleth taught. He was completely silent about the Mosaic legislation. In this matter Qoheleth differed radically from Ben Sira, who identified the speculation about personified wisdom with the law handed down by Moses.[24] Neither Ben Sira nor Qoheleth, however, mentioned specific commandments. Ben Sira did refer to the obligation to support the priests who administered the cult, and it is possible to posit certain Mosaic teachings as the motivation for some of Ben Sira's remarks about parental respect and charitable giving, but other reasons for both are readily available. It is much more difficult to find anything in Qoheleth's teaching that was motivated by the commandments.

Qoheleth seems to have been fond of universal claims; he held an all or nothing attitude. The conclusion that fearing God and keeping the commandments were somehow the entirety of humanity ("the whole of man") accords with the tendency to universalize. What does this mean? Every duty imposed on a person from outside or the complete potential open to anyone who acts autonomously rather than from external compulsion? Voluntary action comes closer to Qoheleth's views elsewhere in the book, for he rejected the comforting belief that God rewards the obedient worshipper.

If the remarks about a divine judgment in the body of the book come from Qoheleth, they provide a reason for adding the twofold imperative about fearing God and keeping the commandments. At some unknown time a shift occurred in which the old view of death as God's judgment on individuals was challenged by belief in a universal assize when all people will be held responsible for their actions. In the book of Joel this judgment day is believed to be a time when the nations who have persecuted the Judeans will be punished severely.

In due time the final judgment was projected onto the stage of eternity and individualized. The two concepts, immediate judgment at death and a delayed judgment until some future moment when all will face their Maker, continued in New Testament times. The parable about the rich man and Lazarus reflects the idea of an immediate judgment at death, while the Apostle Paul thought in terms of a day of universal judgment at a date to be determined by God alone.

As everyone knows, the thought of being judged for one's deeds acted as a powerful motive for disciplined behavior. In case anyone lacked knowledge about what that constituted, the answer was available: "Be religious and observe the teachings attributed to Moses." The word for commandments, *miswoth,* probably has this restricted meaning, although it could be more general. In that case it refers to the mandates issued by wise teachers, of whom Qoheleth was one. Even a limited understanding of the Hebrew word poses difficulty, for it is unlikely that this editor intended readers to observe the whole body of ritual enjoined in the Bible. Lacking further instruction, how would readers have kept this command? We do not know.

The final epilogue concludes by elaborating on this imagined judgment: "Surely God will bring every work into judgment, concerning every secret, good or bad." With this warning, the earlier advice that Qoheleth gave about following the desires of eyes and mind is exposed for what it is, like all deeds in the last judgment. Unlike God's work, which has been shown to be mysterious and even painful, at least for some people, human deeds are subject to scrutiny by a higher power. This idea was not lost to Ben Sira, who warned his students that the Lord will reveal their secrets and overthrow them before the whole congregation (Sir 1:30). A moment's reflection exposes the dilemma presented by the prospect of bringing every deed to light. If Qoheleth is right that God is actually indifferent to human aspirations to live a virtuous life, why this sudden turnaround? Either Qoheleth changed his mind about divine arbitrariness or someone else is the author of the epilogue. Furthermore, if

God treats everyone without regard to conduct, how can anyone prepare for a day of judgment? A consistent God who made known the divine will for humans would enable them to clean up their act so that airing their deeds would not be shameful.

Regardless of the real nature of the epilogues—a framing device or editorial glosses—they illustrate the dramatic impact of Qoheleth's teachings. He has either exposed the true limits of wisdom, or he has shown its transformative power.

Bankruptcy or Resounding Success?

For many interpreters Qoheleth exemplifies wisdom's bankruptcy,[25] its inability to answer ultimate questions. In him the mind came up against the unknown and unknowable. To be sure the intellect is capable of answering many questions, as Qoheleth clearly demonstrated. Nevertheless it can do no more than touch the outermost edges of the hidden mysteries of God.[26] Unaided, the intellect leaves humans at the mercy of a power over which they have no control. Their vulnerability makes them receptive to an alternative belief system. That is why revelation fared so well in the ancient world. Answers are available, according to this worldview. One need only listen for a divine voice.

For other interpreters Qoheleth demonstrated wisdom's resiliency, its openness to alternative views.[27] From this perspective, wisdom opens new vistas, all the while correcting itself in the light of fresh discoveries and failed explanations. Far from exhibiting the weakness of the intellect, Qoheleth revealed its crowning achievement. Always ready to alter his views, Qoheleth pursued questions and let the answers correct all preconceived notions.[28] This latter point is nicely illustrated by his brief story about a poor but wise man (Qoh 9:13–16).

Poor but Wise

The sages who composed the sayings that make up the several collections in the book of Proverbs constructed a fictional world in which intellectual prowess and resolve of will were thought to guarantee success. Resolve of will was measured by tangible qualities such as wealth, health, progeny, and status. By acquiring the virtues of timing, eloquence, patience, and integrity, individuals believed they could influence their destinies for good. Those who refused to shape character in this way were said to have brought misfortune upon themselves.

The wise who promoted this optimistic literary construct were divided over the means by which action produced favorable or unfavorable results. Sometimes their sayings imply that deeds carry within themselves appropriate consequences; at other times they seem to attribute both reward and punishment to deity. On rare occasions they suggest that the divine role is merely that of facilitator, like a midwife who assists the delivery of an infant.[29]

All three modes of matching deed and consequence rest on an assumption that human beings and deity are fundamentally alike. Without a principle of similarity,[30] there could be no knowledge of divinity apart from special disclosure. Such revelation could only initiate from above, since analogy from human thoughts and actions would inevitably abort. The supreme fiction of an orderly universe in which justice prevails arises out of this belief in a correspondence between human and divine character, it being taken for granted that deity valued truth and justice in the same way good people did.

What happens, however, when this comforting view that women and men are made in the divine image (*beselem 'elohim*) is shattered by the conviction that the deity is responsible for shameful acts that are more accurately described as bestial than as humane?[31] That is precisely the situation in which Job found himself when confronted by a deity he no longer recognized. It was also the context for Qoheleth's philosophical search for a more permanent and tangible meaning in life than *hebel*. The shifting worldview either precipitated a crisis or served as catalyst for the creation of a more reliable perspective on the world.[32] Either way the era may correctly be called axial.[33] The social causes for the vanishing dream among sages are complex, as we can gather from an incident that made a lingering impact on Qoheleth: "This also I have observed[34]—wisdom[35] under the sun, and personally significant. A tiny village, sparsely populated, yet a great king came to it, surrounded it, and built mighty siege-works[36] against it. There was found[37] in it a poor man [but] wise, and he could have rescued[38] the city by means of his wisdom but no one thought about that poor man. I say: 'Wisdom is superior to strength, although the wisdom of the poor [man] was scorned, his words unheard'" (9:13–16).

An accusative of specification, *hokmah* ("wisdom") calls attention to the particular anomaly being introduced. The introductory *gam* implies that it does not stand alone ("this *also*"), but it is unclear just what antecedent instances of wisdom Qoheleth had in mind. The immediate context[39] offers two very different insights: the fastest runner does not always win a race, nor does the strongest person necessarily prevail in battle; and wise, understanding, and informed persons do not always receive bread, riches, and favor. The reason: chance may come into play, rendering null and void the qualities on which humans rely for favorable outcomes. The images of fish and fowl being caught in a loathsome net or trap signify a grim outcome for humans.

Hence Qoheleth's language of personal observation brings home the earlier point and makes smooth transition to the familiar threat posed by unchecked power. Thematic words highlight sage and wisdom, here discovered in the unlikeliest of places. A peasant[40] possesses wisdom; the ultimate position of *hakam* almost invites readers to imagine an adversative (poor *but* wise). In his case the acquisition of wisdom has not yielded its anticipated harvest.[41] Wise and therefore prosperous has become poor *but* wise. Contrasting words, great and small, describe competing factions and build up certain expectations with respect to who will win this conflict.

A great king is the subject of at least three verbs in succession. Although normal Hebrew syntax implies that the fourth verb has the same subject as the preceding three verbs, exceptions do occur.[42] Furthermore Qoheleth's linguistic usage frequently goes its own way. One may therefore read *umasa'* as impersonal ("one found"), which makes more narrative sense than thinking that the king who was overseeing the siege could somehow have discovered an intelligent commoner residing inside the wall of the town, and moreover that his advice would have swayed a king to spare a city he was determined to pillage.[43]

Does the poor but wise man do anything, or is he merely acted upon? One's reading of the verb indicating an act of saving reflects a decision about which of the two antecedent points this story illustrates. A potential understanding of the verb ("he could have rescued") accentuates the statement that intelligence does not necessarily produce beneficial results. An actual reading ("he saved") emphasizes the observation that the swift and strong are not always assured victory.[44] If the poor but wise man delivered the city under siege, the populace was singularly ungrateful, and if no one remembered him, how could Qoheleth have heard of the incident? Moreover Qoheleth's memory would have negated the denial that anyone remembered him, unless the story is more personal than meets the eye.[45] If the city fell to the great king, the people's failure to think about a possible rescuer illustrates the fatal flaw of sages: dependence on others' acceptance of their wisdom. Notably the adjective *hakam* is lacking in the end, where only "that poor man" appears.

Qoheleth's personalization of his anecdote, "therefore I said," reasserts conventional belief that intelligence is superior to strength only to controvert it with the reminder that the peasant's wisdom was despised and his advice went unheeded. The two "better than" proverbs that follow this anecdote contrast shouts of a ruler among fools with the words of the wise that are quietly heeded (and spoken?) and declare wisdom to be better than implements of war, although like a little fire in proverbial lore[46] a single errant one can destroy a lot of good. Throughout this section, "time and affliction" hover in the background, like nets and traps.

The requirement of verisimilitude has guided the analysis of Qoheleth's example story to this point. In all likelihood, however, it is a product of his fertile imagination,[47] just like that in 4:13–16, where another poor but wise youth is deemed better than an old but foolish king, who does not know how to be instructed any longer. This "rags to riches" story remotely recalls elements of the narrative about Joseph, although the stress now falls on fading loyalty. Here too conventional wisdom is turned on its head, for age is no longer associated with sagacity, nor is youthfulness linked to lack of understanding.

With a single stroke of the pen, the rhetoric in 9:13–16 becomes one of erasure;[48] expectations vanish like smoke or mist (*hebel*). A tiny village that has every right to rest securely, like Laish in Judg 18:7, found itself at the mercy of a king bent on breaching its defenses, and a commoner stood out as one possessing extraordinary intelligence of a tactical nature. While the deity may be able to frustrate best-laid plans for battle, the determining force in the story about a poor but wise man is chance, and its essential characteristic is lethal.

Perhaps this brief anecdote illustrates the point I wish to make about an axial age better than anything else in Qoheleth's profound reflections about the nature of things, for it concerns beliefs about the good life and about power. It is precisely here that the greatest threat to the sapiential view of the world rests. The abuse of power and its effect on the innocent bring to naught every hope for security, the necessary precondition for successful living. Once the deity is no longer thought to exercise control over the course of human events, lawlessness naturally follows. Catastrophic disasters such as the destruction of Jerusalem threaten long-held convictions about a just deity and lead to a new concept of divinity as remote and hidden, if not altogether alien.[49]

A corollary of this sea change in the concept of deity is agnosticism, which has serious implications for the traditional view of reward and punishment. The disappearance of universal moral order undermined wisdom's raison d'être. In earlier times the deity's glory is said to have consisted in concealing things (or words), a king's glory was in finding them out. In such a world, sages imagined themselves in the service of, and even in the role of, royalty. With Qoheleth, that exalted position was reduced to a farce (1:12–2:26).[50] In this new context life's grandeur had faded, leaving loathsome back-breaking toil and its meager yield (2:18a).[51]

Two words, *hinnam* ("without cause") and *hebel,* signify this fundamental transformation in viewing the world. One derives from the prose introduction to the book of Job, and the other is Qoheleth's favorite expression for reality. *Hinnam* explodes the comfortable assumption that the universe operates according to a calculable moral principle. In its place the adversary substituted an absence of cause—in other words gratuitous action devoid of any discernible reason. *Hebel* robs human conduct of any gain in the final analysis, rendering life totally futile and frequently absurd.[52]

It is not necessary to document the traditional understanding of reality that the authors of Job and Qoheleth undercut by these two important concepts, disinterested righteousness (*hinnam*) and futility (*hebel*). It is embodied in the sacred texts that were gradually emerging in exilic times, especially the Deuteronomic interpretation of causation that pervades priestly, prophetic, and apocalyptic literature as well as the book of Proverbs and the lament tradition. Its most succinct expression occurs in Ps 37:25: "I have been young and also [am] old, but I have not seen the righteous forsaken or his offspring searching for bread." A proper society, by this standard, is one in which the deity enforces a strict system of measured cause and effect. In the psalmist's mind, this was exactly the kind of moral order sustained by the sovereign whom his poetry honors.

Such a simplistic interpretation of human events pronounces judgment on the poor for ignoring instruction (Prov 13:18) and on the sick for religious offense, as Job's friends did. Obedience to divine instruction brings blessing, hence wealth (Prov 10:22); disobedience brings curse according to this way of thinking. It applies both to society and to individuals, at least in official narratives that record the nation's history. Its power rests in a persuasive logic that appeals to utopian dreams, easily reinforced by "testimonials" accumulated over time in which the theory seems to work.[53]

Now and again astute thinkers broke free from this type of reasoning enough to acknowledge an occasional wise person among the poor, as in "A rich man may consider himself intelligent but a perceptive poor man finds him out" (Prov 28:11). More commonly popular wisdom emphasized the vulnerability of the poor and the ease by which they were either ignored or treated contemptuously (Prov 18:23). Therefore kindness to the poor was viewed with favor inasmuch as the creator had fashioned both the affluent and the impoverished (Prov 14:31; 17:5; 19:17; 22:2).

The radical thinker Qoheleth questioned the premises of traditional wisdom when insisting that despite claims to the contrary a *ḥakam* simply cannot know (8:17). Although a proper time for everything exists, in Qoheleth's estimation, the deity has made it impossible for anyone to discover it (3:11).[54] Wisdom may have an advantage over folly, but it is only relative. In the end wisdom yields no lasting profit because death cancels all supposed gain. Everything therefore is futile and shepherding wind (1:14b). The decisive factor governing human lives is chance, another name for a distant deity's arbitrary conduct that is wholly oblivious to a moral norm.

Societal Changes

What social realities contributed to Qoheleth's dismantling of the sages' traditional understanding of theology and anthropology? Answers to this question vary, but three things stand out above the rest, one economic, another political, and a third institutional.[55] Earlier I discussed Qoheleth's historical context. Here I emphasize the social implications of foreign hegemony and the resulting second-class citizenship into which his compatriots had been thrown by a world that seemed to be spinning out of control. Three words capture the social factors succinctly: affluence, revenue, and inheritance.

Affluence

An unprecedented economic volatility may explain Qoheleth's lingering concern for profit, together with his anecdotal references to a miser, a loser at investing, and the hidden costs of an increase in possessions. In a society where money answered everything, the primary goal was to manage wealth wisely. The singular advantages of a monetary economy included, among other things, the availability of disposable funds, a type of liquidity that was unknown under pastoral nomadism and subsistence farming. The radical changes introduced by Persian and Ptolemaic rulers[56] presented rare opportunities to acquire vast sums of money but also to lose heavily in an unpredictable market. The resulting shifts in class and the social turmoil created by reversals of fortune brought secondary effects as well, particularly changes in status. In general three distinct levels existed in Yehud: the affluent, a retainer class, and the peasantry. Belonging to the first group were the higher rank within the priesthood, some scribes, wealthy landowners, tax "farmers" and collectors, and foreign officials. The lower clergy and ordinary scribes made up the majority of the second level, and the third comprised day laborers who toiled to eke out a living. A certain restlessness characterized all three. The rich, never satisfied, feared the loss of their treasures; the middle class hungered for more; and lacking any champion, the peasantry recognized their vulnerability on many fronts.

Revenue

The depoliticization of the priestly class greatly reduced their power from that of Ezra roughly two centuries earlier.[57] Their waning influence can be measured by Qoheleth's virtual silence about them and their responsibilities during the era when the temple cult was believed to have assured divine blessing for an entire people. Like prophets, about whom he said nothing, priests and sages alike depended on esteem among citizens for status. Disenfranchisement and depoliticization brought alienation[58] and relative deprivation, disturbing the natural rhythm of society.

This disenchantment, a rupture in the symbolic universe to which Qoheleth bore witness, was precipitated by governmental policy inaugurated by Persian rulers and continued during Ptolemaic times. Throughout the provinces, spies rendered the articulation of any seditious thought a virtual death sentence. An elaborate bureaucracy involving supervisors, each with a more authoritative boss, extended all the way to the king himself. Their responsibility mainly involved the gathering of revenues, often achieved by farming out taxes to others who increased the official tax burden for personal gain. The potential for abuse of privilege was huge. Qoheleth's lament that justice was absent from the judiciary reveals corruption at the core. Royal grants to favorites, the military, and temple personnel were handed out arbitrarily. Proprietary rights over one's portion were threatened by those on a higher rung of the social ladder.

The heavy levy of taxes was felt most keenly by peasants, especially in years of drought or diseases that reduced the yield from grain fields and olive orchards. A bad year might require peasants to borrow seed money for the next year's planting, often at an exorbitant rate of interest, and failure to repay debt frequently turned them or their children into slaves until the slate was clean.[59] In addition the requirement to fulfill military duty when the foreign ruler conscripted the populace threatened those who could ill afford a temporary, or worse, a permanent loss of valuable workers in the fields and vineyards.

Inheritance

Naturally the most exposed institution was the family. Although Qoheleth said little about it,[60] he often referred to the practice of transferring possessions to an heir at death. His remarks about this process lack any hint of satisfaction over being able to ease the lot of succeeding generations. Worse still they imply that individuals cannot know whether recipients of largesse will be deserving or not. Qoheleth's language contains not the slightest indication of intimate knowledge within the confines of a household, unlike the prose conclusion to the book of Job. For Qoheleth the inability to hold on to hard-earned possessions was conclusive evidence of life's utter absurdity.

The major figure within households received no praise from Qoheleth, who urged her counterpart to enjoy life with "a woman whom you love." This curious language leaves the object of pleasure unclear, whether one's wife or more probably a lover like the girl in Song of Songs.[61] The unflattering assessment of women in 7:26–29 contrasts markedly with the glowing praise in Prov 31:10–31. Qoheleth did not say that all women are more bitter than death, for he described a particular type of woman.[62] Even if in 7:26 he quoted a proverbial saying, the validity of which he questioned, Qoheleth nevertheless proceeded to pronounce a wholly negative judgment on women and an almost equally absolute assessment of men. As we have seen, such a low opinion of human nature in general is well known in the Bible and in ancient Near Eastern literature.[63] Sadly misogyny raised its ugly head in much of the literature of the ancient Near East and became even more obnoxious in Greco-Roman texts.

A Remote Deity and Its Consequences

It is noteworthy that Qoheleth never personified wisdom. In this regard he followed the author of the book of Job, whose distancing of deity invites mediation.[64] Accordingly the poetic dialogue introduces three mysterious figures who Job hoped would come to his assistance (a mediator, a witness, and a redeemer), and Elihu referred to additional ones, an angel and a messenger. Qoheleth's deity is even more remote, but the gulf between creator and creatures is unbroken.[65] For him, "God is in heaven and you are on earth, therefore let your words be few" (5:1b). With respect to power, divine or human, Qoheleth's primary concern assumed a defensive stance, a caution grounded in precedent.

Unlike the teachers in the book of Proverbs, Qoheleth never used "my son" with reference to his audience.[66] Its only occurrence is in the second epilogue. His heightened egotism[67] and general aloofness have led some interpreters to think of him as unmarried, and his compassion for oppressed members of society has been questioned. Although a vibrant intellectual group is reflected in his remarks about hermeneutics, he acknowledged that intellectual pursuits take a heavy toll and ultimately are not worth the effort. Why then did he take such pains to develop a vocabulary that enabled him to engage in philosophical reflection about the meaning of human existence?[68] Why too did he begin to think about the cognitive process? In him readers are far removed from village life presumed in the older collections in the book of Proverbs. Strangely, however, he offered little evidence of residing in an urban environment and even less proclivity for religious practice while living in a city that boasted a functioning temple and cultic personnel.

In short Qoheleth's *hebel* thinking helped to bring about the complete destruction of a sacred canopy already gravely threatened by *hinnam* reasoning in the book of Job. The combination of economic, political, and familial circumstances enabled Qoheleth to achieve a significant breakthrough with respect to the limits of knowledge. His rhetorical "who knows?" and "no one knows," and "one cannot find" reminded listeners and later readers of human vulnerability before death and a remote, arbitrary deity.[69] His world evoked a concession that everything under the sun was *hebel*, even the momentary pleasures available to a lucky few. For them too the darkness of Sheol awaited, symbolized by chance, his word for fate. The plight of the oppressed, for whom there were no comforters, was actually universal.

Attempts to Counter Hinnam *and* Hebel *Thinking*

Such a world devoid of the comfort of a merciful deity was intolerable to the sages who followed. Ben Sira went to great lengths to highlight divine compassion. His incorporation of Israel's narrative tradition made it possible to document divine mercy in sacred memory. To minimize the impact of Qoheleth's concept of a remote deity, he took up the earlier myth of personified *hokmah*, which he nationalized while simultaneously opening it up to all people through linkage to the story of creation. His identification of *hokmah* with the Mosaic torah was an extraordinary claim that Israel's intellectual legacy had universal application. At the same time, as we have seen, Ben Sira freely employed arguments of Stoic philosophy to defend divine justice, specifically the existence of opposites in nature that assured a principle of exact reward and retribution. Above all, however, he replaced Qoheleth's agnosticism with fervent praise.[70]

The unknown author of Wisdom of Solomon, thoroughly Hellenized and writing in elevated Greek like the prologue to Sirach, adopted rhetoric to defend Israel's deity against charges of cruelty to Egyptians. In doing so, he used the story of the exodus as pivotal, showing how in it the same natural elements were harmful to Egyptians and beneficial to the people they had wrongly enslaved. Within a mercy dialogue[71] he argued that Israel's God acted with restraint, giving the Egyptians ample opportunity to repent, and with a punishment characterized by measure for measure. This author even added an erotic dimension to speculation about *hokmah* already present in Prov 8:22–31 and Sir 4:18; 14:20–27, but now linked to King Solomon who had taken her as wife.

Whereas Ben Sira had considered death less odious than Qoheleth did, the author of Wisdom of Solomon could not pretend that it was inconsequential. The demise of a child was for him a wrenching dilemma, but his belief in the soul's immortality and his trust in God's goodness eased the pain of premature death.[72] His reflections on theodicy involve both philosophy and psychology while eventually introducing an eschatological response.[73]

The new circumstances made it possible for Ben Sira and the author of Wisdom of Solomon to reconstruct a sacred canopy, thereby returning to the original enchanted world. Perhaps the heady days under the High Priest Simon II and the overall resurgence of the priesthood played a role for Ben Sira, as did his membership in an increasingly important scribal profession. The author of Wisdom of Solomon lived in a wholly different context, the Alexandrian. His concerns, which are tangential to those surfacing as a direct result of thinking characterized by *hinnam* and *hebel,* are introduced by a distortion of Qoheleth's own words. The wish to capture the present moment was by no means unique to Qoheleth; it has a strong presence in Egyptian literature. One hazards a guess that the social reality he experienced was not restricted to Jerusalem.

The wisdom literature from Qumran took up Qoheleth's emphasis on the deity's remoteness, which it labels "the mystery that is to be," while combining this idea with an apocalyptic expectation, where mediation through a host of angelic beings eased the tension arising from apparent divine inaction.[74]

Israelite sages, like their counterparts in Egypt and Mesopotamia, shaped a worldview in which the intellect possessed the capacity to open up the means of securing the good life. That elevation of human potential was brought down through a combination of rigid doctrine and historical circumstances. The removal of the sacred canopy was largely the work of radical ideas that are summed up in two words: *hinnam* and *hebel.* In this situation of anomie, new social conditions brought unrest at every level of citizenry. Affluence, political instability under foreign rule, and the imperiled family evoked a sense of utter futility. The breakdown of utopian views presented a rare opportunity for those who practiced wisdom to demonstrate its potential for achieving a breakthrough. Qoheleth did precisely that, although his emphasis on life's meaninglessness, the deity's remoteness, and the limits of knowledge was unacceptable to later sages such as Ben Sira and the author of Wisdom of Solomon. The dream of prosperity was not easily abandoned, even for a society that yielded an anecdote about a poor *but* wise man.

Conclusion

We may be unable to decide whether Qoheleth's teachings expose the weakness of intellectual pursuits or mark their finest hour, whether they signal the bankruptcy of wisdom or reveal its ultimate triumph—its power of self-criticism. Our indecision is owing to the ambiguity intrinsic to the book in which the insights are packaged. And the ambiguity accurately represents reality itself, which Qoheleth described with complete honesty.

Nothing in his teachings communicates this ambiguity as powerfully as the brief unit in 11:1–8, which moves from the mundane to the sublime. In it Qoheleth expressed his conviction that life is full of choices and that the outcome of each one is uncertain because of unpredictable forces beyond one's control. Nevertheless individuals confronted with decisions need not despair, he observed, for nature has its temporary consolations for an anticipated bleak ending. Like no other section in the book, this one brings readers down to the places where most people spend their waking hours, at the junction of society and nature, both wholly subject to a mystery that humans have named God.[1] A close look at this unit will remind us of the twists and turns our journey has taken.

Send your bread on the waters, for in many days you may find it.

Give a portion to seven—or even to eight—, for you do not know what misfortune will occur on earth.

If the clouds are full of rain, they empty on the earth; and if a tree falls in the south or in the north, where the tree falls, there it is.

Whoever continually watches the wind does not sow, and whoever keeps on observing the clouds does not harvest.

As you do not know the way of the wind—like a fetus in the womb of a pregnant woman—so you do not know the work of the deity who brings everything into being.

In the morning sow your seed, and toward evening withhold not your hand, for you do not know whether this or that will succeed, or if both of them alike will be favorable.

Now sweet is the light; seeing the sun, pleasant to the eyes.

Even if people live many years let them rejoice in them all, and remember the days of darkness, for they will be many. Everything that comes is futile. (11:1–8)

The down-to-earth language ranges from the staples of life, bread and water, to the simple joy of basking in sunlight. The images recall the complicated task of eking out a living from inhospitable ground, and they point to unfathomable mysteries such as wind and gestation. In doing so, they highlight the contingency of human existence and the hidden activity of God. With nearly embarrassing simplicity, Qoheleth ventured into the realm where life begins and closed where life does, in darkness that stretches into the unknown.

The inability of humans to understand the anomalies of everyday life or to anticipate future events described in 10:14 returns in 11:1–2, 5–6, but a gradual shift from the realm of Ptolemaic officials mentioned in 10:16–19 to farmers referenced in 11:4 and 6 corresponds to the emphasis on simple human pleasures, bread and wine. And the means of acquiring them, money, is set against the backdrop of nature.

The truism in 10:19 that bread effects laughter, wine gladdens the living, and money answers everything provides a transition to the curious advice in 11:1 about sending bread on the water. If the word *lehem* ("bread") in 10:19 refers to actual sustenance, as is likely, does that literal sense carry over into 11:1? If so, it renders the counsel satiric, and when combined with 11:2 ("Give a portion to seven—or even to eight—for you do not know what misfortune will occur on earth"), it indicates different ways of squandering resources. The result of releasing bread on water is obviously soggy bread, and that of spreading it among many is empty hands for the one giving it away.

What if bread has a figurative sense here? This meaning is well attested in the Bible, ranging from an erotic connotation to the spiritual, from contexts of war to romantic interludes. For example Joseph was said to have been denied nothing by Potiphar except the bread his master ate, which Gen 39:9 identifies as his wife. Similarly the aphorism attributed to personified folly in Prov 9:17 owes its poignancy to an erotic double entendre, bread and water: "Stolen water is sweet, clandestine bread, pleasant."

The Targum of Qoheleth, an ancient translation into Aramaic, gives a figurative sense to several words in 11:1–8—specifically those indicating seed, morning and evening, and hand—giving the passage sexual connotations. Figuratively bread suggests two possibilities. Either Qoheleth was advising people to make charitable contributions in the hope of receiving assistance in case their financial situation became shaky, or he was suggesting that they invest liberally in commercial enterprises, especially maritime ventures.

The first interpretation seems to be supported by a similar saying in the Egyptian Instruction of Ankhsheshonky: "Do a good deed and throw it in the water; when it dries you will find it." Things do not dry in water, so a figurative sense of the Egyptian saying is likely. In context it indicates an act of charity. Still how can the rediscovery of a good deed profit anyone? The second interpretation also runs into difficulty, for one expects a different Hebrew word for water, *hayyam* ("the sea").[2] Furthermore an extended sense of *lehem* to mean grain that is loaded on a ship is strange. Above all, however, the aphorism says nothing about profit, the sole purpose of investment.

What did Qoheleth mean? Spontaneous generosity, even self-motivated giving, or diversification of investments? If the Greek practice of generosity in friendship and philanthropy provided the backdrop of Qoheleth's advice,[3] the use of the word *portion* instead of "money" remains unexplained. Risky investments during the Hellenistic period sometimes resulted in huge profits, but Qoheleth had already told the sad tale of someone who lost everything in a risky venture (5:12–16). Would he now have advocated such unpredictable action? In short Qoheleth's advice is far from transparent. And what if Kevin Cathcart is correct in saying that the numerical sequence seven/eight is a magical incantation in Ugaritic literature?[4] Does it have that meaning in Qoheleth's use?

The admonitions about charitable giving or investments concern the interaction of humans and nature. The following verse restricts itself entirely to natural events. Nevertheless the outpouring of rain from saturated clouds and the falling of a tree, presumably during the accompanying windstorm, can have consequences for people. Did Qoheleth mean that human ignorance about the future is just as inevitable as the laws of nature? Or does the word translated "tree" indicate a divining rod as in Hos 4:12? The geographical indicators, south and north, are probably specific rather than a merism to express ubiquity. The reason: trees and divining rods do not fall everywhere. Nor does lightning, a suggested emendation for "tree."

In 11:4 Qoheleth returned to the interplay of humans and nature, but with a twist. Mere observation replaces action. Farmers who watch endlessly for a favorable wind will never sow, and those who observe clouds in search of perfect conditions will never reap. The point made here seems too obvious. Even the dumbest farmer would not be ignorant of Qoheleth's truism.[5] Is something else intended? Who else watches over the wind and clouds? Their maker, the *shomer* ("watcher") of humankind. Did Qoheleth mean that the deity will not attend to human tasks, even though individuals resort to foolish behavior, magical incantation, and divining rods?

If Qoheleth used the idea of watching as a transition to the deity, verse 5 makes the shift complete. The exact meaning of the reference to wind and fetus is not clear. It can describe the mystery of breath entering a fetus, or it can compare the visible effects of the wind to the discernible movement of a fetus within a pregnant woman. Only the effects of divine activity can be seen.

Qoheleth's move from anthropology to theology, from human folly to divine creativity, takes place in the most intimate of places. It occurs precisely where human ignorance is greatest, at the beginning of life. He used a rare word for a pregnant woman (*hammele'a,* "the full one") and doubled the negation of knowledge where a single indication of ignorance would have sufficed.

In verse 6 Qoheleth returned to the mode of exhortation, urging decisive and persistent action in the face of abysmal ignorance about the future. Temporal adverbs ("morning and evening") precede imperatives ("sow and do not hold back"). Ignorance is no excuse to do nothing. Or does the contrast between one kind of action and another link divine and human activity? Sowing seed would then indicate sexual congress, which takes its cue from the reference to God's involvement in gestation.

The theme word, "you do not know,"[6] in 11:2, 5, and 6 comes to rest in the mystery of birth. And the contrasting good and bad in the unit enable Qoheleth's hearers to avoid foolish waste, profligate squandering of resources, inaction, and ceaseless toil. Such endeavor, he argued, is subject to chance that cannot be controlled, whether through magic or gargantuan effort.

Then what should one do? Accept the limits imposed on the intellect and enjoy the sweetness of sunshine. Qoheleth's return to an adjective that he used figuratively in 5:11 (*"Pleasant* is the sleep of a laborer (or slave) whether he eats little or much.") may be dictated by the necessity for a parallel to *tob* ("good"). The emphatic conjunction contrasts a sure thing (many dark days) with the uncertainties that generated the futile activities Qoheleth just ridiculed.

Enjoyment, however, stands under the knowledge that a long sojourn in Sheol awaits everyone. The closing statement minces no words: "All that comes is futile." The ironic contrast between many years and dark days matches the tension underlying the two jussives, "let him rejoice but remember. . . ." It pales before the pathos in 6:3, however, where days and years are joined together to express a period less enviable than the lot of a stillborn. The whole unit reaches a resounding conclusion in a summons to seize the moment but to reflect on the specter of death. Carpe diem and memento mori. As we have already seen, the final unit, 11:9–12:7, treats these two themes.

Thus two themes stand out in this brief unit: human inability to know and the inevitability of random events. Against this depressing background, and the foreground of even more troubling dark days ahead, Qoheleth urged the young to seize every available pleasure. This is not his final word. That belongs to his formulaic assertion: "Everything that comes is futile." And he might have added: "Just as everything that has been and is now."

Qoheleth's Legacy

How have Qoheleth's teachings fared through the centuries? Under Neoplatonic influence, the many contradictions and gaps in his thoughts were given a spiritual or allegorical interpretation. Only with the rediscovery of Aristotle in the thirteenth century did that situation begin to change. An ideal world gave way to the real one; literal readings replacing allegorical readings. The change was dramatic, with a total of thirteen commentaries on Ecclesiastes being written in that century alone.[7] Nevertheless a spiritual interpretation continued along with the revived literal emphasis until the Protestant reformers put their significant influence behind the plain sense of a text.

Because of his allusive language and inconsistency, Qoheleth was partly responsible for the two approaches to his thinking. In this respect he is not alone. The early

Christian theologian Origen considered Ecclesiastes and Song of Songs a pair, with Qoheleth teaching that all knowledge, together with the physical world, deserves contempt, and with Song of Songs progressing toward union with Christ. Jerome's pastoral letter to a certain Blesilla, whom he hoped to persuade to adopt a monastic vocation, emphasized Qoheleth's contempt of the world, which Jerome likened to a prison. In his view Qoheleth's remarks about eating and drinking apply to the sacraments. Jerome's influence prevailed over that of Theodore of Mopsuestia, who gave priority to the literal sense of Qoheleth's words, as did the influential Nicholas of Lyra of a much later period (d. 1345).

Among Jewish interpreters, a similar approach to that in Christian circles is attested, except for the Christology. Tannaitic interpreters and the Targumic authors combined literal (*peshat*) and allegorical (*midrash*) strategies when reading Ecclesiastes. Their midrashic interpretations are mostly allegorical. Rashbam (1085–1155) broke away from this approach, insisting on an exclusively literal interpretation. He also recognized 1:1–2 and 12:8–14 as a frame for the whole book.

During this period of rival approaches to Ecclesiastes, Solomonic authorship was assumed. The emphasis fell on both the contrast between a cosmos in which *hebel* ruled and the future promise of immortality and the tensions in the book. The Protestant reformers dropped the assumption of Solomonic authorship and the negative view of the world. For Luther linguistic considerations ruled out Solomon as author, and the divine affirmation of creation in Genesis excluded contempt of the world. *Hebel,* Luther concluded, applied to the human condition, a proclivity toward sin.

On the Jewish side, Samuel David Luzzatto (Shadal) wrote a rhymed essay in 1823 or 1824 (not published until 1860) in which he said Qoheleth "denies the immortality of the soul, asserts determinism, and recommends carnal pleasures." Luzzatto insisted that Solomon would not have written in such a defective style and certainly not in postexilic language deeply influenced by Aramaic. Later sages, according to Luzzatto, tried to negate Qoheleth's influence by adding 11:9b ("But know that God will bring you into judgment for all these things"), 12:1a ("Remember your creator in the days of your youth"), and 12:7b ("and the spirit returns to God who gave it").

Divine Revelation or Human Advice?

Qoheleth went out of his way to dissuade anyone from thinking that what he said derived from anything other than personal observation. He did not hide behind a claim to speak on behalf of God. He was not the only biblical author who gave voice to human concerns. Those joining him are quite different from each other. Psalmists lifted their voices in lament and/or praise, but what they said is thoroughly human, even to hatred of enemies.[8] The author of Song of Songs celebrated the strong appeal of sexual attraction, a force stronger than death. Poets lamented the destruction of the holy city and the misery ensuing from the invasion by Babylonian soldiers.[9] Even more disturbing is their wondering if God had forsaken the people of the covenant.

Now if these biblical works were written from below, as it were, do they carry authority the way books written from above do?[10] Clearly, Ecclesiastes, Song of Songs, and Psalms are unlike other biblical literature that presents itself as divine revelation. Moreover Qoheleth's philosophical approach of following his eyes to a rational conclusion led to the denial of fundamental teachings that laid claim to divine origin. It would seem, therefore, that the substantial arguments that can be raised against a theory of the inspiration of scripture become insurmountable where Ecclesiastes is concerned. We need to keep in mind several things.

Qoheleth simply described reality as he observed it. The world is irrational, he deduced, for life is all too brief; human effort is without profit; all so-called pleasures are trivial; intellectual pursuits are doomed to fail; and serious gaps in divine justice plague humanity.

Despite his emphasis on personal observation, Qoheleth was open to life's deep mysteries, particularly at the inception of life and its termination. Between these episodic events, human beings encounter random forces that evoke joy and sorrow. Qoheleth openly acknowledged the ambiguities of existence that challenge the controlling principle that shapes the biblical record—the system of rewards and retribution.

Qoheleth's pedagogy is dialogic. He presented two sides of an issue, often leaving his own view lurking in the shadows. His reason may have been a rhetorical tease, or he may not have been able to make up his mind. Time's passage may also have brought changes in the answers he gave to complex questions. Perhaps he even recognized the limitations of his own perspective and chose a rhetoric of erasure.[11]

Qoheleth realized that all things are relative under the sun. Absolutes belong to another world, if they actually exist. That principle applies to wisdom, goodness, and work. All these are only worthwhile up to a point. In the end too much study, excessive righteousness, and endless toil are mere puffs of wind, nothing but *hebel*.

More than any other author, Qoheleth attended to time's passage. We are puppets in a drama until death stills our voice and immobilizes us. Ironically nature outlasts human beings. Not only does time seal human destiny, but it makes possible multiple opportunities to love and hate, laugh and cry, speak and be silent, plant and uproot, sew and rip apart, and so much more.

Qoheleth understood the fragility of human existence. The bloom of youth fades quickly, and a dark future awaits. We may create exquisite metaphors for the transition, but that verbal virtuosity is ultimately silenced by death, symbolized by a shattered lamp and broken cord.

Qoheleth did not flinch in the face of death. He would probably have agreed with the Egyptian sage who suggested that death's real name is "Come."[12] He might even have been like the weary woodcutter who lay down at his cabin to die and called for death. When death came and asked what he could do for the woodcutter, the response was: "I need help reloading this wood; please be quick about it."[13] As in the Arab tale about the poor slave—which is echoed in John O'Hara's first novel, *Appointment at Samarra*—fleeing to another city will not postpone a destiny inscribed in stone.

Because Qoheleth's teachings underscore the human element in scripture, he has been viewed as an intruder in the sacred canon, an entry into sacred space through the back door. Perhaps a better approach is to see Ecclesiastes as a testament to the integrity and courage of an original thinker. It may be that logical persuasion is the finest authority available to mortals. Authority based on anything else is surely *hebel,* transient, and at times even foul.

Contempt for the World

Qoheleth's teachings have led some Christians to one of two options. Some have chosen asceticism, believing that nothing in this life has any real value. By emptying themselves of everything that belongs to earthly existence except for bread and water, they have given themselves wholly to the inner life of devotion to their maker. Contempt for the world, or at least indifference toward what it has to offer, is their way of responding to Qoheleth's assessment of everything as meaningless. Such contempt of the world is not entirely missing from Jewish interpreters of Ecclesiastes. Moshe ben Hayyin Alsheikh (1508–1601) viewed Qoheleth as a call to asceticism and piety, the storing up of good deeds and Torah to carry back to the king's palace. Alsheikh considered the good things of this world nothing compared to the promise of rewards in the eternal realm.[14]

Others have tried to escape from the things of this world into a mystical union with God. Their aim is to become one with the wholly other so that worldly desires no longer enter their minds.[15] Christians were not alone in this endeavor. In the Middle Ages they were joined by Jews who sought unity with their creator above all else.

Neither of these alternatives does justice to Qoheleth's advice about enjoyment. Most Jewish interpreters have been true to the message involving pleasure. His words have even evoked the radical statement that everyone will have to give an account for all the good things they have not enjoyed.[16] The reason: to do less is to be an ingrate. Nevertheless Qoheleth's words about enjoyment were spoken against a backdrop of serious questions about the meaning of everything. They did not grow out of belief in divine goodness.

Much has been made of the fact that Qoheleth believed he lived in a three-storied universe. From this worldview some critics have argued that he thought everything under the sun (on earth and in Sheol) was futile, meaningless, and ephemeral but that above the sun (God's realm) *hebel* does not apply. I have given voice to that optimistic reading of Qoheleth in a poem entitled "Beyond the Sun."[17]

I

Under the sun,
the tangled knots
of human carnage

expose envy, greed,
and bloated ego,
their frayed edges
masking a pained journey
from trust to abuse,
promise to betrayal,
passion to indifference.

2

Above the sun,
a master weaver
twists diverse threads
in many directions
to reveal a pattern
of hope and pardon.

3

Beneath the heavens,
victims cry out
for measured justice,
an eye for an eye,
"A moment's satisfaction
for past wrongs,
finally avenged."

4

Beyond the sun,
no one assesses guilt,
or even merit!
Forgiveness reigns
in a kingdom
that knows no end.

Did Qoheleth ever drop the slightest hint that he viewed the divine realm as a place where the injustices below will be set right? Rarely did he mention the upper story, and, when he did, he emphasized the danger it poses and stressed its distance from where humans reside. Fear, therefore, was for him the proper attitude toward heaven. And one ingredient of fear is wonder, the capacity to stand awestruck before the unknown and unknowable.[18] If Qoheleth championed anything, it is the limit of the intellect to fathom the mysteries of daily existence. That insight into the epistemological dilemma did not stop him from stretching his mind as far as possible. In his thinking, God placed a longing for hidden things—or for permanence—in the mind. Along with the desire, however, came a closed door blocking all access. That door is fashioned by a human's finite nature. One can even say that Qoheleth's depiction of God in 3:11 imputes irony to the deity: "He has made everything beautiful in its time; also he has put the unknown in their mind because of which no one can find out the work God has done from beginning to end."

The Ironic Wink

In my introduction I observed that irony lies in the eye of the beholder. Now at long last, I wish to explain why I chose the subtitle *The Ironic Wink* for this volume. Above all Qoheleth inverted the expectation in Greek drama that the *eiron* pose as less than he is, adopting instead the role of the *alazon*. Qoheleth claimed to be a king who possessed both abundant wealth and wisdom. Then in the epilogue, he is called a sage who sought to write pleasant things. Both assertions are refuted by history and by his teachings, which rule out superior knowledge, reek of skepticism, and abound in reminders of approaching death. Moreover he praised joy in contexts that suggest irony, especially in light of the individual's dependence on God's enabling power to take advantage of good fortune. Indeed nothing prohibits a reader from concluding that these statements about enjoyment are intended ironically.

Because everything is *hebel,* according to Qoheleth, all his ideas partake of this quality, even the judgment that all is futile, transient, or mist. As such, they go up in smoke, every concept deconstructing its opposite. In my view the second epilogue is an example of misreading, a failure to grasp the irony of what precedes it. In the end everything belongs to the category of *hebel,* and those who think religious devotion, fear of God, and keeping of statutes transform existence into a life akin to that in the garden of Eden have failed to recognize the poignancy of Qoheleth's insights. We know better, for he winks in our direction. Or does he? Perhaps the irony is directed at those of us who think we understand him.

Appendix

Intellectual Kinship

This imaginary letter was inspired by Stephen Greenblatt's account of the discovery of Lucretius's De rerum natura. *I am struck by the similarities between Qoheleth and this first-century* B.C.E. *Roman poet. Like the letter, Octavia is fictional.*

You may be surprised to receive another letter from me, Octavia, for it has been only a few days since I last wrote to you. The reason for this letter is my excitement over discovering a remarkable meditation on death that is in some ways akin to my own *De rerum natura,* which you know so well. I came across the work quite by accident. During a leisurely dinner with a Jewish merchant from Alexandria, we fell into talking about the nature of the universe. At one point he mentioned a scroll that had recently been translated into Greek from its original Hebrew. He said it was about death and that it recommends pleasure as the highest good. My curiosity thoroughly aroused, I had to see the manuscript for myself. Although it was not easy to obtain a copy, I did so at considerable expense. I must say that the silver was well spent.

My initial impression was that the work was neither poetry nor prose but a combination of the two. In this respect it is different from the hexameters of my meditation. The author claims to be a king, but certain things suggest that this assertion is fiction. The treatise resembles a diatribe with opposing views juxtaposed so as to make it difficult to tell which one represents the author's thinking. A single thesis runs through the entire work: everything is ephemeral, futile, a mere breath. A secondary thesis is the denial of any profit in life.

The author has drunk deeply at the fountain of Greek philosophy. He accepts Thales's explanation for the basic elements of the universe—earth, air, fire, and water. He agrees with Monimus that everything is mist, like a puff of wind, and he relies on Epicurus and Stoic understanding of the universe as a balance of opposites that are perfectly structured in the most elegant manner possible.

And yet he thinks everything is in motion. The wind goes this way and that. The sun pursues its rounds. Rivers rush toward the sea, and people talk incessantly. Has he not come close to my view that the particles making up the universe are in constant flux? To be sure I argue that a single element, an atom, is the fundamental building block of the universe. These invisible particles move endlessly, and the overall structure is always changing as particles realign themselves in a limited number of shapes.

Above all a swerve made the universe possible. In this regard I disagree with him and his mentors, who attribute the origin of things to the gods. To me gods are a delusion, no different from angels, ghosts, and demons. The author may not think of gods as a delusion, but they seem to serve little if any purpose for him other than to instill fear by their thoroughly irrational behavior. The idea of providence is thus a pipe dream. In that view he is surely right.

What is the place of human beings in this world? This Jewish philosopher understands that we are no different from beasts. Why? Because we all die and then decompose. He rightly challenges those who think humans are immortal and animals are not. While he and I may differ about the impetus for action—envy of others as opposed to the struggle to survive—we agree that the highest goal of life is the pursuit of pleasure and reduction of pain. As I see it, he appears to be caught in a paradox. While insisting on a deterministic fate, he encourages people to observe the golden mean and thus to act in a prudent manner, being neither too virtuous nor too evil.

What about death? Must it be feared? The learned author puts together an exquisite collage of images that evokes wonder at the mystery of death. Wonder, not fear at the prospect of dying, is a healthy attitude to the event that permits the invisible particles to form themselves into additional shapes. This brilliant thinker faces death without fear because he realizes that all is mere breath, every striving futile, empty, and meaningless. To think otherwise is to fall victim to the greatest illusion of all, that the intellect can guarantee success and well-being.

Words fail me, my sister, to describe what a profound effect this meditation on death has had on me. It is as if I have found a kindred spirit like you.

Your loving brother,
Lucretius

Notes

Introduction

1. Richard Lattimore, *Themes in Greek and Latin Epitaphs* (Urbana: University of Illinois Press, 1962), 75.

2. Tony Augarde, ed. *The Oxford Dictionary of Modern Quotations* (Oxford & New York: Oxford University, 1991), 129. The quotation is from Jiddu Krishnamurti.

3. Among modern commentators, Choon-Leong Seow is unique in retaining the translation "vanity" for this word despite the change in meaning from the Latin *vanitas*. See Seow's *Ecclesiastes* (New York: Doubleday, 1997).

4. Jerry A. Gladson, *The Five Exotic Scrolls of the Hebrew Bible* (Lewiston, N.Y.: Edwin Mellen, 2009), provides an informative introduction to these megilloth.

5. There are many introductions to this literature, including James L. Crenshaw, *Old Testament Wisdom* (3d ed.; Louisville: Westminster John Knox, 2010); Leo G. Perdue, *The Sword and the Stylus* (Grand Rapids: Eerdmans, 2008), and *Wisdom Literature* (Louisville: Westminster John Knox, 2007); John J. Collins, *Jewish Wisdom in the Hellenistic Age* (Louisville: Westminster John Knox, 1997); and Gerhard von Rad, *Wisdom in Israel* (Nashville: Abingdon, 1972).

6. I remain skeptical about the existence of wisdom psalms. See my discussions in *The Psalms* (Grand Rapids: Eerdmans, 2001), 87–95.

7. The best commentary on these sayings is in Michael V. Fox's *Proverbs 1–9* (New York: Doubleday, 2000) and *Proverbs 10–31* (New Haven: Yale University Press, 2009). For research prior to 1995, see R. N. Whybray, *The Book of Proverbs* (Leiden: Brill, 1995). Katharine J. Dell, *The Book of Proverbs in Social and Theological Context* (Cambridge: University Press, 2006), endeavors to integrate wisdom into the general context of the rest of the Hebrew Bible.

8. Two different approaches to this book are my *Reading Job: A Literary and Theological Commentary* (Macon: Smyth & Helwys, 2011), and J. Gerald Janzen's *At the Scent of Water: The Ground of Hope in the Book of Job* (Grand Rapids: Eerdmans, 2009).

9. Augustinus Gianto, "Human Destiny in Emar and Qoheleth," in *Qohelet in the Context of Wisdom* (ed. Antoon Schoors; Bibliotheca ephemeridum theologicarum lovaniensium 156; Louvain: University Press, 1998), 473–79.

10. Karel van der Toorn, "Did Ecclesiastes Copy Gilgamesh?" *Biblical Review* 16 (2000): 23–30, evaluates Qoheleth's relationship with Mesopotamian, Egyptian, and

Greek sources. He concludes that Qoheleth definitely borrowed a proverb about a three-fold cord from Mesopotamia and that there are striking similarities with Siduri's advice from the Gilgamesh epic, although Egyptian Harper Songs also emphasize some of the same themes. According to van der Toorn, Qoheleth's thought world is much like that of the Greek thinkers of his day.

11. Quoted in Stephen Greenblatt, *The Swerve: How the World became Modern* (New York: Norton, 2011), 80.

12. This citation is taken from Ray Waddle, *Against the Grain: Unconventional Wisdom from Ecclesiastes* (Nashville: Upper Room, 2005), xv.

13. The Balcones Poetry Prize for 2011 went to Mark Jarman for *Bone Fires: New and Selected Poems.*

14. Despite the title, this book of poetry is a powerful analysis of the mystery of transcendence as well as human ignorance about God's existence and workings.

15. Mark Jarman, *Questions for Ecclesiastes* (Ashland, Oreg.: Story Line Press, 1997), 54.

16. Waddle, *Against the Grain,* 156.

17. Bertrand Russell, "A Free Man's Worship," in *The Meaning of Life* (ed. E. D. Klemke; 2d ed.; New York & Oxford: Oxford University, 2000), 76.

18. Arthur Schopenhauer, "On the Vanity of Existence," ibid., 67.

19. Cited by R. W. Hepburn, in "Questions about the Meaning of Life," ibid., 276.

20. Jacques Ellul, *Reason for Being: A Meditation on Ecclesiastes* (Grand Rapids: Eerdmans, 1990), 31.

21. Ibid., 117.

22. Ibid., 208.

23. Robert Gordis, *Koheleth: The Man and His World* (New York: Schocken, 1968), 58.

24. Ibid., 302.

25. Ibid., 3.

26. Ibid., 132.

27. Albert Camus, "The Absurdity of Human Existence," in *The Meaning of Life,* 98.

28. "Let no man say that I have said nothing new; my arrangement of matter is new. In playing tennis we both use the same ball, but one of us places it better" (Blaise Pascal, *Pensées* [New York: Modern Library, 1947], 359, aphorism 676). What Pascal says about the books of Job and Ecclesiastes may not be new, but it is apropos: "Solomon and Job have known best and spoken best of man's misery; the one the most fortunate, the other the most unfortunate of men; the one knowing by experience the emptiness of pleasure; the other, the reality of sorrow" (ibid., 193, aphorism 357).

29. The quote is from Wayne C. Booth, *A Rhetoric of Irony* (Chicago & London: University of Chicago Press, 1974), 91.

30. Ibid., 177–78.

31. Ibid., 244.

Chapter 1. Authorial Deceit

1. Elias Bickerman, *Four Strange Books of the Bible: Jonah/Daniel/Koheleth/Esther* (New York: Schocken, 1967), 158–67.

2. This interpretation is derived from an extended sense of the Greek *ekklesiastes* to indicate one who assembled people and was not just a member of an assembly.

3. The shift from first to third person has convinced most scholars that at least one and probably two editorial additions occur at 12:9–14.

4. It is generally acknowledged that the adversary's function was to make sure that human goodness sprang from higher motives than fear or desire for gain. Although in the divine service, the provocateur has a sinister side that may explain the later development of this figure into the devil.

5. The translations throughout the present book are my own.

6. The Hebrew text on which this study of Qoheleth is based is the Leningrad Codex B19A from 1008 c.e. A critical edition, *Biblica Hebraica Quinta,* was published in 2004.

7. Patrick W. Skehan, *Studies in Israelite Poetry and Wisdom* (Washington: Catholic Biblical Association, 1971), 42–43.

8. Frank Zimmerman, *The Inner World of Qohelet* (New York: Ktav, 1973). This book is marred by a psychologizing tendency that takes great liberties with the text.

9. Michael V. Fox. *A Time to Tear Down & a Time to Build Up: A Rereading of Ecclesiastes* (Grand Rapids: Eerdmans, 1999), 160–61.

10. Translation and notes of these two works attributed to Solomon are in volume 2 of James H. Charlesworth, ed., *The Old Testament Pseudepigrapha* (2 vols.; Garden City, N.Y.: Doubleday, 1985). R. B. Wright translated Psalms of Solomon (1639–70) while Charlesworth is responsible for Odes of Solomon (725–71).

11. In some ritual texts the seven sages mediated knowledge to humans prior to the flood, and they were succeeded by four sages, called *ummanu,* the last of whom is a human being. At the head of this chain of wisdom is Ea (or Enki in the Sumerian version), the god of wisdom. "From him the line of wisdom descends through the *apkallu* and *ummanu* down to human scholars," according to Richard J. Clifford in *The Wisdom Literature* (Nashville: Abingdon, 1998), 25–26.

12. James L. Crenshaw, "Sipping from the Cup of Wisdom," in *Jesus and Philosophy: New Essays* (ed. Paul K. Moser; Cambridge: University Press, 2009), 41–62, and Karel van der Toorn, "Sources in Heaven: Revelation as a Scholarly Construct in Second Temple Judaism," in *Kein Land für sich allein* (ed. Ulrich Hübner and Ernst Axel Knauf; Freiburg: Freiburg and Göttingen University Press / Vandenhoeck & Ruprecht, 2002), 265–77.

13. Ellen van Wolde, ed., *Job 28: Cognition in Context* (Biblical Interpretation Series 64; Leiden: Brill, 2003); Alison Lo, *Job 28 as Rhetoric: An Analysis of Job 28 in the Context of Job 22–31* (Vetus Testamentum Supplements 97; Atlanta: Society of Biblical Literature, 2003); and Scott C. Jones, *Rumors of Wisdom* (Beiheft zur Zeitschrift für die Alttestamentliche Wissenschaft 398; Berlin & New York: de Gruyter, 2009).

14. Surprisingly the Hebrew Bible rarely, if ever, alludes to Adam (and Eve) after the primal myth in Gen 1–11. A change takes place in Sirach and in Fourth Ezra (Second Esdras).

15. Possibly the most controversial view has been put forth by Silvia Schroer, *Wisdom Has Built Her House: Studies on the Figure of Sophia in the Bible* (Collegeville: Liturgical,

2000). She thinks "*Hokmah* is a counterpart for YHWH, a divine counterpart . . . the God of Israel in the image of a woman and in the language of the goddesses" (29).

16. Richard J. Clifford and John J. Collins, "Introduction: The Theology of Creation Traditions," in *Creation in the Biblical Traditions* (ed. Clifford and Collins; Catholic Biblical Quarterly Monograph Series 24; Washington: Catholic Biblical Association, 1992), 1–15. In the ancient world, beginnings shaped the subsequent course of things, hence the importance of stories about creation.

17. James L. Crenshaw, *Education in Ancient Israel: Across the Deadening Silence* (Anchor Bible Reference Library; New York: Doubleday, 1998); David M. Carr, *Writing on the Tablet of the Heart: Origins of Scripture and Literature* (New York: Oxford University Press, 2004); and Karel van der Toorn, *Scribal Culture and the Making of the Hebrew Bible* (Cambridge, Mass.: Harvard University Press, 2007).

18. The word *midrash* is derived from the verb *darash,* "to seek out," and refers to Jewish commentary, often homiletical, on a biblical text. An alternative to the free-flowing reading is *peshat,* which adheres closely to the literal, simple, historical sense.

19. Above all by Peter Höffken, "Das EGO des Weisen," *Theologische Zeitschrift* (1985): 121–34.

20. Jennifer L. Koosed, *Gleaning Ruth: A Biblical Heroine and Her Afterlives* (Columbia: University of South Carolina Press, 2011) throws new light on the agrarian context of this exquisite tale.

21. T. A. Perry, *The Honeymoon Is Over: Jonah's Argument with God* (Peabody, Mass.: Hendrickson, 2006); like Perry's other books, this one abounds in fascinating readings, often highly conjectural. That judgment particularly applies to *God's Twilight Zone: Wisdom in the Hebrew Bible* (Peabody, Mass.: Hendrickson, 2008).

22. "They gave themselves [the papyrus roll as a lector] priest, the writing board as a son-he-loves, (books of) wisdom (as) their pyramids, the reed-pen (as) their child, and the back of a stone for a wife. From great to small were made into his children. (As) for the scribe, he is the foremost of them" ("In Praise of Learned Scribes"). This attitude includes disdain for all other professions, as in "The Satire on the Trades." Both texts are found in James B. Pritchard, ed., *Ancient Near Eastern Texts Relating to the Old Testament* (3d ed. with supplement; Princeton: Princeton University Press, 1969), 431–34—hereafter cited as *ANET.* Miriam Lichtheim's translation of "The Satire on the Trades" is in William W. Hallo, ed., *The Context of Scripture* (3 vols.; Leiden & Boston: Brill, 2003), 1:122–25. The professions that are satirized include sculptor, smith, carpenter, jewel maker, barber, reed cutter, potter, mason, gardener, farmer, weaver, arrow maker, courier, stoker, cobbler, washerman, bird catcher, and fisherman.

23. The "Instruction of Amenemope" concludes as follows: "It has come to its end / In the writing of Senu, son of the God's Father, Pa-miu." "The Satire on the Trades" ends this way: "It has come to a happy ending in success."

24. "I, Saggil-kinam-ubbib, the exorcist, am an adorant of the god and the king."

25. Johannes C. de Moor, "Theodicy in the Texts of Ugarit," in *Theodicy in the World of the Bible* (ed. Antti Laato and de Moor; Leiden & Boston: Brill, 2003), 108–50. On the four occurrences of the word *haqam* ("wise") in Ugaritic literature and the role of sages at Ugarit, see Ignacio Marquez Rowe, "Scribes, Sages, and Seers in Ugarit and Syria," in

Scribes, Sages, and Seers: The Sage in the Eastern Mediterranean World (ed. Leo G. Perdue; Forschungen zur Religion und Literatur des Alten und Neuen Testaments 219; Göttingen: Vandenhoeck & Ruprecht, 2008), 95–108.

26. Harold C. Washington, *Wealth and Poverty in the Instruction of Amenemope and the Hebrew Proverbs* (Society of Biblical Literature Dissertation Series 142; Atlanta: Scholars, 1994), notes that Egyptian scribes multiplied according to the demands of society. He uses Meir el-Medinah just south of Thebes as a prime example of a small town in the fourteenth century B.C.E. that witnessed a rapid growth of local scribes because of the need for their expertise.

27. J. Edward Wright, *The Early History of Heaven* (Oxford: Oxford University, 2000), traces the development of belief in life after death. The biblical concepts relating to an afterlife are treated in James H. Charlesworth et al., *Resurrection: The Origin and Future of a Biblical Doctrine* (New York: T. & T. Clark, 2006).

28. Shannon Burkes, *Death in Qoheleth and Egyptian Biographies of the Late Period* (Society of Biblical Literature Dissertation Series 170; Atlanta: Society of Biblical Literature, 1999). Common complaints run through the late Egyptian biographies: I am too young for death; I am without fault; death seizes the young rather than the old who walk in his vicinity; and I thirst although water surrounds me.

29. James L. Crenshaw, "The Shadow of Death in Qoheleth," in *Israelite Wisdom: Theological and Literary Essays in Honor of Samuel Terrien* (ed. John Gammie et al.; Missoula, Mont.: Scholars, 1978), 205–16; republished in my *Urgent Advice and Probing Questions* (Macon: Mercer University, 1995), 573–85.

30. Charlesworth, ed., *The Old Testament Pseudepigrapha*, 1:773–995. The following testaments are translated and annotated: Twelve Patriarchs, Job, Three Patriarchs, Moses, Solomon, and Adam.

31. Ruediger Safranski, *Nietzsche: A Philosophical Biography* (New York: Norton, 2002), is an excellent introduction to this complex thinker.

32. *The Oxford Dictionary of Modern Quotations*, 229–30.

33. James C. VanderKam, *Enoch: A Man for all Generations* (Columbia: University of South Carolina Press, 1995).

34. From many recent studies on apocalyptic, for its originality and scope, I single out that by Anathea E. Portier-Young, *Apocalypse against Empire: Theologies of Resistance in Early Judaism* (Grand Rapids: Eerdmans, 2011).

35. On the prophetic concept of a day of Yahweh, see James L. Crenshaw, *Joel* (New York: Doubleday, 1995), 47–50, and the relevant commentary throughout. Scholars have pointed to the darkening of sun and moon as evidence of apocalyptic thought in Qoheleth.

36. There is evidence that some Jews continued to use the Septuagint even into the Common Era.

37. F. J. Backhaus, "Kohelet und die Ironie," *Biblische Notizen* 101 (2000): 29–55, distinguishes ironies of style from allusive irony and an ironic base but does not think the irony is radical enough to reach atheism or absurdity. See also Harold Fisch, "Qoheleth: A Hebrew Ironist," in *Poetry with a Purpose: Biblical Poetics and Interpretation* (Bloomington: Indiana University Press, 1988), 158–78; Carolyn J. Sharp, "Ironic Representation,

Authorial Voice, and Meaning in Qoheleth," *Biblical Interpretation* 12 (2004): 37–68; Ramond Sophie, "Y a-t-il de l'ironie dans le livre de Qohélet?" *Vetus Testamentum* 60 (2010): 621–40; and I. Spangenberg, "Irony in the Book of Qohelet," *Journal for the Study of the Old Testament* [hereafter cited as *JSOT*] 72 (1996): 57–69.

Chapter 2. Veiled Truth?

1. Disturbed by the misogyny in this brief unit, interpreters have recently argued that (1) Qoheleth was referring to the foreign/strange woman warned against in Proverbs, (2) was quoting an opinion with which he disagreed, (3) conceded that the aphorism is erroneous, (4) admitted that he had not been able to confirm the negative view of woman, (5) actually referred to personified Wisdom, both elusive and unattainable, and (6) placed the emphasis on woman's strength. Representatives of these views are discussed in my *Old Testament Wisdom,* 146n6.

2. Two different approaches to the biblical story about David are Marti J. Steussy, *David: Biblical Portraits of Power* (Columbia: University of South Carolina, 1999), and Robert Pinsky, *The Life of David* (New York: Schocken, 2005).

3. Although the adjective *ḥakam* ("wise") is used to describe this woman, it does not seem to have the meaning of a professional sage. Some interpreters, however, think of her as a member of this elite group, despite the rarity of *ḥakam* used in this sense. Furthermore the woman merely said what Joab instructed her to say. At most she was a talented actress.

4. The most elaborate theory of this genre is that of T. A. Perry, *Dialogues with Kohelet: The Book of Ecclesiastes* (University Park: Pennsylvania State University, 1993). The problem of recognizing quotations is addressed by Michael V. Fox, "The Identification of Quotations in Biblical Literature," *Zeitschrift für die Alttestamentliche Wissenschaft* 92 (1980): 416–31.

5. Perry distinguishes between the Presenter (which he calls *P*) and Kohelet (labeled *K*) as the man of faith versus the man of experience respectively. Lloyd Geering, *Such Is Life: A Close Encounter with Ecclesiastes* (Salem, Oreg.: Polebridge Press, 2009), enters into dialogue with Qoheleth.

6. There are actually four different "speakers": a young man, a young woman, her brothers, and the daughters of Jerusalem. Ariel and Chana Bloch, *The Song of Songs* (Berkeley: University of California, 1995), use different fonts to make this fact clear.

7. R. N. Whybray, "The Identification and Use of Quotations in Ecclesiastes," *Vetus Testamentum Supplements* 32 (1981): 435–51.

8. Krüger, *Qoheleth* (Minneapolis: Fortress, 2004), thinks Qoheleth's initial reflections expressing hatred of the world (1:12–2:26) describe the Hellenistic Zeitgeist and that the central section, 3:1–4:12, develops a theological alternative (74). He says the text in 8:1–5 is so ambiguous that it practically deconstructs itself (157).

9. No interpreter has succeeded in decoding the structure of Ecclesiastes despite many attempts, a large number of which are ingenious. I discuss the possibilities in my commentary in the Old Testament Library (*Ecclesiastes* [Philadelphia & London: Westminster, 1987]).

10. George Aaron Barton, *The Book of Ecclesiastes* (Edinburgh: T. & T. Clark, 1908), illustrates this approach. He identified the following editorial glosses: 4:5; 5:3, 7a; 7:1a, 3, 5, 6–9, 11, 12, 19; 8:1; 9:17, 18; 10:1–3, 8–14a, 15, 18, 19.

11. Jeffrey H. Tigay, *The Evolution of the Gilgamesh Epic* (Philadelphia: University of Pennsylvania Press, 1982).

12. The most troublesome of these relate to divine justice. For example, in 11:9b one reads "But know that God will bring you into judgment for all these," although Qoheleth just urged people to walk in the ways of their heart and in the sight of their eyes. Similarly 8:12–13 states as a certainty that traditional doctrine about divine justice is accurate, despite assertions to the contrary elsewhere. Admittedly one is reluctant to give up the belief that justice will become reality some day. In a forthcoming treatment of this problem by Stuart Weeks, "Divine Judgment and Reward in Ecclesiastes," Qoheleth's ambivalent attitude is emphasized.

13. Fox, *A Time to Tear Down & a Time to Build Up,* 18–20.

14. Kurt Galling, *Der Prediger* (Handbuch zum Alten Testament 1, 18; 1940; Tübingen: J. C. B. Mohr, 1969).

15. *The Oxford Dictionary of Modern Quotations,* 35.

16. Ibid., 226.

17. James L. Crenshaw, "Qoheleth's Quantitative Language," in *The Language of Qohelet in Its Context: Essays in Honour of Prof. A. Schoors on the Occasion of his Seventieth Birthday* (ed. Angelika Berlejung and Pierre van Hecke; Orientalia lovaniensia analecta 164; Leuven: Uitgeverij Peeters, 2007), 1–22; republished in my *Prophets, Sages, & Poets* (St. Louis: Chalice, 2006), 83–94, 224–30.

18. Only here is a feminine verb used with Qoheleth as subject. Hence Perry writes, "By compensation or identification, Kohelet feminizes his name, as if to say: I am not more reliable than women are" (*Dialogues with Kohelet,* 132).

19. James L. Crenshaw, "The Problem of Theodicy in Sirach: On Human Bondage," *Journal of Biblical Literature* 94 (1975): 49–64; republished in my *Urgent Advice and Probing Questions,* 155–74.

20. Norbert Lohfink, *Qoheleth* (Minneapolis: Fortress, 2003), 122, thinks "this" whole series could summarize the biographical ideal of a young Greek: "success in sport as a youth, then a military career, eventually setting up a family, accumulation of wealth, public influence in the polis."

21. Michael V. Fox, "Frame-Narrative and Composition in the Book of Qohelet," *Hebrew Union College Annual* 48 (1977): 83–106.

22. Tremper Longman III, *The Book of Ecclesiastes* (Grand Rapids: Eerdmans, 1998), and Eric S. Christianson, *A Time To Tell: Narrative Strategies in Ecclesiastes* (JSOT Supplementary Series 28; Sheffield: Sheffield Academic, 1998). The latter is informed by sophisticated literary theory.

23. *Ecclesiastes* (Philadelphia: Jewish Publication Society, 2004), 13, even concedes that the phrase "and to grasp folly" in 2:3 may be a pious gloss. In *A Time to Tear Down & a Time to Build Up,* 358, Fox admits that verses 12:13–14 are a postscript standing outside the conjectured frame.

24. Edward L. Greenstein, "Sages with a Sense of Humor: The Babylonian Dialogue between a Master and His Servant and the Book of Qoheleth," in *Wisdom Literature in Mesopotamia and Israel* (ed. Richard J. Clifford; Atlanta: Society of Biblical Literature, 2007), 55–65.

25. Raymond C. Van Leeuwen, "The Background to Proverbs 30:4a," in *Wisdom, You Are My Sister* (ed. Michael L. Barré; Catholic Biblical Quarterly Monograph Series 29; Washington, D.C.: Catholic Biblical Association of America, 1995), 102–21, posits a myth about ascending to heaven and returning. The Mesopotamian hero Adapa is reputed to have reached heaven and returned to earth with secrets revealed to him by the gods.

26. Von Rad, *Wisdom in Israel,* 248 and 311, gives voice to both views, presumably because he changed his mind at some point.

27. Qoheleth's language exposes the thin line between dialogue and monologue for him. At issue is the extent to which his allusions to conversation with the heart resemble Egyptian dialogue with the heart. In my view he simply indicated internal reflection about the merits of an argument.

Chapter 3. Elusive Essence

1. The Masoretic Text has thirty-eight uses of *hebel,* but many scholars emend *hakkol* ("everything") in 9:2 to *hebel.* The Hebrew characters for the letters *b* and *k* are similar.

2. Besides the illuminating discussion of *hebel* in Michael V. Fox, *Qohelet and His Contradictions* (JSOT Supplementary Series 18; Sheffield: Almond, 1989), 29–51, I have found these works to be useful: Ethan Dor-Shav, "Ecclesiastes, Fleeting and Timeless," *Azure* 18 (5765/2004): 67–87, and Douglas B. Miller, *Symbol and Rhetoric in Ecclesiastes: The Place of Hebel in Qoheleth's Work* (Academia Biblica 2; Atlanta: Society of Biblical Literature, 2002). I cannot accept Miller's conservative conclusions about Qoheleth's message.

3. Baruch A. Levine, "The Appeal to Personal Experience in the Wisdom of Qoheleth," in *From Babel to Babylon* (ed. Joyce Rilett Wood, John E. Harvey, and Mark Leuchter; New York: T. &. T. Clark, 2006), 332–45.

4. Responses to a perceived delay in punishing the wicked and rewarding the virtuous are in many ways predictable; see James L. Crenshaw, *Defending God: Biblical Responses to the Problem of Evil* (New York: Oxford University, 2005); See my "Theodicy," *Anchor Bible Dictionary* (ed. David Noel Freedman; 6 vols., New York: Doubleday, 1992), 6:444–47, and "Theodicy," *New Interpreter's Dictionary of the Bible* (ed. K. D. Sakenfeld; 5 vols., Nashville: Abingdon, 2006–9), 5:551–55.

5. He may have been criticizing a new idea that has its roots in Hellenism.

6. Norbert Lohfink, "Kohelet 1, 2 'Alles ist Windhauch'—universale oder anthropologische Aussage?" in *Studien zu Kohelet* (Stuttgarter Biblische Aufsatzbände Altes Testament 26; Stuttgart: Katholisches Bibelwerk, 1998), 125–42.

7. In "Qoheleth's Quantitative Language," I discuss the striving toward philosophical universalism in his thinking, a point that Peter Machinist makes differently in "Fate,

miqreh, and Reason: Some Reflections on Qohelet and Biblical Thought," in *Solving Riddles and Untying Knots* (ed. Ziony Zevit, Seymour Gitin, and Michael Sokoloff; Winona Lake: Eisenbrauns, 1995), 159–74.

8. Fox, *A Time to Tear Town & a Time to Build Up,* 30: "*Hebel* in Qohelet means 'absurd' understood in the sense described at length in Albert Camus's classic description of the absurd, *The Myth of Sisyphus.*" The absurd is irrational, an affront to reason, meaningless.

9. In Jewish tradition Abraham actually sacrificed Isaac, whose body was carried by angels to paradise and nursed for three years in the dew of heaven. Shalom Spiegel's *The Last Trial* (New York: Schocken, 1967) is an exquisite analysis of this legend about Gen 22.

10. Mark S. Smith wrote in "Rephaim," *Anchor Bible Dictionary,* 5:674–76, that the Bible treats Rephaim in two categories: descriptions of the dead in the underworld and references to a group or nation of giants or warriors.

11. The second century c.e. Roman ruler Marcus Aurelius used the expression "things as smoke" in the context of great men who have died. In his *Meditations* (New York: Book of the Month Club, 1996), 89, he remarked: "For thus continuously thou wilt look at human things as smoke and nothing at all. . . . But thou, in what a brief space of time is thy existence."

12. James L. Crenshaw, "Beginnings, Endings, and Life's Necessities in Biblical Wisdom," *Prophets, Sages, & Poets,* 95–103, 230–33 (originally in *Wisdom Literature of Mesopotamia and Israel*).

13. The ale wife, Siduri, gives this advice:

> The life thou pursuest thou shalt not find.
> When the gods created mankind,
> Death for mankind they set aside,
> Life in their own hands retaining.
> Thou, Gilgamesh, let full be thy belly,
> Make thou merry by day and by night.
> Of each day make thou a feast of rejoicing,
> Day and night dance thou and play!
> Let thy garments be sparkling fresh,
> Thy head be washed; bathe thou in water.
> Pay heed to the little one that holds on to thy hand.
> Let thy spouse delight in thy bosom!
> For this is the task of /mankind/.

(*ANET,* 90)

14. In recent commentaries there seems to be a trend toward a positive interpretation of Qoheleth's thought, as opposed to earlier pessimistic treatments. See, for example, Krüger, *Qoheleth* (2004); Seow, *Ecclesiastes* (1997); Bartholomew, *Reading Ecclesiastes* (1998); and Ludger Schwienhorst-Schönberger, *Kohelet* (2004) and "Gottes Antwort in

der Freude. Zur theologie göttlicher Gegenwart im Buch Kohelet" *Bibel und Kirche* 54 (1999). None of these goes as far as R. N. Whybray, "Qoheleth, Preacher of Joy," *JSOT* 23 (1982): 87–98.

15. I am reminded of Montaigne's comment about the inherent limitations to every claim about absolutes ("mon être universel comme Michel de Montaigne," *Essais,* 3:2).

16. The existence of antithetic meanings for the verb *barak* in the prologue to the book of Job rests on the two instances in which the antagonist assured Yahweh that an afflicted servant would curse him to his face. The other five uses of the verb (four in the prologue and one in the epilogue) are better explained as the usual "bless." Only two of these are considered problematic: the wife's urging Job to bless God and die, just as a condemned Achan was instructed to give glory to God, and Job's thinking his children might have sinned inadvertently and then blessed Yahweh without having atoned for the offense. This understanding of his words is more charitable than the suspicion that they have deliberately transgressed.

17. In addition to the standard commentaries, the following special studies of Psalm 39 address specific issues. Otto Kaiser, "Psalm 39," *Gottes und der Menschen Weisheit* (Beiheft zur Zeitschrift für die Alttestamentliche Wissenschaft 261; Berlin: de Gruyter, 1998), 71–83; Richard J. Clifford, "What Does the Psalmist Ask for in Psalms 39:5 and 90:12?" *Journal of Biblical Literature* 119 (2000): 59–66; W. A. M. Beuken, "Psalm 39," *Heythrop Journal* 19 (1978), 1–11; Ellen F. Davis, "Prisoner of Hope," in *The Art of Reading Scripture* (ed. Davis and Richard B. Hays; Grand Rapids: Eerdmans, 2003), 300–305.

18. "Conceal your heart, control your mouth" ("Ptahhotep" 618). "A man may be ruined by his tongue / Beware and you will do well" ("Any" 7, 8). "Do not sever your heart from your tongue . . ." ("Amenemope" 10, 16, compare "Insinger" 25, 21). "Keep firm your heart, steady your heart, do not steer with your tongue; If a man's tongue is the boat's rudder / The Lord of All is yet its pilot" ("Amenemope" 18, 3–5). "You may trip over your foot in the house of a great man; you should not trip over your tongue" ("Ankhsheshonq" 10, 7). Similar advice can be found in Mesopotamian wisdom and in Ahiqar.

19. On the biblical attitude to those who acted as if God were not, see my *Defending God,* 27–40, 203–8.

20. James T. Robinson, *Samuel Ibn Tibbon's Commentary on Ecclesiastes* (Texts and Studies in Medieval and Early Modern Judaism 20; Tübingen: Mohr Siebeck), 112–41, explains the way Ibn Tibbon used dialectic to good effect.

21. I examined the formula "Do not say" and its peculiar relationship to theodicy in "The Problem of Theodicy in Sirach," 49–64.

22. The search for the primary meaning of *hebel* continues in Dominic Rudman, "The Use of *Hebel* as an Indicator of Chaos in Ecclesiastes," in *The Language of Qohelet in Its Context,* 121–41. Dor-Shav, "Ecclesiastes, Fleeting and Timeless," 74, opts for vapor or mist.

23. The *Hebrew and English Lexicon of the Old Testament* (ed. Francis Brown, Samuel R. Driver, and Charles A. Briggs; Oxford: Clarendon Press, 1907), 364, lists "shew inactivity" as a meaning for the hiphil (causative) of *hashah.*

24. That is, even the person who can stand transfixed is actually no more than a vapor.

25. As Masoretic Text stands, the picture is that of a fantasm, an image that quickly slips away. I understand the preposition *bet* as essentia, meaning "as an image."

26. The elliptical style of the poet reaches a high point here. Its meaning conveys the utter futility of human enterprises, which ultimately amount to nothing, for possessions succumb to time just like people.

27. "This double expression of existential complaint offers an exact frame to the core verse, 'My hope is in thee' (v 8b) . . . this core verse functions like the prow of a ship in high seas" (Samuel Terrien, *The Psalms: Strophic Structure and Theological Commentary* [Grand Rapids: Eerdmans, 2003], 330–31).

28. Although some interpreters understand this verse as present, it seems better to take it as the poet's reflecting back on a previous condition and offering a justification for silence, one that points straight to Yahweh.

29. According to Berakot 32b (a tractate from the Babylonian Talmud), supplication moves on an ascending scale (prayer, crying aloud, tears). The last of these, tears can pass through any door, for the gates of tears are always open. The Psalmist, however, is less sanguine than some rabbis.

30. Robert Alter, *The Book of Psalms* (New York: Norton, 2007), 140, sees this verse as an "instance of the so-called breakup pattern in which a hendiadys ('sojourner and set-tler' meaning 'resident alien') is split up with each of the component terms set into one of the two parallel versets."

31. Amos Hakham, *The Bible: Psalms with Jerusalem Commentary* (3 vols.; Jerusalem: Mosad Harav Kook, 2003), 1:308n4, attributes this view to some commentators, although he thinks *nis'ab* means "certain, established."

32. Kaiser, "Psalm 39." He also relies heavily on uniformity of consonants in each colon.

33. Any attempt to ascertain the date of a biblical psalm requires decisions about so many unknowns as to render the conclusion highly tenuous; see my *The Psalms* and my "Foreword: The Book of Psalms and Its Interpreters," in Sigmund Mowinckel, *The Psalms in Israel's Worship* (Grand Rapids: Eerdmans, 2004), xix–xliv.

34. H. A. Brongers, "Bemerkungen zum Gebrauch des adverbialen *we'attah* im Alten Testament," *Vetus Testamentum* 15 (1965): 289–99.

35. John Goldingay, *Psalms 1–41* (vol. 1 of *Psalms;* Grand Rapids: Baker Academic, 2006), 557–58, implausibly translated *hodi'eni* as "acknowledge" and thinks the poet is asking for strength to accept a short life.

36. Alter, *The Book of Psalms,* 137, thinks the dominance of triadic versets, as opposed to the usual dyadic, expresses a powerful psychological tension, introducing an element of surprise and destabilizing what has gone before it.

37. The many studies of this psalm have not exhausted its riches—see my *The Psalms,* 109–27.

38. This is not the only instance of ellipsis in the psalm (compare v. 6, "they hustle—a breath" and vv. 2a and 5b). On the basis of *mehamon* in Ps 37:16 and *hehamon* in 1 Chr 29:16, one could construe *yehemayun* as a distortion of an original reference to wealth.

39. Alter, *The Book of Psalms,* views the preposition on "from good" as an indicator of deprivation, but this interpretation is unlikely since the silence is voluntary.

40. As late as IQ412 15 (a fragment from Qumran), the poet advised doors of protection for the tongue, and the Epistle of James compares the tongue to a fire and considers it an instrument of poison (vv. 6–8), a small member that controls humans the way rudders guide ships. Here too the idea of bits in the mouths of horses is mentioned in the context of keeping the tongue in check.

41. James L. Crenshaw, "Deceitful Minds and Theological Dogma: Jer. 17:5–11," in *Prophets, Sages & Poets,* 73–82, 222–24; also published in *Utopia and Dystopia in Prophetic Texts* (ed. Ehud Ben Zvi; Helsinki: Finnish Exegetical Society; Göttingen: Vandenhoeck & Ruprecht, 2006), 105–21; P. J. Tomson, "'There Is No One Who Is Righteous, Not Even One': Kohelet 7, 20 in Pauline and Early Jewish Interpretation," in *The Language of Qohelet in Its Context,* 183–202.

42. Practitioners of various divinatory techniques sought to read the future and in doing so to gain both prestige and monetary profit. Apocalyptic literature takes a much wider sweep by focusing on changes of universal magnitude: new heavens and a new earth.

43. A text from Emar, Enlil and Namzitarra, reckons life to be 120 years (compare Gen 6:3). Like Qoheleth, this author saw life as fleeting; the closing lines read: "the days of man are approaching, day to day they verily decrease, year after year they verily decrease. One hundred twenty years are the years of mankind—verily it is their bane" (J. Klein, "The 'Bane' of Humanity: A Lifespan of One Hundred Twenty Years," *Acta Sumerologica* 12 [1990]: 57–70).

44. This shift mirrors that from silence to speech, perhaps also from trust to sharp attack.

45. Chr 29:15 brings together several ideas that appear in Psalm 39, specifically resident alien and sojourner, all our ancestors, days like a shadow, and absence of hope. The Epistle of Hebrews 11:13 applies the category of sojourners to a long list of biblical heroes. According to Lev 25:23, the earth belongs to Yahweh, its inhabitants being sojourners and resident aliens.

46. See James L. Crenshaw, "Flirting with the Language of Prayer (Job 14:13–17)," in *Worship and the Hebrew Bible: Essays in Honor of John T. Willis* (ed. Patrick Graham, Rick Marrs, and Steven McKenzie; JSOT Supplementary Series 284; Sheffield: JSOT, 1999), 110–23; republished in my *Prophets, Sages, & Poets,* 6–13, 201–3.

47. Rudman, "The Use of *Hebel* as an Indicator of Chaos in Ecclesiastes," 121–22, 133, does not include Ps 39:12, limiting the concrete use to two, and even then, he writes, "a figurative use is evident."

48. Deut 32:21 has *hebel* in parallelism with "not god," suggesting that idols have no real vitality. Several examples of *hebel* emphasize the powerlessness of idols (Jer 10:3, 8, 15; 14:22; 16:19; Jonah 2:9). According to 2 Kgs 17:15, Israelites who turned to *hahebel* became worthless themselves (*wayyehbalu*).

49. The *mem* thus becomes the participial prefix to the verb *halak* ("to walk"). Other interpreters think the word for "in the image" derives from a root that means shadow.

50. The exquisite poem in 1:4–11 begins with the clause "a generation dies [literally 'goes'] and another comes." Similarly 6:4 says that the stillbirth "comes in futility and departs, its name covered by darkness."

51. On this negative particle, see Crenshaw, "Qoheleth's Quantitative Language," 1–22; Antoon Schoors, *The Preacher Sought to Find Pleasing Words: A Study in the Language of Qohelet* (Orientalia lovaniensia analecta 41; 2 vols. Louvain: Peeters, 1992, 1994), 1: 151f; and Bo Isaksson, *Studies in the Language of Qoheleth with Special Emphasis on the Verbal System* (Acta Universitatis Upsaliensis, Studia Semitica Upsalensia, 10; Uppsala, 1987), 172–74.

52. According to Goldingay, *Psalms, 1–41*, 556, "*'alam* never occurs to describe voluntary silence except as an attribute to Yahweh's servant who is silent under attack (Isa 53:7), though Job also apparently kept silence for a week (2:13). The parallel verb *hashah* is likewise never used to describe voluntary silence except in Ecclesiastes' meditation (3:7)." The relevance of Job 2:13 escapes me, for it does not employ the verb *'alam*.

53. Antoon Schoors, "God in Qoheleth," in *Schöpfungsplan und Heilsgeschichte: Festschrift für Ernst Haag* (ed. Renate Brandscheidt and Theresia Mende; Trier: Paulinus, 2002), 251–70, and "Theodicy in Qohelet," in Laato and Moor, ed., *Theodicy in the World of the Bible*, 375–409.

54. The role of joy in Qoheleth is widely debated, with R. Norman Whybray and Norbert Lohfink leading the way to a positive understanding of joy as a divine gift. Others, including me, cannot reconcile the prevailing mood of the book and its haunting refrains that emphasize life's emptiness with anything approximating joy. For the opposite view, see Whybray, "Qoheleth, Preacher of Joy"; Lohfink, "Qoheleth 5, 17–19—Revelation by Joy," *Catholic Biblical Quarterly* 52 (1990): 625–35; and Schwienhorst-Schönberger, "Gottes Antwort in der Freude. Zur theologie göttlicher Gegenwart im Buch Kohelet," 156–63. On the problem see Hans-Peter Müller, "Theonome Skepsis und Lebensfreude—Zu Koh 1, 12–3, 15," *Biblische Zeitschrift* 30 (1986): 1–19. In *Ecclesiastes* (Grand Rapids: Eerdmans, 2011), Peter Enns finds little joy in Qoheleth's teachings. Enns conjectures that Qoheleth was angry with God (39), maintained distance and even indifference toward God (66), enjoined fear of God, "not a healthy, covenantal fear" (84), and viewed the king as capricious and unjust, behind whom is an equally capricious and unjust God (89). Enns thinks Qoheleth's problem "touches on the trustworthiness, even goodness, of God" (122). By contrast, Eunny P. Lee, *The Vitality of Enjoyment in Qoheleth's Rhetoric* (Beiheft zur Zeitschrift für die Alttestamentliche Wissenschaft 353; Berlin: de Gruyter, 2005), discovers far more joy in Qoheleth's thought than I consider likely.

55. Gen 8:21; 17:17; 24:45; 27:41; Deut 7:17; 8:17; 9:4; 15:9; 18:21; 1 Sam 27:1; 1 Kgs 12:26; Pss 10:6, 11, 13; 14:1; 53:2; 77:6; Qoh 1:16; 2:1, 15; 3:17, 18; Isa 14:13; 47:8, 10, Jer 5:24; 13:22; Zeph 1:12; Ob 3; Est 6:6. Qoh 9:1 has "I laid it to my heart."

56. Fox, *A Time to Tear Down & a Time to Build Up*, 176 ("Note how his heart is treated as a distinct 'person' in 1:17 and 7:25," presumably in addition to 2:1). In his discussion of the heart in Qoheleth's thought, Fox refers to a similar concept in the Egyptian "Memphite Theology" (77–78). Robert D. Holmstedt, "*'ani* and *libbi*: The Syntactic Encoding

of the Collaborative Nature of Qoheleh's Experiment," *Journal of Hebrew Scriptures* 9 (2009): 1–27, thinks Qoheleth did not always agree with his inner conversation partner.

57. Arguing that this expression and related expressions ("put to my heart") imply intentional movement, Pierre van Hecke, "The Verbs *ra'â* and *šma'* in the Book of Qohelet. A Cognitive-Semantic Perspective," in *The Language of Qohelet in Its Context,* 215n51, considers it less likely that listening, a passive state, is meant. He overlooks the possibility that listening as an intellectual activity is highly intentional.

58. The extent of detachment in Qoheleth has assumed fresh perspective as a result of Fox's interpretation of the frame narrative as a device that distinguishes a speaker, Qoheleth, from the narrator who keeps at a safe distance because of Qoheleth's radical teaching.

59. The claim that the historical paradigm has been replaced by a literary one may be exaggerated, for even the current interest in reception history combines both history and literature. The extensive intertextual studies by André Robert in the first half of the twentieth century were inspired by an interest in the influence of earlier literature on successive generations, not by Julia Kristeva.

60. Hope, that is, can be sustained only as long as there is life. The psalmist's final words of death and nonbeing emphatically authenticate the claim that human existence is fleeting, like breath itself.

61. In this analysis of Psalm 39, I have omitted the superscription that mentions Jeduthun, like Psalm 62, which also distinguishes words and thoughts (v. 5). According to 2 Chr 5:12, Jeduthun, a Levite singer, was present along with Asaph and Heman when Solomon dedicated the temple.

Chapter 4. Ocular Deception

1. Levine, "The Appeal to Personal Experience in the Wisdom of Qoheleth"; Antoon Schoors, "Words Typical of Qohelet," in *Qohelet in the Context of Wisdom,* 26–33; and Jennifer L. Koosed, *(Per)mutations of Qohelet: Reading the Body in the Book* (Library of Hebrew Bible/Old Testament Studies; New York: T. & T. Clark, 2006), 37–45.

2. There is an unmistakable pun on the word *heshbon,* but the form here can refer to instruments of warfare. It definitely has a negative connotation for Qoheleth.

3. On the significance of the body for Qoheleth, see Koosed, *(Per)-mutations of Qohelet.*

4. In *The Wisdom Books: Job, Proverbs, and Ecclesiastes* (New York: Norton, 2010), Robert Alter's interpretation of the hasty remark as a vow is probably confirmed by the next four verses (362), but the warning may also refer to prayer.

5. In 11:5 Qoheleth coined a word for a pregnant woman from this same verb.

6. The word for scales of measurement is similar to the verb for hearing.

7. A distinction between hearing and heeding is necessary.

8. According to Ptahhotep:

> Useful is hearing to a son who hears;
> If hearing enters the hearer,
> The hearer becomes a listener,
> Hearing well is speaking well.

Useful is hearing to one who hears,
Hearing is better than all else.
It creates good will.
How good for a son to grasp his father's words,
He will reach old age through them.
He who hears is beloved of god,
He whom god hates does not hear. . . .

(*Ancient Egyptian Literature;* ed. Miriam Lichtheim,
3 vols.; Berkeley: University of California Press, 1973,
1976, 1980, 1: 74—hereafter cited as *AEL*).

9. Note the use of hearing in the instruction about the fundamental obligations imposed by Yahweh on the covenanted people in Deut 6:4–9 (the Shema').

10. Carol A. Newsom, "Woman and the Discourse of Patriarchal Wisdom: A Study of Proverbs 1–9," in *Gender and Difference in Ancient Israel* (ed. Peggy L. Day; Minneapolis: Fortress, 1989), 142–60.

11. "And now, my sons, listen to me, happy are those who keep my ways. Heed instruction and become wise; do not neglect it. Happy is the person who hears me, watching at my gates every day, watching by my doors. For the one who finds me finds life and receives favor from Yahweh, but whoever offends me does violence to himself. Everyone who despises me loves death" (Prov 8:32–36).

12. Susan Niditch, *Oral World and Written Word: Ancient Israelite Literature* (Louisville: Westminster John Knox, 1996), illustrates the difficulty of finding adequate criteria for distinguishing oral from written tradition. She rightly recognizes the persistence of orality alongside writing in ancient Israel until quite late.

13. Once the monarchy ceased in Israel, the need for trained scribes was less acute than before. With the emergence of mercantile interests and rise of a wealthy class, the scribal profession found a ready clientele once again.

14. Note the title of Antoon Schoors's magisterial study of the language of Qoheleth: *The Preacher Sought to Find Pleasing Words.* The first of the two volumes deals with grammar, the second with vocabulary.

15. James L. Crenshaw, "Transmitting Prophecy across Generations," in *Prophets, Sages, & Poets,* 167–72, 248–53; first published in *Writings and Speech in Israelite and Ancient Near Eastern Prophecy* (ed. Ehud ben Zvi and Michael H. Floyd; Society of Biblical Literature Symposium Series 10; Atlanta: Society of Biblical Literature, 2000), 31–44.

16. Ellen F. Davis, *Swallowing the Scroll: Textuality and the Dynamics of Discourse in Ezekiel's Prophecy* (JSOT Supplementary Series 78; Sheffield: Almond, 1989), argues that with Ezekiel a decisive shift to the text occurs, placing revelation on a back burner. Perhaps nostalgia gains dominance as a result.

17. Various interpreters have recognized many similarities between the book of Job and Isa 40–55.

18. "As to Hezekiah, the Jew, . . . I made a prisoner in Jerusalem, his royal residence, like a bird in a cage . . . [he] did send me, later, to Nineveh . . . 30 talents of gold, 800 talents of silver, precious stones, antinomy, large cuts of red stone, couches (inlaid) with ivory . . . his own daughters. . . ." (*ANET,* 288).

19. James L. Crenshaw, "Clanging Symbols," in *Urgent Advice and Probing Questions,* 371–82; first published in *Justice and the Holy* (ed. D. A. Knight and P. J. Paris; Philadelphia: Fortress, 1989), 51–64.

20. I have examined ancient rhetoric in two essays: "Wisdom and Authority: Sapiential Rhetoric and its Warrants," in *Urgent Advice and Probing Questions,* 326–43—first published in *Vetus Testamentum Supplements* 32 (1982): 10–29—and "The Contest of Darius' Guards in 1 Esdras 3:1–5:3," in *Urgent Advice and* Probing *Questions,* 222–34; first published in *Images of Man and God* (ed. B. O. Long; Sheffield: Almond, 1981), 74–89, 119–20.

21. In this "detective novella," the prophet Daniel managed to discover the truth and condemn the accusers to die.

22. The evidence of Stoic influence has been examined recently by S. L. Mattila, "Ben Sira and the Stoics: A Re-examination of the Evidence," *Journal of Biblical Literature* 119 (2000): 473–501.

23. Crenshaw, "Qoheleth's Quantitative Language."

24. James L. Crenshaw, "Qoheleth in Historical Context," *Biblica* 88 (2007): 285–99.

25. Harsh discipline and a pedagogy in which rote memory prevailed made ancient education less than enviable, as ample scribal texts indicate. Even the hieroglyph for a teacher—a raised arm holding a cane for whipping a child—reveals the nature of education in Egypt.

26. On Qumran see Matthew J. Goff, *Discovering Wisdom: The Sapiential Literature of the Dead Sea Scrolls* (Vetus Testamentum Supplements 116; Leiden: Brill, 2007).

27. Machinist, "Fate, *miqreh,* and Reason," and Martin Rose, "Qohelet als Philosophe und Theologe: Ein biblische Votum für *Universitas,"* in *Universitas in Theologia—Theologia in Universitate* (ed. Matthias Kreig und Martin Rose; Zurich: Theologische, 1997), 177–99.

28. Joseph Blenkinsopp, "Ecclesiastes 3:1–15: Another Interpretation," *JSOT* 66 (1995): 55–64, thinks 3:2–8 is an embedded Stoic poem, with 3:9–11 a commentary on it.

29. On this psalm see my *The Psalms,* 109–27.

30. James L. Crenshaw, "The Expression *mi yodea'* in the Hebrew Bible," in *Urgent Advice and Probing Questions,* 279–91; first published in *Vetus Testamentum* 36 (1986): 274–88.

31. It could be argued that God sees everything by virtue of being in heaven and that Qoheleth understood this idea as a motive for doing good.

32. Hans-Peter Müller, "Wie sprach Qohälät von Gott?" *Vetus Testamentum* 18 (1968): 507–21, emphasizes the importance of the verb "to give" in Qoheleth's discourse.

33. Dominic Rudman, *Determinism in the Book of Ecclesiastes* (JSOT Supplementary Series 316; Sheffield: Academic Press, 2001).

34. Choon-Leong Seow, "The Social World of Ecclesiastes," in *Scribes, Sages, and Seers,* 189–217; and Mark Sneed, "The Social Location of the Book of Qoheleth," *Hebrew Studies* 39 (1998): 41–51. Elsa Tamez, *When the Horizons Close: Rereading Ecclesiastes* (Eugene, Oreg.: Wifp & Stock, 2000), 11, refers to the many changes that took place under Ptolemaic rule: military tactics, the method of exercising power from Alexandria, the administration of the kingdom and its finances, the minting of coins, management

in Egypt and the provinces, agricultural technology, large-scale commerce, philosophical discussion, and inventions in mathematics and physics.

35. Thus leading to the further breakdown of the family structure.

36. For insight into the consequences of empires, see Portier-Young, *Apocalypse against Empire.*

37. Leonidas Kalugila, *The Wise King* (Coniectanea biblica Old Testament Series 15; Lund: Gleerup, 1980).

38. James L. Crenshaw, "The Missing Voice," in *A Biblical Itinerary: In Search of Method, Form, and Content* (ed. E. E. Carpenter; JSOT Supplementary Series 240; Sheffield: Academic Press, 1997), 133–43. The contents page of this volume omits my name and the article title.

39. It now appears that a son's voice is heard in a text from Emar (Gianto, "Human Destiny in Emar and Qoheleth," 478): "The son opened his mouth to speak, addressing his father, the counselor. 'I have silently listened to the word of my father. Let me speak now.'"

40. Bel and the Dragon found its way into the Septuagint. It is a tale about exposing a priestly fraud and destroying the idol that has been the object of elaborate food offerings eaten by priests.

41. The Apocalypse of Abraham mercilessly pokes fun at idols that fall in the fire, lose a head, suffer all manner of abuse, and are completely helpless. See R. Rubinkiewicz, "The Apocalypse of Abraham," in *The Old Testament Pseudepigrapha,* 1:681–705.

42. Treated at length in my *Prophetic Conflict: Its Effect upon Israelite Religion* (Beiheft zur Zeitschrift für die Alttestamentliche Wissenschaft 124; Berlin: de Gruyter, 1971), reprinted by the Society of Biblical Literature in 2007.

43. The book of Tobit can be found in the Septuagint. It is a story about a devout Tobit, who suffers blindness for doing good deeds and eventually regains his sight through the agency of an angel, who leads Tobit's son to retrieve money and in the process to obtain a wife.

44. Martin Hengel, *Judaism and Hellenism* (Philadelphia: Fortress, 1974).

45. James Muilenburg, "A Qoheleth Scroll from Qumran," *Bulletin of the American Schools of Oriental Research* 135 (1954): 20–28.

46. Choon-Leong Seow, "Linguistic Evidence for the Dating of Qoheleth," *Journal of Biblical Literature* 115 (1996): 643–66, opts for a date in the late fifth or early fourth century.

Chapter 5. Surreptitious Givens

1. Jerome S. Bruner, *On Knowing* (Cambridge, Mass.: Belknap Press of Harvard University Press, 1966), 132–37.

2. The changing approaches to the Bible indicate shifting interests: historical criticism, form and redaction criticism, literary, feminist, deconstructionist analysis, and so forth.

3. Michael V. Fox, "Qohelet's Epistemology," *Hebrew Union College Annual* 58 (1987): 137–55.

4. James L. Crenshaw, "Qoheleth's Understanding of Intellectual Inquiry," in *Qohelet in the Context of Wisdom,* 205–24.

5. I use this infelicitous translation to emphasize the ownership of the poverty.

6. Biblical poetry consists of lines in parallelism, normally two or three cola, sometimes called stichs. The types of parallelism vary from synonymous to antithetic, and even to synthetic, a type of progression by incremental steps.

7. An ivory from Nimrud depicts a woman peering out a window; see *ANET,* 39, no. 131.

8. On the deity's use of suffering as a disciplinary tactic, see my "Divine Discipline in Job 5:17–18, Proverbs 3:11–12, Deuteronomy 32:39, and Beyond," in *Reading Job Intertextually* (ed. Katharine Dell and Will Kynes; London: T. & T. Clark, 2012).

9. Crenshaw, "Deceitful Minds and Theological Dogma: Jer 17:5–11," in *Prophets, Sages, & Poets,* 73–82, 222–24; first published in *Utopia and Dystopia in Prophetic Texts,* 105–21.

10. David Penchansky and Paul L. Redditt, eds., *Shall Not the Judge of All the Earth Do What Is Right? Studies on the Nature of God in Tribute to James L. Crenshaw* (Winona Lake: Eisenbrauns, 2000).

11. Books 2 and 3 of Psalms (42–89) show a preference for the divine name Elohim over Yahweh, but inconsistency abounds.

12. See my *Reading Job: A Literary and Theological Commentary* (Macon: Smyth & Helwys, 2011).

13. Jon S. Levenson, *Creation and the Persistence of Evil* (San Francisco: Harper & Row, 1988).

14. *ANET,* 60–72, and Hallo, ed., *The Context of Scripture,* 1:390–403. Although labeled a creation epic by modern scholars, Enuma Elish is really an account of the elevation of Marduk as supreme god at the temple Esagila.

15. See the translation by Lichtheim in *AEL,* 1: 51–57.

16. James L. Crenshaw, "The Eternal Gospel (Eccl 3:11)," in my *Urgent Advice and Probing Questions,* 548–72.

17. Edward L. Greenstein, "The Poem on Wisdom in Job 28 in Its Conceptual and Literary Contexts," in *Job 28: Cognition in Context,* 253–80, argues that God is the one who performs the amazing deeds described in this poem.

18. For these interpreters the meaning is believed to be a desire for something permanent in a transient world, a longing for a reality that transcends the finite.

19. W.H. Schmidt, "br'; to create," in *Theological Lexicon of the Old Testament* (ed. Ernst Jenni and Claus Westermann; trans. Mark E. Biddle; 3 vols. Peabody, Mass.: Hendrickson, 1994), 1:253–56, considers the verb cultic and late; its occurrences are primarily in Deutero-Isaiah, the priestly account of creation, and Psalms. Helmer Ringgren, "*Bara',*" in *Theological Dictionary of the Old Testament* (ed. G. Johannes Botterweck and Helmer Ringgren; trans. John T. Willis; 15 vols.; Grand Rapids: Eerdmans 1974–2006, 2:248, calls attention to the peculiar use of this verb in Isa 45:7 to specify darkness and evil as Yahweh's creations, probably as a polemic against Persian dualism.

20. In Hebrew infinitive constructs can be translated as a temporal clause. An example is Gen 1:1, which should be rendered in English "When God began to create the heavens and the earth, the earth was waste and void."

21. I am not convinced by Krüger's remark that Qoheleth meant that the world is perfect and therefore needs no adjusting (*Qoheleth,* 89).

22. Troubling descriptions of God in the Bible have evoked considerable response lately. See Crenshaw, *Defending God;* Jack Miles, *God: A Biography* (New York: Knopf, 1995); and Eric A. Seibert, *Disturbing Divine Behavior: Troubling Old Testament Images of God* (Minneapolis: Fortress, 2009).

23. Schoors, "God in Qohelet."

24. Qoheleth thinks of Sheol, not a Freudian return to the mother's womb. In Egypt the underworld was designated as "there," and Job's remark is simply a synonym for Sheol.

25. Erich Auerbach, *Mimesis* (trans. Willard R. Trask; Princeton: Princeton University, 1953).

26. James L. Crenshaw, "Three Things You Must Know to Escape the Clutches of the Evil One," in *Testimonies of Vocation* (ed. William E. Rogers; Greenville: Furman University, 2011), 1–14.

27. Seow, *Ecclesiastes,* 351–52, explains how all three meanings may have been intended, with priority given to cistern in the metaphorical sense of wife.

28. The poet's admiration for the beauty of the heavens and the awe they inspire is boundless.

29. Qoheleth's allusion to the divine gift of life breath maintains distance through mystery. No human can replicate the deity's work.

30. I am convinced that fear in Qoheleth's use differs from that in Proverbs, where it is the first step in the learning process. For Qoheleth fear had an element of dread.

31. In Job 22:5–9 Eliphaz accused Job of exacting pledges from brothers without cause, stripping the naked, withholding water and bread, and abusing widows and orphans. This same Job had been declared innocent by God and the narrator.

32. "Does the Almighty delight in your innocence? Does he gain when you perfect your ways?" (Job 22:3). With this question Eliphaz rejected the basic concept of God in the Bible.

33. "But I know that my redeemer is alive and afterward he'll rise upon the dust" (Job 19:25). The Baal episode in Canaanite literature has a similar exclamation about the god who has been resuscitated. Job, however, dismissed the possibility of surviving death.

34. Ben Sira used a formula of debate, one that often was associated with theodicy; see my "The Problem of Theodicy in Sirach," 156–60.

35. *ANET,* 142–49 ("If Hurringa to my house I take, / Bring the lass into my court. / Her double I'll give in silver, / and her treble in gold," 145).

36. Fox, *A Time to Tear Down & a Time to Build Up,* 229, emends "messenger" to read "God." Seow, *Ecclesiastes,* 201, conjectures that Qoheleth was referring to a priest, as does Krüger, *Qoheleth,* 109, with reference to Mal 2:7. That text, however, calls priests messengers of God in a context of instruction and has nothing to do with death.

37. "When your envoy comes to fetch you . . . do not say, 'I am young to be taken.' For you do not know death. When death comes he steals the infant who is in his mother's arms, just like him who reached old age" (*AEL,* 2:138). *ANET,* 420, translates the first line as: ". . . when thy messenger comes to take thee."

38. Fox, *Ecclesiastes,* 61, thinks Qoheleth was referring to himself as the quintessential wise man who was yet unable to fathom the nature of events. Bartholomew, *Ecclesiastes,* 293, considers this text epistemology ironized.

Chapter 6. Victorious Time

1. Jacobus Wilhelm Gericke, "Possible Allusions to Ancient Near Eastern Solar Mythology in Qohelet: A Comprehensive Enquiry" (Ph.D. diss., University of Pretoria, 2002).

2. *ANET,* 79.

3. Greek influence such as *hyph' helio* is therefore unlikely.

4. The term *mishpat* normally means "statute," but Judg 13:12 uses it in the sense of procedure.

5. The unexpected result of action is carried to an extreme in Amos 5:18–20 (fleeing from a lion, one encounters a bear, or on escaping to enter the safety of one's house, is bitten by a poisonous snake).

6. One can say that the deity faces a dilemma. Human survival depends on divine patience, but delayed punishment encourages the wicked to offend bravely.

7. Its use in Robert Kennedy's funeral illustrates this point.

8. "For every tick, there's a tock, / every beginning, an ending. / If time stops on a tick, / Does all hope disappear? / If time's on a straight line, / Is there a mid-point, / an intersection of a cross?" Crenshaw, "Anticipation," *Dust and Ashes* (Eugene, Oreg.: Cascade Books, 2010), 39.

9. See the discussion of catalogs in Yair Hoffman, *A Blemished Perfection: The Book of Job in Context* (JSOT Supplementary Series 213; Sheffield: Academic Press, 1996), 84–114.

10. Strictly speaking, that is not true. Suicide is an exception to it.

11. Nature plays a huge role in Qoheleth's teaching from beginning to end (1:4–11 and 11:6 [8]–12:7).

12. In Hebrew poetry, as in most modern poetry, rhyme plays no part.

13. In ancient Mesopotamia and in Egypt, onomastica, or lists of nouns, were widespread.

14. Priestly divination was widely practiced in Mesopotamia, and wisdom applied specifically to bettering one's life through studying the livers of sacrificed animals and through oneiromancy, telling the future by means of dreams.

15. The beginnings of such instruction occur in Tobit 12:6–9 and the Apostle Paul frequently listed virtues and vices in his letters to churches.

16. Blenkinsopp, "Ecclesiastes 3:1–15: Another Interpretation."

17. Hengel, *Judaism and Hellenism;* Collins, *Jewish Wisdom in the Hellenistic Age.*

18. Ben Sira described divine majesty with rational precision but ended in wonder, just as the praise of the God of truth does in 1 Esd 4:34–41.

19. Fox, *Ecclesiastes,* 21, points out that the interpretation is arbitrary and that "gathering" does not mean refraining from something.

20. Perhaps it could refer to the placing of stones on a game board and removing them at the appropriate time.

21. Jack Sasson, *Jonah* (New York: Doubleday, 1990), is both original and thorough.

22. The name *Bethlehem* is a combination of two nouns, "house" and "bread."

23. For analysis of death in Qoheleth's thought, see Kathryn Imray, "Qoheleth's Philosophy of Death" (Ph.D. diss., Murdoch University, 2009).

24. Although both he and Gilgamesh killed the monster Humbaba, guardian of the forest, only Enkidu suffered the dire consequences. Otherwise the story would have aborted.

25. The biblical story of the flood is derived from this earlier myth. The similarities between the two accounts make this conclusion compelling.

26. Anat, a warrior goddess, is described in one text as walking knee-deep in blood and gore, and on returning home she imagines that the furniture is additional prey (*ANET,* 136): "She binds the heads to her back, / Fastens the hands in her girdle. / She plunges knee deep in knight's blood, / Hip deep in the gore of heroes."

27. Ibid., 101–3.

28. The story about King Saul's resorting to the medium of Endor to summon Samuel's spirit from the grave is the only biblical instance of anyone returning from Sheol, and Samuel groused about it.

29. On the importance of this text in the Bible and in the Passover liturgy in contemporary Jewish worship, see my *Defending God.*

30. The description of old age in the Instruction of Ptahhotep rivals that of Qoheleth. It reads:

> Age is here, old age arrived, feebleness came, weakness grows, childlike one sleeps all day. Eyes are dim, ears deaf, strength is waning through weariness, the mouth, silenced, speaks not, the heart, void, recalls not the past, the bones ache throughout. Good has become evil, all taste is gone, what age does to people is evil in everything. The nose, clogged, breathes not, painful are standing and sitting. (*AEL,* 1:62–63)

31. Others read "Remember your creator."

32. If the darkening of moon and stars is part of apocalyptic drama, it is certainly muted. For a different view, see J. Gerald Janzen, "Qohelet on 'Life under the Sun,'" *Catholic Biblical Quarterly* 70 (2008): 465–83. He thinks Qoheleth fell for apocalyptic and eschatological views but became "jaundiced" when expectations did not materialize.

33. James L. Crenshaw, "Youth and Old Age in Qoheleth," in *Urgent Advice and Probing Questions,* 535–47; first published in *Hebrew Annual Review* 10 (1986): 1–13.

34. The poet Abir beautifully described life as oil in a lamp; death arrives when the lamp has no more fuel.

35. The human condition consists of dust and ashes; see my *Dust and Ashes.*

36. The Targum on Isa 14:18 has "house of eternity" and Tob 3:6 varies the expression to "eternal abode" (*topos aionios*).

37. Lohfink, *Qoheleth,* 101–2, thinks the original reference is to strength and from that to bitter. He quotes a saying of Sermonides: "Yes, this [woman] is the greatest plague that Zeus has made, and he has bound us to them with a fetter which cannot be broken."

38. James L. Crenshaw, "Love Is Stronger than Death: Intimations of Life Beyond the Grave," in *Resurrection,* 53–78.

39. Compare the Descent of Inanna, who is stripped of all clothes and jewelry as she passes through the seven gates of the underworld. This Sumerian myth was the model for Ishtar's descent into the underworld (*ANET,* 51–57, 106–9).

40. Martin Buber, "The Heart Determines (Psalm 73)," in *On the Bible* (New York: Schocken, 1968), 199–210.

41. Crenshaw, *The Psalms,* 109–27.

42. Crenshaw, *Defending God,* 141–77.

43. "You accursed wretch, you dismiss us from this present life, but the King of the universe will raise us to an everlasting renewable life. . . . For our brothers after enduring a brief suffering have drunk of ever-flowing life under God's covenant" (2 Macc 7:9, 36).

44. David Winston, *The Wisdom of Solomon* (Garden City, N.Y.: Doubleday, 1979).

Chapter 7. Tasty Nectar

1. Compare the Harper's Song from the tomb of King Intef. After some remarks about the dead, who are as though they had never been, it reads: "Hence rejoice in your heart! Forgetfulness profits you, follow your heart as long as you live! Put myrrh on your head, dress in fine linen, anoint yourself with oils fit for a god. Heap up your joys, let your heart not sink!" (*AEL,* 1:196–97).

2. The royal fiction imitates stories of Mesopotamian kings who boast about their accomplishments in construction and horticulture, as well as the accumulation of the trappings of wealth. All is not mere bragging, as the hanging gardens of Babylon attest. William P. Brown, *Ecclesiastes* (Louisville: John Knox, 2000), 32, remarks that any king worth his salt had to excel in handling the sword in one hand and the garden spade in the other.

3. Ironically the author's reputation has persisted for more than two thousand years.

4. The sages often used "better than" comparisons, sometimes with puns as in 7:1. Several such comparisons are grouped together in this chapter (7:1, 2, 3, 5, and 8).

5. H. Lewis Ginsberg, *Studies in Kohelet* (New York: Jewish Theological Seminary of America, 1950), and "Supplementary Studies in Kohelet," *Proceedings of the American Academy of Jewish Research* (1952): 35–62, recognized two different meanings of *'amal* in Qoheleth, "toil" and "wages," the result of labor.

6. Martin Rose, "De la 'crise de la sagesse' à la 'sagesse de la crise,'" *Revue de théologie et de philosophie* 131 (1999): 133, remarks that Qoheleth's faint praise of pleasure is a poor substitute for other grand confessions of Yahweh. What else, Rose adds, could Qoheleth have said about the God who had failed to protect Judah and Israel, Jerusalem, and the anointed and had even sent his people into exile?

7. The difference is a single character in Hebrew.

8. According to Martin A. Shields, *The End of Wisdom: A Reappraisal of the Histori-cal and Canonical Function of Ecclesiastes* (Winona Lake: Eisenbrauns, 2006), Qoheleth's

heterodoxy was so alarming that the epilogue was composed to warn students not to subscribe to the path of wisdom, which had proven itself bankrupt, with Qoheleth as the perfect example of its folly.

9. Qoheleth thus found himself in the same situation as the poet who composed the Mesopotamian "I Will Praise the Lord of Wisdom," who wrote: "I wish I knew that these things would be pleasing to one's god! What is good for oneself may be offense to one's god, what in one's own heart seems despicable may be proper to one's god, who can know the will of the gods in heaven? Who can understand the plans of the underworld gods? Where have humans learned the way of a god?" The prayer of Judith in the Apocrypha is similar. Basically she says: "You can not plumb the depths of the human heart, how then can you fathom God's mind?"

10. This noun is derived from the verb "to do" or "to make" and ranges from divine creative activity to mundane acts of ordinary workers.

11. The myth of a fall lies behind the description of hubris in Isa 14:3–23 and Ezek 28:1–19.

12. Note the expansive characterization of Job as a person of integrity and wholeness, one who is religious and who turns away from evil (Job 1:1).

13. In the first sentence of *Speak, Memory,* Nabokov wrote: "Common sense tells us that our existence is but a crack between two eternities of darkness."

14. The Babylonian Theodicy accuses the gods of endowing humans with lies. According to Enuma Elish, people were created out of the blood of the dead god Kingu for the sole purpose of feeding the gods by means of the cultic apparatus.

15. The Egyptian Insinger Papyrus repeats a theme about fate again and again, with slight variants. It reads: "The fate and fortune that come, it is the god who sends them," and "Fate and fortune go and come when he commands them" (*AEL,* 1:186–217).

16. The sages give a vivid account of the effects of too much strong drink (Prov 23:29–35), to which may be compared the humorous description of the power of wine in 1 Esd 3:18–24.

17. According to C. J. Labuschagne, "*'nh* I to answer," *Theological Lexicon of the Old Testament*, 2:926–30, the primary sense of the verb is "to react."

18. Lohfink, "Qoheleth 5:17–19—Revelation by Joy."

19. Seow, *Ecclesiastes,* 224–25, calls the word multivalent and interprets it to mean that God has made it possible to forget about one's ephemeral life.

20. Or it can result in denial; see Ernest Becker, *The Denial of Death* (New York: Free Press, 1973). Neil Gilman, *The Death of Death* (Woodstock, Vt.: Jewish Lights Publishing, 1997), cannot be accused of denying the reality of death.

21. Ginsberg, *Studies in Kohelet.* In a forthcoming article, "Qoheleth's Hatred of Life: A Passing Phase or an Enduring Sentiment?," I argue that *'amal* symbolizes the human condition in the story of disobedience by Adam and Eve just as it does in the book of Job. In contrast Qoheleth uses *hebel* to indicate the human condition.

22. Sir 38:24–34 ("Without them a city cannot be established, and man can neither sojourn nor live there," verse 32).

23. Abraham raised the vexing issue of divine justice in Gen 18:25 with this question: "Shall not the Judge of all the earth act justly?" See my "The Sojourner Has Come to Play the Judge: Theodicy on Trial," in *Prophets, Sages & Poets,* 195–200, 261–64.

24. Moyna McGlyn, *Divine Judgment and Divine Benevolence in the Book of Wisdom* (Wissenschaftliche Untersuchungen zum Neuen Testament 2, Reihe 139; Tübingen: Mohr Siebeck, 2001).

25. The Egyptians would have viewed things differently, for no reasonable explanation can be given for the deaths of all their firstborn sons.

26. Charlesworth, ed., *The Old Testament Pseudepigrapha,* 1: 872–902 (especially chapter 10, 887–88).

27. The commander in chief (God) explains to Abraham: "But I made the world, and I do not want to destroy any one of them; but I delay the death of the sinner until he should convert and live."

28. If this assurance of justice comes from Qoheleth, it reveals the conflict within his mind about an issue that the book of Job explored at great length.

29. The prayer is found in the Septuagint. It contains the striking image of bending the knee of the heart.

30. That silence becomes unbearable when contemplating modern horrors. At what unspeakable cost was Hitler given time to repent? And what of the many other modern genocides?

31. Qoheleth voiced a well-known complaint in the ancient world about social reversals, made visible by slaves riding on horses and nobles going on foot.

32. The subject is unclear. It could be human beings rather than the deity.

33. Dogs were scavengers, not domestic pets. The saying reflects disdain for the lowly canine.

34. It has been said that all meaningful thought begins with the idea of death. E. M. Forster wrote: "Death destroys a man; the idea of Death saves him" (*The Oxford Dictionary of Modern Quotations,* 83).

35. Interpreters differentiate between instructions that take the form of imperatives and "sentences" that simply make a statement. The bulk of Proverbs belongs to the latter category.

36. Instead of writing "your wife," Qoheleth used the cumbersome phrase "the woman whom you love." Gordis, *Koheleth,* 306, says that Qoheleth "was certainly no apologist for the marriage institution."

37. The contrast between the present light and anticipated darkness is striking.

38. The context specifies visible reminders attached to one's garment as a warning not to follow the wanton desires of the eyes and mind.

39. See my "From the Mundane to the Sublime (Reflections on Qoh 11:1–8)," in my *Prophets, Sages & Poets,* 61–72, 217–22.

40. E. Ruprecht, "*smh* to rejoice," *Theological Lexicon of the Old Testament,* 3:1272–77, emphasizes the original sense of shining and the Dionysian superabundance in the uses of this verb.

41. R. Ficker, "*rnn* to rejoice," *Theological Lexicon of the Old Testament,* 3:1240–43, notes that the majority of uses of this verb are to praise Yahweh, such as *gil, "*to rejoice,"

according to Claus Westermann, ibid., 1:312–14. On rejoicing as an epiphenomenon, see Gary A. Anderson, *A Time to Mourn, a Time to Dance* (University Park: Pennsylvania State University Press, 1991).

Chapter 8. Flawed Genius

1. For some interpreters, Fox and Shields for example, Qoheleth exemplifies dangerous teachings that the framing narrative warns against. Others think that the first epilogue is admiring, if realistic, about the effects of such unorthodox thoughts and that the second epilogue seeks to direct readers' attention to more traditional views.

2. Expertise in weaving, design, jewel making, and so forth is called wisdom. There is also a shady side to wisdom, counsel that brings death (the crafty serpent in the Garden of Eden; Jonadab who advised Amnon on how to seduce his half sister, Tamar; and Hushai, who persuaded Absalom to delay his attack on a fleeing David).

3. R. N. Whybray, *The Intellectual Tradition in the Old Testament* (Beiheft zur Zeitschrift für die Alttestamentliche Wissenschaft 135; Berlin: de Gruyter, 1974), thinks the wise were wealthy landholders.

4. Girls were not normally given scribal training. The teachings in Proverbs specifically apply to boys or young men.

5. The books of Job and Ecclesiastes were both probably written for advanced students or for adults with an intellectual bent.

6. Crenshaw, *Education in Ancient Israel.*

7. Although the rhetoric is Greek, it nevertheless has utility in describing aspects of Hebrew literature.

8. In "A Dispute between a Man and His Ba," death is compared to the scent of lotus blossoms and myrrh, longing for home while in a lengthy captivity, recovery from illness, and a smooth pathway (*AEL,* 1:168). It is no surprise, then, that death can be called "shepherd."

9. The Twenty-third Psalm has made the metaphor of God as shepherd familiar to many. William L. Holladay, *The Psalms through Three Thousand Years: Prayerbook of a Cloud of Witnesses* (Minneapolis: Fortress, 1993), discusses the reasons for the rise in the popularity of Psalm 23 in the late nineteenth and early twentieth centuries.

10. In contrast with the Mesopotamian tradition about the seven wise men from primordial times, who received divine secrets that they transmitted to humans.

11. Fox, *Ecclesiastes,* 84, translates as follows: "The words of sages are like goads / and {those of} the masters of collections are like implanted nails, stuck in by a shepherd."

12. That is also the difficulty that Job complained about.

13. Is this an attack on Qoheleth for adding his teachings to a growing canon (Proverbs and Job), or does it indicate concern over other works, some of which eventually were labeled Apocrypha and Pseudepigrapha?

14. Ignorance about the future invariably presents an opportunity for people to profit by claiming special insight, whether from studying the stars and constellations or from immediate revelation. The modern "Left Behind" series of publications reveal the persistence of this phenomenon.

15. Michael E. Stone, *Fourth Ezra* (Minneapolis: Fortress, 1990), stresses the transforming visions in this powerful cry of distress.

16. One way to shield Yahweh from objectionable acts and ideas is to shift the blame to lesser figures such as Uriel and Satan.

17. See my "Impossible Questions, Sayings, and Tasks," in *Urgent Advice and Probing Questions,* 265–78.

18. The danger was both immediate—punishment by a teacher—and punishment in later life—the consequence of wrong thinking.

19. Note that the word is "heard," not "said."

20. Too many alternatives were being offered to those willing to think for themselves, including mystery religions.

21. The "whole of a human being" is ambiguous. According to Franz Delitzsch, *Commentary on the Song of Songs and Ecclesiastes* (Edinburgh: T. & T. Clark, 1877), 200, "these two stars do not turn the night into day."

22. As implied by the King James Version.

23. Rudolf Otto, *The Idea of the Holy* (New York: Oxford University Press, 1958).

24. Sir 24:33 seems to imply that Ben Sira thought of his own teachings as inspired prophecy. In other words he mediated revelation in the same way personified wisdom does.

25. Hartmut Gese, "The Crisis of Wisdom in Koheleth," in *Theodicy in the Old Testament* (ed. James L. Crenshaw; Issues in Religion and Theology 4; Philadelphia: Fortress / London: SPCK, 1983), 141–53; and Shields, *The End of Wisdom.*

26. Michael Fishbane, *The Garments of Torah* (Bloomington: Indiana University Press, 1989).

27. Above all, Krüger, *Qoheleth.*

28. B. L. Berger, "Qohelet and the Exigencies of the Absurd," *Biblical Interpretation* 8 (2001): 141–79, uses the apt phrase "a rhetoric of erasure." Gary D. Salyer, *Vain Rhetoric: Private Insight and Public Debate in Ecclesiastes* (Sheffield: Academic Press, 2001), prefers "vain rhetoric" because "I" discourses imply their own limitation and invite dialogic dissension with their major premises and conclusions (390).

29. Klaus Koch, "Gibt es ein Vergeltungsdogma im Alten Testament?," *Zeitschrift für Theologie und Kirche* 52 (1955): 1–42; abridged English translation in *Theodicy in the Old Testament,* 57–87. Koch stated the issue in extreme terms by which deeds carry within themselves the appropriate consequences. Scholars have responded by assigning a much larger role to Yahweh in the nexus between cause and effect than Koch envisioned.

30. Van der Toorn, "Sources in Heaven," 265–77, has explained the rise of revelation and elitism as a product of the breakdown of the principle of similarity between gods and humans. Joyce Rilett Wood, "When Gods Were Men," in *From Babel to Babylon,* 285–98, thinks editors began in the mid-sixth century b.c.e. to make a sharp distinction between humans and deity that was nonexistent until then: "gods and goddesses of the ancient world, whether Near Eastern or east Mediterranean, were created in our image, so that an almost perfect parallel can be drawn between them and us" (285).

31. Attempts to paint a more attractive picture of Yahweh reveal the depth of concern to negate the effect of questionable conduct attributed to the deity. These efforts are discussed in my *Defending God.*

32. Gese, "The Crisis of Wisdom in Koheleth," and Rose, "De la 'crise de la sagesse' à la 'sagesse de la crise.'"

33. William S. Morrow, *Protest against God: The Eclipse of a Biblical Tradition* (Hebrew Bible Monographs 4; Sheffield: Sheffield Phoenix Press, 2006), associates the distancing of deity with an axial age, roughly exilic and early postexilic times, when Yahweh came to be viewed as both remote and unfathomable.

34. Levine, "The Appeal to Personal Experience in the Wisdom of Qoheleth," distinguishes three uses of the verb *ra'ah* in Qoheleth's discourse: seeing as observation of events and phenomena; seeing as reflecting on the meaning of "happenings"; and seeing as perceiving, realizing.

35. No textual basis for deleting *hokmah* ("wisdom") exists. It may function as an accusative of specification emphasizing the anomaly to be discussed. See Paul Joüon and Takamitsu Muraoka, *A Grammar of Biblical Hebrew* (Subsidia Biblica 27; Rome: Editrice Pontificio Istituto Biblico, 2006), 126g.

36. Qoh 7:26 refers to snares, and in 9:12 the singular form occurs. Two manuscripts have a word that differs orthographically in the letter *r*, easily confused with *d* (compare Septuagint, Symmachus, Peshitta, and Vulgate).

37. According to regular syntax of Hebrew, the sequence of verbs should have the same subject, the first change coming with "and he delivered." For an impersonal reading ("one found"), see *Gesenius' Hebrew Grammar* (ed. E. Kautzsch; Oxford: Clarendon Press, 1910), 144d.

38. The verb for "deliverance" can be understood as either actual or potential. For unrealized possibility in verbs, see *Gesenius' Hebrew Grammar*, 106p.

39. The commentaries (such as Krüger, Seow, Schwienhorst-Schönberger, Fox, and Crenshaw) address the difficulties involved in ascertaining discrete literary units in Qoheleth's observations.

40. In biblical Hebrew *misken* ("poor man," "commoner") is limited to Ecclesiastes, where it occurs four times (4:13; 9:15 [bis] 9:16).

41. Verse 7:15 calls attention to such a miscarriage of justice that Qoheleth personally observed. From this he concluded that it is a mistake to strive for membership with the devout or even to be particularly astute.

42. Isaksson, *Studies in the Language of Qoheleth,* and Schoors, *The Preacher Sought to Find Pleasing Words.* Isaksson reads *umillat* as "he might have saved the city," but Schoors refuses to exclude either interpretation, actual or potential.

43. One could think of an unmentioned person coming upon the poor man and bringing him into the king's presence or some other such explanation that the narrative leaves in the dark.

44. Opposite interpretations are given, for example by Krüger, *Qoheleth,* 178–80, and Seow, *Ecclesiastes,* 308–11. Krüger opts for an actual deliverance of the city while Seow prefers a potential reading of the verb.

45. In that case Qoheleth would have been the commoner. Samuel Ibn Tibbons interpreted this story as "a journey of the soul," an allegory with universal application.

46. "Do not disdain a small document, a small fire, a small soldier" ("The Instruction of 'Ankhsheshonq," 16, 25).

47. Levine, "The Appeal to Personal Experience in the Wisdom of Qoheleth," 340, disagrees. For him the story was based on a personal observation that caused Qoheleth to ponder its significance.

48. Berger, "Qoheleth and the Exigencies of the Absurd," 174.

49. Hans-Peter Müller, "Der unheimliche Gast. Zum Denken Kohelets," *Zeitschrift für Theologie und Kirche* 84 (1987): 440–64, and "Neige der althebräischen »Weisheit« Zum Denken Qohäläts," *Zeitschrift für die Alttestamentliche Wissenschaft* 90 (1978): 238–64.

50. Roberto Vignolo, "Wisdom, Prayer and Kingly Pattern: Theology, Anthropology, Spirituality of Wis 9," in *Deuterocanonical and Cognate Literature Yearbook 2005: The Book of Wisdom in Modern Research* (ed. Angelo Passaro and Giuseppe Bellia; Berlin: de Gruyter, 2005), 255–82.

51. In the royal fiction the king is described as personally involved in the toil that produced buildings, gardens, canals, and so forth. Qoheleth claimed to have arrived at the view that his work and its fruit are loathsome in the final analysis.

52. Dor-Shav, "Ecclesiastes, Fleeting and Timeless," 67–87, captures the vibrancy of Qoheleth's use of *hebel*.

53. Crenshaw, "Deceitful Minds and Theological Dogma."

54. I remain convinced that *ha'elem* ("the hidden") is a superior reading to the Masoretic Text *ha'olam* ("eternity"), Qoheleth's primary concern being the unfathomable nature of the cognitive gift.

55. On Qoheleth's environment see Seow, "The Social World of Ecclesiastes"; and my "Qoheleth in Historical Context," *Biblica* 88 (2007): 285–99. For a social-scientific approach, see Sneed, "The Social Location of the Book of Qoheleth," 41–51, and *The Politics of Pessimism in Ecclesiastes: A Social Science Perspective* (Atlanta: Society of Biblical Literature, 2012). According to Sneed, Qoheleth resisted the excessive rationalism of earlier sages who claimed to know much about God and his ways. In doing so Qoheleth returned to a concept of a truly unknowable God, one who is capricious and holy. Qoheleth's pessimism enabled his compatriots to cope in a world in which the deity failed to live up to expectations.

56. Seow's defense of a date for Qoheleth during the Persian era, based largely on linguistic grounds, has failed to persuade recent commentators, in part because language is not like a meteor, which flashes for a brief moment and then burns itself up. Even if a cluster of vocabulary items identical to Qoheleth's use first appeared in the late fifth and early fourth centuries B.C.E., its immediate disappearance is wholly unlikely. For Seow's argument, see "Linguistic Evidence and the Dating of Qoheleth," *Journal of Biblical Literature* 115 (1996): 643–66. Robert Harrison, "Qoheleth in Socio-Historical Perspective" (Ph.D. diss., Duke University, 1991), defends a Hellenistic date, which is accepted by most interpreters. The broader context has been studied recently by Christoph Uehlinger, "Qohelet im Horizont mesopotamischer, levantinischer und ägyptischer Weisheitsliteratur der persischen und hellenistischen Zeit," in *Das Buch Kohelet: Studien zur Struktur, Geschichte, Rezeption und Theologie* (ed. Ludger Schwienhorst-Schönberger; BZAW 254; Berlin & New York: de Gruyter, 1996), 155–247, and Reinhold Bohlen, "Kohelet in Kontext Hellenistischer Kultur," in ibid., 249–73.

57. Seow's use of Nehemiah's memoir to document international trade at an early date could be pushed back to texts from the time of Isaiah or Ezekiel. The desire to possess more things hardly began in Qoheleth's day, even if the later minting of coins facilitated commerce.

58. Frank Crüsemann, "The Unchangeable World: The 'Crisis of Wisdom' in Koheleth," in *The God of the Lowly* (ed. Willy Schottroff and W. Stegemann; Maryknoll, N.Y.: Orbis, 1984), 57–77, depicts Qoheleth's alienation from less privileged members of society.

59. "The increase of indenture of persons is a consequence of problems of self-sufficiency in the household economy and is typically related to the growth of commerce and production outside traditional family or 'lineage' modes of production" (Carol Meyers, *Discovering Eve: Ancient Israelite Women in Context* [New York: Oxford University, 1988], 192). In harsh times, when money was in high demand, interest rates escalated. The records from Egypt reveal instances of extraordinary rates of interest on loans in cash, in at least one case reaching 120 percent per annum.

60. Similar reticence has characterized biblical interpreters for the most part, recently overcome by the joint venture of Carol Meyers, Joseph Blenkinsopp, John J. Collins, and Leo G. Perdue (*Families in Ancient Israel* [Louisville: Westminster/John Knox, 1997]).

61. The expression "Enjoy life with the woman you love" is similar to "and I found more bitter than death the woman who is a snare, whose heart is a net, whose hands are bonds" (Qoh 7:26) in that the references to woman require further elucidation. One expects the *'ishshah* ("wife") in Qoh 9:9 to end with the second-person pronominal suffix, indicating possession.

62. Thomas Krüger, "'Frau Weisheit' in Koh 7, 26," *Biblica* 73 (1992): 394–403, introduces the idea of personified wisdom to recent interpretations of the verse as a popular proverb that Qoheleth refuted. See, for example, Norbert Lohfink, "War Kohelet ein Frauenfiend?" in *La Sagesse de l'Ancien Testament* (ed. Maurice Gilbert; Bibliotheca ephemeridum theologicarum lovaniensium 51; Louvain: University Press, 1979), 259–87.

63. As in the following:

> Enlil, king of the gods, who created teeming mankind,
> Majestic Ea, who pinched off their clay,
> The Queen who fashioned them, Mistress Mami,
> Gave twisted words to the human race,
> They endowed them in perpetuity with lies and falsehood.
>
> ("The Babylonian Theodicy")

64. Only Job 28:12–28 even remotely resembles speculation about a feminine embodiment of divine perception; see van Wolde, ed., *Job 28: Cognition in Context.*

65. "The way of wisdom provides no guarantee, and projects no reciprocity in the human-divine encounter" (Levine, "The Appeal to Personal Experience in the Wisdom of Qoheleth," 344).

66. The second epilogue does adopt this usual type of addressing listeners (12:12). It has an ancient pedigree ("The Instruction of Suruppak," 31; *The Context of Scripture,* 569).

67. Höffken, "Das EGO des Weisen."

68. Machinist, "Fate, miqreh, and Reason," and Rose, "Qohelet als Philosophe und Theologe."

69. Müller, "Wie sprach Qohälät von Gott?"; Schoors, "God in Qoheleth," 251–70, and "Theodicy in Qohelet," in *Theodicy in the World of the Bible,* 375–409.

70. Johannes Marböck, *Weisheit im Wandel: Untersuchungen zur Weisheitstheologie bei Ben Sira* (Bonner biblische Beiträge 37; Bonn: Hanstein, 1971).

71. Moyna McGlynn, *Divine Judgment and Divine Benevolence,* 25–53.

72. Michael Kolarcik, *The Ambiguity of Death in the Book of Wisdom 1–6: A Study of Literary Structure and Interpretation* (Analecta biblica 127; Rome: Pontifical Biblical Institute, 1991).

73. Crenshaw, "The Problem of Theodicy in Sirach," and Collins, *Jewish Wisdom in the Hellenistic Age,* 133–232.

74. Goff, *Discerning Wisdom.*

Conclusion

1. Crenshaw, "From the Mundane to the Sublime." Robert Wright, *The Evolution of God* (New York: Little, Brown, 2009), traces the changing concept of deity from earliest times to the present.

2. Seow, *Ecclesiastes,* 334, recognizes the difficulty of interpreting this verse as pertaining to transport over the seas.

3. Jeremy Corley, "Friendship According to Ben Sira," in *Der Einzelne und seine Gemeinschaft bei Ben Sira* (BZAW 270; Berlin: de Gruyter, 1998), 65–71.

4. Kevin Cathcart, "Notes on Micah, 5, 4–5," *Biblica* 49 (1968): 511–14.

5. Even farmers are divinely instructed, according to Isa 28:25–29.

6. On the basis of this and other thematic refrains, Addison D. G. Wright argued for a precise structure to Ecclesiastes, but his argument is forced at too many places to be persuasive ("The Riddle of the Sphinx: The Structure of the Book of Qoheleth," *Catholic Biblical Quarterly* 30 [1968]: 313–34).

7. Bartholomew, *Ecclesiastes,* 29.

8. Eric Zenger, *A God of Vengeance: Understanding the Psalms of Divine Wrath* (Louisville: Westminster John Knox, 1996).

9. Nancy C. Lee, *Lyrics of Lament: From Tragedy to Transformation* (Minneapolis: Fortress, 2010).

10. In a forthcoming article, "Qoheleth and Scriptural Authority," I examine the assumptions generally used to support a view of biblical inspiration.

11. Berger, "Qohelet and the Exigencies of the Absurd."

12. See *AEL,* 3:63 ("As for death, 'Come!' is his name"). The Tale of the Eloquent Peasant has this praise of death: "A thirsty man's approach to water, an infant's mouth reaching for milk, thus is a longed-for death seen coming, thus does his death arrive at last" (*AEL,* 1:182).

13. Jerome R. Mintz, *Legends of the Hasidim* (Chicago: University of Chicago, 1968), is a treasure trove of such stories. The tale of the woodcutter is from Jean de la Fontaine, *Fables.*

14. Fox, *Ecclesiastes,* xxvi–xxvii.

15. See Vladimir Losky, *The Mystical Theology of the Eastern Church* (Crestwood, N.Y.: St. Vladimir's Seminary, 1976).

16. Ironically Christians have been burdened with the concept of a fall and original sin, which for some makes the idea of enjoyment seem sinful.

17. Crenshaw, *Dust and Ashes.*

18. Perry, *God's Twilight Zone,* 157–73, and William P. Brown, "Wisdom's Wonder: A New Hermeneutical Lens for the Sapiential Literature of the Hebrew Bible," a paper presented in 2011 at the national meeting of the Society of Biblical Literature in San Francisco.

Selected Bibliography

Books

Adams, Samuel L. *Wisdom in Transition: Act and Consequence in Second Temple Instructions.* Leiden: Brill, 2008.

Anderson, William H. U. *Qoheleth and Its Pessimistic Theology: Hermeneutical Struggles in Wisdom Literature.* Mellen Biblical Press Series 54. Lewistown: Mellen Biblical Press, 1997.

Alter, Robert. *The Wisdom Books: Job, Proverbs, and Ecclesiastes.* New York: Norton, 2010.

Bartholomew, Craig G. *Reading Ecclesiastes: Old Testament Exegesis and Hermeneutical Theory.* Analecta Biblica 139. Rome: Editrice Pontificio Istituto Biblico, 1998.

———. *Ecclesiastes.* Grand Rapids: Baker Academic, 2009.

Barton, George A. *The Book of Ecclesiastes.* Edinburgh: T. & T. Clark, 1908.

Berlejung, Angelika, and Pierre van Hecke, eds. *The Language of Qohelet in its Context.* Orientalia lovaniensia analecta 164. Louvain: Peeters, 2007.

Bickerman, Elias. *Four Strange Books of the Bible: Jonah/Daniel/Koheleth/Esther.* New York: Schocken, 1967.

Braun, Rainer. *Kohelet und die frühhellenistische Popularphilosophie.* Beiheft zur Zeitschrift für die Alttestamentliche Wissenschaft 130. Berlin: de Gruyter, 1973.

Brown, William P. *Ecclesiastes.* Louisville: John Knox, 2000.

Burkes, Shannon. *Death in Qoheleth and Egyptian Biographies of the Late Period.* Atlanta: Society of Biblical Literature, 1999.

Christianson, Eric S. *A Time to Tell: Narrative Strategies in Ecclesiastes.* Journal for the Study of the Old Testament Supplementary Series 280. Sheffield: Academic Press, 1998.

Collins, John J. *Jewish Wisdom in the Hellenistic Age.* Old Testament Library. Louisville: Westminster John Knox, 1997.

Crenshaw, James L. *Ecclesiastes.* Old Testament Library. Philadelphia: Westminster, 1987.

———. *Urgent Advice and Probing Questions: Collected Writings on Old Testament Wisdom.* Macon: Mercer University, 1995.

———. *Education in Ancient Israel: Across the Deadening Silence.* Anchor Bible Reference Library. New York: Doubleday, 1998.

———. *Defending God: Biblical Responses to the Problem of Evil.* New York: Oxford University Press, 2005.

————. *Prophets, Sages & Poets.* St. Louis: Chalice, 2006.

————. *Dust and Ashes: Poems.* Art for Faith's Sake 3. Eugene, Oreg.: Cascade Books, 2010.

————. *Old Testament Wisdom.* 3d ed. Louisville: Westminster John Knox, 2010.

Eaton, Michael A. *Ecclesiastes.* Tyndale Old Testament Commentaries. Leicester: Inter-Varsity Press, 1983.

Ellul, Jacques. *Reason for Being: A Meditation on Ecclesiastes.* Grand Rapids: Eerdmans, 1990.

Enns, Peter. *Ecclesiastes.* The Two Horizons Old Testament Commentary. Grand Rapids: Eerdmans, 2011.

Fox, Michael V. *Qohelet and His Contradictions.* Journal for the Study of the Old Testament Supplementary Series 71. Sheffield: Almond, 1989.

————. *A Time to Tear Down & a Time to Build Up: A Re-reading of Ecclesiastes.* Grand Rapids: Eerdmans, 1999.

Galling, Kurt. *Der Prediger.* Handbuch zum Alten Testament 1, 18; 1940. Tübingen: J. C. B. Mohr, 1969.

Geering, Lloyd. *Such Is Life! A Close Encounter with Ecclesiastes.* Salem, Oreg.: Polebridge Press, 2010.

Ginsberg, H. Lewis. *Studies in Kohelet.* New York: Jewish Theological Seminary of America, 1950.

Ginsburg, Christian D. *The Song of Songs and Coheleth.* 1857. New York: Ktav, 1970.

Gordis, Robert. *Koheleth: The Man and His World.* New York: Schocken, 1968.

Harrison, Robert. "Qoheleth in Socio-historical Perspective." Ph.D. diss., Duke University, 1991.

Imray, Kathryn. "Qoheleth's Philosophies of Death." Ph.D. diss., Murdoch University, 2009.

Isaksson, Bo. *Studies in the Language of Qoheleth with Special Emphasis on the Verbal System.* Acta Universitatis Upsaliensis, Studia Semitica Upsalensia, 10. Uppsala, 1987.

Jarman, Mark. *Questions for Ecclesiastes.* Ashland, Oreg.: Story Line Press, 1997.

————. *Unholy Sonnets.* Ashland, Oregon: Story Line Press, 2000.

Johnston, Robert K. *Useless Beauty: Ecclesiastes through the Lens of Contemporary Film.* Grand Rapids: Baker Academic, 1984.

Ingram, Doug. *Ambiguity in Ecclesiastes.* London: T. & T. Clark, 2006.

Kidner, Derek. *A Time to Mourn and a Time to Dance.* Downers Grove, Ill.: Inter-Varsity Press, 1976.

Koh, Y. V. *Royal Autobiography in the Book of Qoheleth.* Beiheft zur Zeitschrift für die Alttestamentliche Wissenschaft 369. Berlin & New York: de Gruyter, 2006.

Koosed, Jennifer L. *(Per)mutations of Qohelet: Reading the Body in the Book.* Library of Hebrew Bible/Old Testament Studies. New York: T. & T. Clark, 2006.

Krüger, Thomas. *Qoheleth: A Commentary.* Edited by Klaus Baltzer. Translated by O. C. Dean Jr. Hermeneia. Minneapolis: Fortress, 2004.

Laurent, Françoise. *Les biens pour rien en Qohéleth 5,9–6,6 ou la traversee d'un contraste.* Beiheft zur Zeitschrift für die Alttestamentliche Wissenschaft 323. Berlin: de Gruyter, 2002.

Lee, Eunny P. *The Vitality of Enjoyment in Qohelet's Theological Rhetoric.* Beiheft zur Zeitschrift für die Alttestamentliche Wissenschaft 353. Berlin: de Gruyter, 2005.

Limburg, James. *Encountering Ecclesiastes. A Book for Our Time.* Grand Rapids: Eerdmans, 2006.

Loader, J. A. *Ecclesiastes: A Practical Commentary.* Text and Interpretation. Grand Rapids: Eerdmans, 1986.

————. *Polar Structures in the Book of Qohelet.* Beiheft zur Zeitschrift für die Alttestamentliche Wissenschaft 152. Berlin & New York: de Gruyter, 1999.

Lohfink, Norbert. *Studien zu Kohelet.* Stuttgarter Biblische Aufsatzbände Altes Testament 26. Stuttgart: Katholisches Bibelwerk, 1998.

Longman, Tremper, III. *The Book of Ecclesiastes.* New International Commentary on the Old Testament. Grand Rapids: Eerdmans, 1998.

Loretz, Oswald. *Qohelet und der alte Orient. Untersuchungen zu Stil und theologischer Thematik des Buches Qohelet.* Freiburg: Herder, 1964.

Macdonald, Duncan Black. *The Hebrew Philosophical Genius: A Vindication.* Princeton: Princeton University Press, 1936.

McNeile, A. H. *An Introduction to Ecclesiastes.* Cambridge: Cambridge University Press, 1904.

Miller, Douglas B. *Symbol and Rhetoric in Ecclesiastes: The Place of Hebel in Qohelet's Work.* Academica Biblica 2. Atlanta: Society of Biblical Literature, 2002.

Murphy, Roland E. *Ecclesiastes.* Word Commentary. Dallas: Word, 1992.

Ogden, Graham. *Qoheleth.* Sheffield: Academic Press, 1987.

Perdue, Leo G. *Wisdom Literature.* Louisville: Westminster John Knox, 2007.

————. *The Sword and the Stylus.* Grand Rapids: Eerdmans, 2008.

————, ed. *Scribes, Sages, and Seers. The Sage in the Eastern Mediterranean World.* FRLANT 219. Göttingen: Vandenhoeck & Ruprecht, 2008.

Perry, T. A. *Dialogues with Qohelet: The Book of Ecclesiastes.* University Park: Pennsylvania State University Press, 1993.

Rad, Gerhard von. *Wisdom in Israel.* Nashville: Abingdon, 1972.

Rudman, Dominic. *Determinism in the Book of Ecclesiastes.* Journal for the Study of the Old Testament Supplementary Series 316. Sheffield: Academic Press, 2001.

Salyer, Gary D. *Vain Rhetoric: Private Insight and Public Debate in Ecclesiastes.* Journal for the Study of the Old Testament Supplementary Series 327. Sheffield: Academic Press, 2001.

Schoors, Antoon. *The Preacher Sought to Find Pleasing Words.* 2 vols. Orientalia lovaniensia analecta 41. Louvain: Peeters, 1992, 1994.

————. ed. *Qohelet in the Context of Wisdom.* Bibliotheca ephemeridum theologicarum 156. Louvain: University Press, 1998.

Schwienhorst-Schönberger, Ludger. *Kohelet.* Herders Theologischer Kommentar zum Alten Testament. Freiburg: Herders, 2004.

Seow, Choon-Leong. *Ecclesiastes.* Anchor Bible 18c. New York: Doubleday, 1997.

Shapiro, Rami. *The Way of Solomon: Finding Joy and Contentment in the Wisdom of Ecclesiastes.* San Francisco: Harper San Francisco, 2000.

Shields, Martin A. The *End of Wisdom: A Reappraisal of the Historical and Canonical Function of Ecclesiastes*. Winona Lake, Ind.: Eisenbrauns, 2006.

Sneed, Mark R. *The Politics of Pessimism in Ecclesiastes: A Social-Science Perspective*. Ancient Israel and its Literature 12; Atlanta: Society of Biblical Literature, 2012.

Tamez, Elsa. *When the Horizons Close. Rereading Ecclesiastes*. Eugene, Oreg.: Wipf & Stock, 2006.

Troxel, Ronald L., Kelvin G. Friebel, and Dennis R. Magary, eds. *Seeking out the Wisdom of the Ancients. Essays Offered to Honor Michael V. Fox on the Occasion of His Sixty-fifth Birthday*. Winona Lake, Ind.: Eisenbrauns, 2005.

Waddle, Ray. *Against the Grain: Unconventional Wisdom from Ecclesiastes*. Nashville: Upper Room, 2005.

Whybray, R. N. *Ecclesiastes*. Grand Rapids: Eerdmans, 1989.

———. *Ecclesiastes*. Old Testament Guides. Sheffield: JSOT Press, 1989.

Witzenrath, Hagia. *Süss ist das Licht . . . Eine literaturwissenschaftliche Untersuchung zu Kohelet 11,7–12,7*. Arbeiten zu Text und Sprache im Alten Testament 11 Band. St. Ottilien: Eos, 1979.

Wright, Benjamin G., III, and Lawrence M. Wills, eds. *Conflicted Boundaries in Wisdom and Apocalypticism*. Symposium Series 35. Atlanta: Society of Biblical Literature, 2005.

Zimmerman, Frank. *The Inner World of Qohelet*. New York: Ktav, 1973.

Articles

Anderson, William H. U. "Ironic Correlations and Scepticism in the Joy Statements of Qoheleth." *Scandinavian Journal of the Old Testament* 14 (2000): 67–100.

Bentjes, Pancratius C. "Who Is Like the Wise? Some Notes on Qohelet 8:1–15." Pages 303–15 in *Qohelet in the Context of Wisdom*. Edited by Antoon Schoors. Louvain: University Press, 1998.

Berger, Benjamin I. "Qohelet and the Exigencies of the Absurd." *Biblical Interpretation* 8 (2001): 141–79.

Blenkinsopp, Joseph. "Ecclesiastes 3:1–15: Another Interpretation." *Journal for the Study of the Old Testament* 66 (1995): 55–64.

Bohlen, Reinhold. "Kohelet in Kontext Hellenistischer Kultur." Pages 249–73 in *Das Buch Kohelet: Studien zur Struktur, Geschichte, Rezeption und Theologie*. Edited by Ludger Schwienhorst-Schönberger. Beiheft zur Zeitschrift für die Alttestamentliche Wissenschaft 254. Berlin & New York: de Gruyter, 1996.

Bolin, Thomas M. "Rivalry and Resignation: Girard and Qoheleth on the Divine-Human Relationship." *Biblica* 86 (2005): 245–59.

Brown, William P. "'Whatever Your Hand Finds to Do': Qoheleth's Work Ethic." *Interpretation* 55 (2001): 271–84.

Carasik, Michael. "Qohelet's Twists and Turns." *Journal for the Study of the Old Testament* 28 (2003): 192–209.

Christianson, Eric S. "Qoheleth and the Existential Legacy of the Holocaust." *Heythrop Journal* 38 (1997): 35–50.

Crenshaw, James L. "The Eternal Gospel (Eccl 3:11)." Pages 23–55 in *Essays in Old Testament Ethics*. Edited by Crenshaw and John T. Willis. New York: Ktav, 1974.

―――. "The Expression 'mi yodea' in the Hebrew Bible." *Vetus Testamentum* 36 (1986): 274–88.

―――. "Youth and Old Age in Qoheleth." *Hebrew Annual Review* 10 (1986): 1–13.

―――. "Ecclesiastes, Odd Book In." *Bible Review* 6 (1990): 28–33.

―――. "Ecclesiastes, Book of." Pages 271–80 in vol. 2 of *Anchor Bible Dictionary*. Edited by David Noel Freedman. 6 vols. New York: Doubleday, 1992.

―――. "Prohibitions in Proverbs and Qoheleth." Pages 115–24 in *Priests, Prophets, and Scribes*. Edited by Eugene Ulrich, John W. Wright, Robert P. Carroll, and Philip R. Davies. Sheffield: JSOT Press, 1992.

―――. "Qoheleth's Understanding of Intellectual Inquiry." Pages 204–24 in *Qohelet in the Context of Wisdom*. Edited by Antoon Schoors. Louvain: University Press, 1998.

―――. "From the Mundane to the Sublime (Reflections on Qoh 11:1–8)." Pages 61–72, 217–22, in Crenshaw, *Prophets, Sages & Poets*. St. Louis: Chalice, 2006.

―――. "Qoheleth in Historical Context." *Biblica* 88 (2007): 285–99.

―――. "Qoheleth's Quantitative Language." Pages 1–22 in *The Language of Qohelet in Its Context: Essays in Honour of Prof. A. Schoors on the Occasion of his Seventieth Birthday*. Edited by Angelika Berlejung and Pierre van Hecke. Orientalia lovaniensia analecta 164. Leuven: Peeters, 2007.

―――. "Qoheleth and Scriptural Authority," forthcoming.

Crüsemann, Frank. "The Unchangeable World: The 'Crisis of Wisdom' in Koheleth." Pages 57–77 in *God of the Lowly*. Edited by Willy Schottroff and Wolfgang Stegemann. Translated by Matthew J. O'Connell. Maryknoll: Orbis, 1984.

Dell, Katharine J. "Ecclesiastes as Wisdom: Consulting Early Interpreters." *Vetus Testamentum* 44 (1994): 301–29.

Dor-Shav, Ethan. "Ecclesiastes, Fleeting and Timeless." *Azure* 18 (5765/2004): 67–87.

Fischer, Stefan. "Qohelet and 'Heretic' Harpers' Songs." *Journal for the Study of the Old Testament* 98 (2002): 105–21.

Fox, Michael V. "Frame-Narrative and Composition in the Book of Qohelet." *Hebrew Union College Annual* 48 (1977): 83–106.

―――. "Qohelet's Epistemology." *Hebrew Union College Annual* 58 (1987): 137–55.

―――. "Wisdom in Qoheleth." Pages 115–31 in *In Search of Wisdom*. Edited by Leo G. Perdue, Bernard Brandon Scott, and William Johnston Wiseman. Louisville: Westminster John Knox, 1993.

―――. "The Inner Structure of Qohelet's Thought." Pages 225–38 in *Qohelet in the Context of Wisdom*. Edited by Antoon Schoors. Louvain: University Press, 1998.

―――. "Time in Qohelet's 'Catalogue of Times.'" *Journal of Northwest Semitic Languages* 24 (1998): 25–39.

George, Mark K. "Death as the Beginning of Life in the Book of Ecclesiastes." Pages 280–93 in *Strange Fire: Reading the Bible after the Holocaust*. Edited by Tod Linafelt. New York: New York University Press, 2000.

Gese, Hartmut. "The Crisis of Wisdom in Koheleth." Pages 141–53 in *Theodicy in the Old Testament*. Edited by James L. Crenshaw. Issues in Religion and Theology 4. Philadelphia: Fortress / London: SPCK, 1983.

Gianto, Augustinus. "Human Destiny in Emar and Qoheleth." Pages 473–79 in *Qohelet in the Context of Wisdom*. Edited by Antoon Schoors. Louvain: University Press, 1998.

———. "Ecclesiastes." Pages 178–85 in vol. 2 of *The New Interpreter's Dictionary of the Bible*. Edited by Katharine Doob Sakenfeld. 5 vols. Nashville: Abingdon, 2006–9.

Ginsberg, H. Lewis. "Supplementary Studies in Kohelet." *Proceedings of the American Academy of Jewish Research* (1952): 35–62.

Greenstein, Edward L. "Sages with a Sense of Humor: The Babylonian Dialogue between a Master and His Servant and the Book of Qoheleth." Pages 55–65 in *Wisdom Literature in Mesopotamia and Israel*. Edited by Richard J. Clifford. Atlanta: Society of Biblical Literature, 2007.

Good, E. M. "The Unfilled Sea: Style and Meaning in Ecclesiastes 1:2–11," Pages 59–73 in *Israelite Wisdom: Theological and Literary Essays in Honor of Samuel Terrien*. Edited by John J. Gammie, W. A. Brueggemann, W. L. Humphreys, and J. W. Ward. Missoula: Scholars Press, 1978.

Gordis, Robert. "Quotations in Wisdom Literature." *Jewish Quarterly Review* 30 (1939): 123–47.

Harrison, C. Robert. "Qoheleth among the Sociologists." *Biblical Interpretation* 5 (1997): 160–80.

Hirshman, Marc. "Qohelet's Reception and Interpretation in Early Rabbinic Literature." Pages 87–99 in *Studies in Ancient Midrash*. Edited by James L. Kugel. Cambridge, Mass.: Harvard University Center for Jewish Studies, 2001.

Höffken, Peter. "Das EGO des Weisen." *Theologische Zeitschrift* (1985): 121–34.

Holm-Nielsen, Svend. "The Book of Ecclesiastes and the Interpretation of It in Jewish and Christian Theology." *Annual of the Swedish Theological Institute* 10 (1976): 38–96.

Holmstedt, Robert D. "'*ani* and *libbi:* The Syntactic Encoding of the Collaborative Nature of Qoheleh's Experiment." *Journal of Hebrew Scriptures* 9 (2009): 1–27

Janzen, J. Gerald. "Qohelet on 'Life under the Sun.'" *Catholic Biblical Quarterly* 70 (2008): 465–83.

Jarick, John. "The Hebrew Book of Changes: Reflections on *Hakkol Hebel* and *Lakkol Zeman* in Ecclesiastes." *Journal for the Study of the Old Testament* 90 (2000): 79–99.

Jong, Stephan de. "A Book on Labour: The Structuring Principles and the Main Theme of the Book of Qohelet." *Journal for the Study of the Old Testament* 54 (1992): 107–16.

———. "God in the Book of Qohelet: A Reappraisal of Qohelet's Place in the Old Testament Theology." *Vetus Testamentum* 47 (1997): 154–67.

Krüger, Thomas. "'Frau Weisheit' in Koh 7, 26." *Biblica* 73 (1992): 394–403.

Kugel, James L. "Qohelet and Money." *Catholic Biblical Quarterly* 51 (1989): 32–49.

Levine, Baruch A. "The Appeal to Personal Experience in the Wisdom of Qoheleth." Pages 332–45 in *From Babel to Babylon*. Edited by Joyce Rilett Wood, John E. Harvey, and Mark Leuchter. New York: T. & T. Clark, 2006.

Levine, Etan. "The Humor in Qohelet," *Zeitschrift für die Alttestamentliche Wissenschaft* 109 (1997): 71–83.

Lohfink, Norbert. "War Kohelet ein Frauenfeind?" Pages 259–87 in *La Sagesse de l'Ancien Testament.* Edited by Maurice Gilbert. Bibliotheca ephemeridum theologicarum lovaniensium 51. Louvain: University Press, 1979.

————. "Qoheleth 5:17–19—Revelation by Joy," *Catholic Biblical Quarterly* 52 (1990): 625–35.

Machinist, Peter. "Fate, *miqreh,* and Reason: Some Reflections on Qohelet and Biblical Thought." Pages 159–75 in *Solving Riddles and Untying Knots.* Edited by Ziony Zevit, Seymour Gitin, and Michael Sokoloff. Winona Lake: Eisenbrauns: 1995.

McKenna, John E. "The Concept of *Hebel* in the Book of Ecclesiastes." *Scottish Journal of Theology* 45 (1992): 19–28.

Miller, Douglas B. "Qoheleth's Symbolic Use of *hbl.*" *Journal of Biblical Literature* 117 (1998): 437–54.

Muilenburg, James. "A Qoheleth Scroll from Qumran." *Bulletin of the American Schools of Oriental Research* 135 (1954): 20–28.

Müller, Hans-Peter. "Wie sprach Qohälät von Gott?" *Vetus Testamentum* 18 (1968): 507–21.

————. "Neige der althebräischen »Weisheit« Zum Denken Qohäläts." *Zeitschrift für die alttestamentliche Wissenschaft* 90 (1978): 238–64.

————. "Theonome Skepsis und Lebensfreude—Zu Koh 1, 12–3, 15." *Biblische Zeitschrift* 30 (1986): 1–19.

————. "Der unheimliche Gast. Zum Denken Kohelets." *Zeitschrift für Theologie und Kirche* 84 (1987): 440–64.

Murphy, Roland E. "Qoheleth's Quarrel with the Fathers." Pages 235–45 in *From Faith to Faith.* Edited by Dikran Y. Hadidian. Pittsburgh: Pickwick, 1979.

————. "On Translating Ecclesiastes." *Catholic Biblical Quarterly* 53 (1991): 571–79.

Newsom, Carol A. "Job and Ecclesiastes." Pages 177–94 in *Old Testament Interpretation Past, Present, and Future.* Edited by James Luther Mays, David L. Petersen, and Kent Harold Richards. Nashville: Abingdon, 1995.

Ogden, Graham S. "Qoheleth IX 1–16." *Vetus Testamentum* 32 (1982): 158–69.

————. "Qoheleth XI 1–6." *Vetus Testamentum* 33 (1983): 222–30.

————. "The Mathematics of Wisdom: Qoheleth IV 1–12," *Vetus Testamentum* 34 (1984): 446–53.

Polk, Timothy. "The Wisdom of Irony: A Study of *Hebel* in Its Relation to Joy and the Fear of God in Ecclesiastes." *Studia Biblica et Theologica* 6 (1976): 3–17.

Rose, Martin. "Qohelet als Philosophe und Theologe: Ein biblische Votum für *Universitas.*" Pages 177–99 in *Universitas in Theologia—Theologia in Universitate.* Edited by Matthias Kreig und Martin Rose. Zurich: Theologische, 1997.

————. "De la 'crise de la sagesse' à la 'sagesse de la crise.'" *Revue de théologie et de philosophie* 131 (1999): 115–34.

Rudman, Dominic. "A Contextual Reading of Ecclesiastes 4:13–16." *Journal of Biblical Literature* 116 (1997): 57–73.

Schoors, Antoon. "Kohelet: A Perspective of Life after Death," *Ephemerides theologicae lovanienses* 61 (1985): 295–303.

————. "Words Typical of Qohelet." Pages 17–39 in *Qohelet in the Context of Wisdom.* Edited by Antoon Schoors. Louvain: University Press, 1998.

————. "God in Qohelet." Pages 251–70 in *Schöpfungsplan und Heilsgeschichte: Fest-schrift für Ernst Haag*. Edited by Renate Brandscheidt and Theresia Mende. Trier: Paulinus, 2002.

————. "Theology in Qohelet." Pages 375–409 in *Theodicy in the World of the Bible*. Edited by Antti Laato and Johannes C. de Moor. Leiden: Brill, 2003.

Schultz, R. L. "A Sense of Timing: A Neglected Aspect of Qoheleth's Wisdom." Pages 257–67 in *Seeking Out the Wisdom of the Ancients. Essays Offered to Honor Michael V. Fox on the Occasion of His Sixty-fifth Birthday*. Edited by Ronald L. Troxel, Kelvin G. Friebel, and Dennis R. Magary. Winona Lake, Ind.: Eisenbrauns, 2005.

Schwienhorst-Schönberger, Ludger. "Gottes Antwort in der Freude. Zur theologie göttlicher Gegenwart im Buch Kohelet." *Bibel und Kirche* 54 (1999):156–63.

Seow, Choon-Leong. "Qohelet's Autobiography." Pages 275–87 in *Fortunate the Eyes That See*. Edited by Astrid B. Beck, Andrew H. Bartelt, Paul R. Raabe, and Chris A. Franke. Grand Rapids: Eerdmans, 1995.

————. "Linguistic Evidence and the Dating of Qoheleth." *Journal of Biblical Literature* 115 (1996): 643–66.

————. "Qohelet's Eschatological Poem." *Journal of Biblical Literature* 118 (1999): 209–34.

————. "The Social World of Ecclesiastes." Pages 189–217 in *Scribes, Sages, and Seers*. Edited by Leo G. Perdue. Göttingen: Vandenhoeck & Ruprecht, 2008.

Sharp, Carolyn J. "Ironic Representation, Authorial Voice, and Meaning in Qohelet." *Biblical Interpretation* 12 (2004): 37–68.

Sherwood, Yvonne. "'Not with a Bang but a Whimper': Shrunken Apocalypses of the Twentieth Century and the Book of Qoheleth." Pages 94–116 in *Apocalyptic in History and Tradition*. Edited by Christopher Rowland and John Barton. London: Sheffield Academic Press, 2002.

Smelik, Klaus. "God in the Book of Qoheleth." Pages 177–81 in *The Language of Qohelet in Its Context*. Edited by Angelika Berlejung and Pierre van Hecke. Orientalia lovaniensia analecta 164. Louvain: Peeters, 2007.

Sneed, Mark. "The Social Location in the Book of Qoheleth." *Hebrew Studies* 39 (1998): 41–51.

————. "(Dis)closure in Qohelet: Qohelet Deconstructed." *Journal for the Study of the Old Testament* 27 (2002): 115–26.

Tamez, Elsa. "Ecclesiastes 3:1–8: A Latin American Perspective." Pages 75–79 in *Return to Babel*. Edited by Priscilla Pope-Levison and John R. Levison. Louisville: Westminster John Knox, 1999.

Tomson, P. J. "'There Is No One Who Is Righteous, Not Even One': Kohelet 7, 20 in Pauline and Early Jewish Interpretation." Pages 183–202 in *The Language of Qohelet in Its Context*. Edited by Angelika Berlejung and Pierre van Hecke. Orientalia lovaniensia analecta 164. Louvain: Peeters, 2007.

Uehlinger, Christoph. "Qohelet im Horizont mesopotamischer, levantinischer und ägyptischer Weisheitsliteratur der persischen und hellenistischen Zeit." Pages 155–247 in *Das Buch Kohelet: Studien zur Struktur, Geschichte, Rezeption und Theologie*. Edited by

Ludger Schwienhorst-Schönberger. Beiheft zur Zeitschrift für die Alttestamentliche Wissenschaft 254. Berlin & New York: de Gruyter, 1996.

Van der Toorn, Karel. "Did Ecclesiastes Copy Gilgamesh?" *Biblical Review* 16 (2000): 23–30.

Van Hecke, Pierre. "The Verbs *ra'â* and *šma'* in the Book of Qohelet. A Cognitive-Semantic Perspective." Pages 203–20 in *The Language of Qohelet in Its Context*. Edited by Angelika Berlejung and Pierre van Hecke. Orientalia lovaniensia analecta 164. Louvain: Peeters, 2007.

Whybray, Roger N. "The Identification and Use of Quotations in Ecclesiastes." *Vetus Testamentum Supplements* 32 (1981): 435–51.

———. "Qoheleth, Preacher of Joy." *Journal for the Study of the Old Testament* 23 (1982): 87–98.

———. "Qoheleth as a Theologian." Pages 239–65 in *Qohelet in the Context of Wisdom*. Edited by Antoon Schoors. Louvain: University Press, 1998.

Wood, Joyce Rilett. "When Gods Were Men." Pages 285–98 in *From Babel to Babylon*. Edited by Joyce Rilett Wood, John E. Harvey, and Mark Leuchter. New York: T. & T. Clark, 2006.

Wright, Addison D. G. "The Riddle of the Sphinx: The Structure of the Book of Qoheleth." *Catholic Biblical Quarterly* 30 (1968): 313–34.

Index of Biblical and Extrabiblical Literature

Subject Index

About the Author

JAMES L. CRENSHAW is the Robert L. Flowers Professor Emeritus of Old Testament at Duke University Divinity School and a Guggenheim fellow in 1984–1985. Crenshaw's most recent books include *Reading Job: A Literary and Theological Commentary; The Psalms: An Introduction, Defending God: Biblical Responses to the Problem of Evil* and *Prophets, Sages & Poets.*

2014. 03. 04   45. 00 (to. 50)